GLOBAL PORTFOLIOS
QUANTITATIVE STRATEGIES FOR MAXIMUM PERFORMANCE

GLOBAL PORTFOLIOS
QUANTITATIVE STRATEGIES FOR MAXIMUM PERFORMANCE

Edited by
Robert Z. Aliber
Brian R. Bruce

BUSINESS ONE IRWIN
Homewood, Illinois 60430

Project editor: Jean Lou Hess
Production manager: Diane Palmer
Compositor: Alexander Graphics Limited
Typeface: 11/13 Times Roman
Printer: The Book Press, Inc.

Library of Congress Cataloging-in-Publication Data

Global portfolios: quantitative strategies for maximum performance /
   edited by Robert Z. Aliber, Brian R. Bruce.
     p.   cm.
   Includes bibliographical references and index.
   ISBN 1-55623-337-X
    1. Portfolio management.   2. Securities.   I. Aliber, Robert Z.
  II. Bruce, Brian R.
  HG4529.5.G56   1991
  332.6—dc20   90–47349

Printed in the United States of America
1 2 3 4 5 6 7 8 9 0 BP 8 7 6 5 4 3 2 1

NOTES ON THE AUTHORS

Robert Z. Aliber is professor of international economics and finance at the Graduate School of Business, University of Chicago.

Robert D. Arnott is president and chief investment officer with First Quadrant Corporation.

Edgar W. Barksdale is chairman of RCB International.

Gary L. Bergstrom is president of Acadian Asset Management, Inc.

Fischer Black is a partner of Goldman, Sachs & Co.

Gary P. Brinson, CFA, is president and managing partner of Brinson Partners.

Remi J. Browne, CFA, is a vice president with State Street Bank and Trust Company.

Brian R. Bruce is a vice president with State Street Bank and Trust Company and editor of *Investing Magazine*.

John R. Chisholm, CFA, is a senior vice president with Acadian Asset Management, Inc.

David F. DeRosa is a vice president with Alliance Capital Management.

Hans L. Erickson is director of research for The DAIS Group, Inc.

H. Gifford Fong is president of Gifford Fong Associates.

Ronald D. Frashure, CFA, is an executive vice president with Acadian Asset Management, Inc.

William L. Green is managing director of RCB International.

Roy D. Henriksson is a senior vice president with Kidder Peabody Inc.

Roger G. Ibbotson is professor in the practice of finance, Yale School of Management and president of Ibbotson Associates.

Philippe Jorion is an associate professor at the Graduate School of Business, Columbia University.

Paul D. Kaplan is chief economist of Ibbotson Associates.

Denis S. Karnosky is managing partner of Brinson Partners.

Dean LeBaron, CFA, is a trustee of Batterymarch Financial Management.

Larry L. Martin, CFA, is a vice president with State Street Bank and Trust Company.

Joseph J. Mezrich is a vice president with Salomon Brothers Inc.

Christopher N. Orndorff, CFA, is a portfolio manager at Payden & Rygel.

Andrew Rudd is president and CEO of BARRA.

Laurence B. Siegel is managing director of Ibbotson Associates.

Rex A. Sinquefeld is chairman of Dimensional Fund Advisors.

Eric H. Sorensen is director of quantitative analysis for Salomon Brothers Inc.

Lawrence S. Speidell is a trustee of Batterymarch Financial Management.

Eric M. P. Tang is president of Portfolio Management Technology.

Lee R. Thomas is a member of the management committee at Investcorp Bank, E. C.

Heydon D. Traub, CFA, is a vice president with State Street Bank and Trust Company.

Peter G. Vann is manager, risk management, at Westpac Investment Management Pty Limited.

James R. Vertin, CFA, is principal of Alpine Counselors.

FOREWORD

For many observers, the recent explosion of U.S. investor participation in global investment has been a startling phenomenon. For those well versed in the fundamentals of portfolio theory, however, this development has represented a logical and necessary evolutionary step in the maturing of investment understanding. Effective diversification is the crucial keystone of realistic investment planning and efficient asset allocation. Global investment, therefore, is a required basic element of any serious investment program.

The global investment ball is rolling—and rolling with increasing momentum. This fact confronts the investor with the realization that successful participation in this desirable expansion of the investment frontier means dealing effectively with the complexities and the operational decision making that such involvement entails. Pragmatically, as shown time and time again by experience in coping with the realities of domestic investment, the concepts and techniques of quantitative analysis and problem solving can be of fundamental assistance in maximizing the productivity and controlling the hazards of global investment exposure. In fact, it is difficult to believe that the opportunities and risks of global market involvement can be effectively addressed in any way other than through the systematic, disciplined, and objective approaches that are part and parcel of the quantitative milieu.

The serious global investor will find in this book—brought together in one place for the first time—a wealth of useful information, comment, opinion, strategies, and assistance distilled from experience and focused specifically on this evolving subject area. Whether new to the game or already involved, every reader will find something of importance here. In particular, the quantitative methods illustrated in this volume represent the next step forward in effective global investment practice; no one can afford not to be aware of them. Money managers, plan sponsors, enlightened individual investors, foundation and endowment investment committees, consultants, and actuaries all are standing at the threshold of an era in which effective investment is clearly a global matter. To realize on the vast opportunities this fact entails—and to do so in a manner consistent with the risk-taking capacity of the specific investor involved—is no easy task. This compendium of outstanding thought and exposition will provide the guidance and help generate the insight and understanding that successful global investment requires.

James R. Vertin

Contents

Foreword, *James R. Vertin*   vii

1   Introduction to Quantitative Global Investing, *Robert Z. Aliber and Brian R. Bruce*   1

PART 1
ASSET ALLOCATION

2   Global Asset Allocation Policy, *Gary P. Brinson and Denis S. Karnosky*   21

3   A Disciplined Approach to Global Asset Allocation, *Robert D. Arnott and Roy D. Henriksson*   33

4   Global Asset Allocation, *Lee R. Thomas*   62

5   Quantitative Asset Allocation Forecasting: Uncovering the "Efficient Frontier," *Eric H. Sorensen and Joseph J. Mezrich*   76

6   Implementing the Asset Allocation Decision, *Edgar W. Barksdale and William L. Green*   101

PART 2
OPTIMAL BOND PORTFOLIOS

7   International Bonds: The Asset Class, *Philippe Jorion*   113

8   International Bond Portfolio Performance: Measurement and Attribution, *H. Gifford Fong and Eric M. P. Tang*   125

9   Methods to Enhance Passively Managed Global Bond Portfolios, *Christopher N. Orndorff*   136

10 Definition and Control of Risk Measures for Active Portfolio Bond Management and the Role of Options, *Peter Vann*   158

PART 3
OPTIMAL EQUITY PORTFOLIOS

11 World Equities: The Past and the Future, *Roger G. Ibbotson, Laurence B. Siegel, and Paul D. Kaplan*   173

12 Global Passive Management, *Brian R. Bruce, Heydon D. Traub, and Larry L. Martin*   197

13 Applied Portfolio Optimization, *Hans L. Erickson*   211

14   The Returns on Performance-Based International Equity
     Portfolios, *Robert Z. Aliber*   227

15   Stock Return Anomalies in Non-U.S. Markets, *Gary L. Bergstrom,
     Ronald D. Frashure, and John R. Chisholm*   241

16   The Gains from International Small-Company Diversification, *Rex
     A. Sinquefield*   254

17   International Investing: The Case for the Emerging Markets,
     Andrew Rudd   264

18   The Universal Valuation Model: A Blueprint for Global Investment
     Strategy, *Dean LeBaron and Lawrence S. Speidell*   285

PART 4
THE FOREIGN EXCHANGE EXPOSURE DECISION

19   Universal Hedging: Optimizing Currency Risk and Reward in
     International Equity Portfolios, *Fischer Black*   303

20   Currency Risks in International Equity Portfolios, *Lee R. Thomas* 318

21   An Introduction to Currency Insurance, *David F. DeRosa*   326

22   The Case for Not Hedging, *Remi J. Browne*   339

INDEX   343

GLOBAL PORTFOLIOS
QUANTITATIVE STRATEGIES FOR MAXIMUM PERFORMANCE

CHAPTER 1

INTRODUCTION TO QUANTITATIVE GLOBAL INVESTING

Robert Z. Aliber
Brian R. Bruce

The proposition that the total return to a diversified international portfolio of equities is higher than the total return to a diversified portfolio of domestic U.S. equities has become increasingly accepted over the last 20 years. Similar statements can be made about the relationship between the total return on a diversified international portfolio of equities and the total returns on a diversified portfolio of Canadian equities or of British equities or of Swiss equities or of German equities. The counterpart proposition, that the risk of a diversified international portfolio of equities is lower than the risk of a diversified portfolio of domestic equities, also has been accepted.

That the returns are higher on a diversified international portfolio of equities than on a diversified portfolio of domestic equities is valid for investors resident in many countries and reflects the significant differences among countries in the rates of return on domestic equities. As a general proposition, the rates of return on the equities of firms headquartered in ''younger'' countries are higher than the rates of return on the equities of firms headquartered in ''older'' countries, where younger and older refer to when a country began to industrialize; presumably, the firms headquartered in younger countries have been experiencing more rapid growth in their sales, assets, and profits. The proposition about the lower risk is effective for investors resident in every country and reflects that changes in the prices of equities in individual countries are less than perfectly correlated with changes in prices of equities in other countries.

Similarly, the rate of return on a diversified portfolio of bonds denominated in the U.S. dollar, the Canadian dollar, the British pound, and other national currencies is higher than the rate of return on a portfolio of bonds denominated in the U.S. dollar, while the risk of the U.S. dollar bond portfolio would be higher than the risk of the diversified portfolio of bonds denominated in the U.S. dollar and other national currencies. And this conclusion about the higher rate of return on the diversified portfolio of bonds denominated in different national currencies is valid for investors resident in many countries, while the conclusion about the reduced risk of such portfolios is valid for investors resident in every country. The higher rates of return on bonds denominated in the Canadian dollar, the British pound, and numerous other foreign currencies might reflect one or several possible factors—that these countries are likely to experience more rapid economic growth, that the price of the U.S. dollar in terms of the currencies of these countries will increase, and that borrowers in these countries are deemed riskier than U.S. borrowers.

The statement that the rates of return are higher on diversified international portfolios of equities and of bonds than on diversified portfolios of U.S. equities and U.S. dollar bonds implicitly adjusts for any losses that investors might incur as a result of changes in the price of the foreign currencies or the costs they might incur to hedge their foreign exchange exposure and avoid these losses.

The statements about the rate of return on a diversified international portfolio of equities and the rate of return on a diversified international portfolio of bonds can be combined into a statement that the rate of return on a diversified international portfolio of both international equities and bonds would exceed the rate of return on a diversified portfolio of U.S. equities and U.S. dollar bonds. And the risk of the international portfolio of equities and bonds would be lower than the risk of a U.S. domestic portfolio of equities and bonds. A set of comparable statements can be made for investors resident in many foreign countries.

That U.S. investors can increase their rate of return by international diversification reflects how the rates of return on the equities and the bonds in many foreign countries have exceeded the rates of return on U.S.

equities and U.S. dollar bonds. The rates of return on U.S. government bonds and on comparable bonds of other governments are shown in Table 1–1, and the rates of return on U.S. corporate bonds and on corporate bonds of firms headquartered in various other counries are shown in Table 1–2. The rates of return on both sets of bonds are shown as local currency returns and U.S. dollar equivalent returns; the U.S. dollar returns on bonds denominated in a particular foreign currency reflect an adjustment to the local currency return for the average annual change in the price of the U.S. dollar in terms of their foreign currency during the designated investment period.

Until the late 1970s, the interest rates on U.S. dollar bonds were below the interest rates on bonds denominated in most foreign currencies; in the 1980s, in contrast, interest rates on bonds denominated in the German mark and in the Japanese yen were below interest rates on U.S. dollar bonds. The variability in the relationship between the rate of return on U.S. dollar bonds and the U.S. dollar equivalent of the rate of return on bonds denominated in a particular foreign currency has increased as a result of the changes in the price of the U.S. dollar in terms of the foreign currency. Thus, in the 1950s and 1960s, the currencies of many foreign countries were devalued relative to the U.S. dollar, which led to a decrease in the excess of the rate of return on the bonds denominated in these foreign currencies over the rate of return on U.S. dollar bonds. In the 1970s, in contrast, many foreign currencies appreciated relative to the U.S. dollar, and so the excess of the rate of return on foreign bonds increased over the rate of return on U.S. dollar bonds. In the 1980s, foreign currencies depreciated in the first half of the decade and then appreciated relative to the U.S. dollar. Therefore, the comparison of the rates of return on U.S. dollar bonds with the U.S. dollar equivalent of the rates of return on bonds denominated in individual foreign currencies is especially sensitive to changes in the relationship between the price of the U.S. dollar in terms of the foreign currency at the beginning and at the end of the investment period.

The rates of return on the equities of firms headquartered in the United States and 22 foreign countries are shown in Table 1–3 both in terms of local currency returns and U.S. dollar equivalent returns. The rates of return on the equities of firms headquartered in many foreign countries, especially Japan and other countries in the Far East, have been substantially above the rate of return on U.S. equities.

TABLE 1–1
Summary Statistics of Annual Rates of Return on Long-Term Government Bonds

Country	Period	Rate of Return in Local Currency			Rate of Return in U.S. Dollars		
		Compound Annual Return	Arithmetic Mean Return	Standard Deviation of Return	Compound Annual Return	Arithmetic Mean Return	Standard Deviation of Return
United States	1961–89	6.18%	6.70%	11.17%	6.18%	6.70%	11.17%
Canada	1961–89	7.64	7.94	8.58	7.08	7.42	8.99
Japan	1967–89	7.58	7.76	6.37	11.99	13.33	17.80
Great Britain	1961–89	8.80	9.83	15.97	6.75	8.51	21.07
Germany	1961–89	7.09	7.31	7.01	10.48	11.34	14.25
France	1961–89	8.00	8.39	9.33	7.40	8.41	15.51
Italy	1961–89	8.80	9.88	15.95	6.16	8.04	21.59
Netherlands	1965–89	7.24	7.46	7.21	9.99	10.92	14.97
Switzerland	1965–89	4.33	4.51	6.28	8.72	9.93	16.85
Australia	1961–89	7.12	7.69	11.19	5.84	6.56	12.72

Source: Ibbotson Associates.

TABLE 1–2
Summary Statistics of Annual Rates of Return on Corporate Bonds

Country	Period	Rate of Return in Local Currency			Rate of Return in U.S. Dollars		
		Compound Annual Return	Arithmetic Mean Return	Standard Deviation of Return	Compound Annual Return	Arithmetic Mean Return	Standard Deviation of Return
United States	1961–86	6.65%	7.04%	9.48%	6.65%	7.05%	9.48%
Canada	1961–86	7.92	8.24	8.70	6.57	6.87	8.28
Japan	1961–86	8.49	8.65	6.08	11.93	12.68	13.52
Great Britain	1961–86	9.59	10.53	15.08	6.92	8.21	17.50
Germany	1961–86	8.72	9.03	8.97	11.97	12.55	11.80
France	1961–86	9.16	9.60	10.12	8.01	9.01	15.77
Italy	1961–86	10.35	11.46	16.16	7.08	8.96	21.44
Netherlands	1961–86	6.71	6.98	7.89	8.96	9.67	12.96
Australia	1961–86	7.86	8.00	5.79	11.02	11.76	13.44

Source: Ibbotson Associates.

The data in Table 1–3 can be readily expanded to show local currency and the U.S. dollar equivalent of the local currency returns for various holding periods. The national equity portfolios with the highest average annual rate of return change from one holding period to the next. Moreover, large differences exist between the local currency returns and their U.S. dollar equivalent because of the change in the price of the U.S. dollar in terms of these foreign currencies.

TABLE 1–3
Summary Statistics of Annual Rate of Return on National Equities: Total Returns in Local Currencies

Country	Period	Compound Annual Return	Arithmetic Mean Return	Standard Deviation of Return
Australia	1969–88	10.46%	13.98%	29.37%
Austria	1969–88	7.08	9.06	24.47
Belgium	1969–88	15.73	17.32	19.56
Canada	1969–88	10.89	12.17	17.13
Denmark	1969–88	15.03	19.91	38.22
France	1969–88	14.16	21.70	44.11
Germany	1969–88	7.93	10.56	25.05
Hong Kong	1970–88	18.30	30.46	55.11
Ireland	1981–88	22.91	27.36	36.37
Italy	1969–88	11.52	17.19	40.06
Japan	1969–88	18.07	20.99	29.35
Malaysia	1981–88	5.32	8.56	28.15
Mexico	1982–88	92.16	129.47	125.30
Netherlands	1969–88	10.98	13.31	23.85
New Zealand	1981–88	16.05	25.03	52.20
Norway	1969–88	13.99	22.21	51.45
Singapore	1970–88	20.20	29.53	53.94
South Africa	1981–88	5.64	9.18	31.42
Spain	1969–88	15.91	19.05	29.22
Sweden	1969–88	15.18	17.93	26.32
Switzerland	1969–88	4.19	6.42	22.28
United Kingdom	1969–88	13.28	18.31	37.86
United States	1969–88	9.52	10.99	17.82

Source: For 1960 through 1980, adapted from data in *Capital International Perspective*, The Capital Group, Geneva, Switzerland, various issues. (Now updated by Morgan Stanley and made available as *Morgan Stanley Capital International Perspective*.) For 1981 through 1988, adapted from data published in connection with the FT-Actuaries World Indices™, which are jointly compiled by The Financial Times Limited, Goldman Sachs & Co., and County NatWest/Wood Mackenzie & Co., Ltd. in conjunction with the Institute of Actuaries and the Faculty of Actuaries.

NATIONAL DIFFERENCES IN EQUITY MARKET VALUES

The market values of equities of firms headquartered in the United States and various other countries are shown in Table 1–4, together with the ratios of market values to national income. The differences in the market values of the equities of firms headquartered in individual countries are striking. The market value of the equities of the firms headquartered in the United States and Japan account for 70 percent of the combined market values. Together the market values of the firms headquartered in the United States, Japan, Great Britain, Canada, Germany, and France account for nearly 90 percent of the combined market values. At the end of 1989, the market value of equities of firms headquartered in Japan was

TABLE 1–4
Market Value and National Income, by Country, 1975–1988 (Market Value and National Income)

	1988 Market Value	1988 National Income	Ratios of Market Values to National Income			
			1975	1980	1985	1988
United States	2,481	4,486	45	47	46	55
Canada	221	390	32	46	40	57
Japan	3,840	1,926	27	34	58	199
Great Britain	718	593	37	40	64	121
Germany	241	88	13	9	24	27
France	229	715	11	9	13	31
Italy	135	597	8	7	13	23
Switzerland	148	138	35	46	78	107
Sweden	89	131	15	11	27	68
Netherlands	88	173	20	16	36	50
Spain	117	188	30	8	10	62
Belgium	58	112	15	10	22	52
Denmark	26	77	8	7	21	34
Norway	17	71	5	5	16	24
Austria	8	91	4	3	5	8
Hong Kong	74	45	115	173	100	164
Singapore/ Malaysia	43	50	34	74	41	34
Australia	134	176	30	41	38	33

Source: International Financial Statistics.

almost as large as the combined market values of firms headquartered in the United States, Great Britain, Canada, and Germany—even though the national income of Japan is 30 percent of the combined national incomes of the United States and these three other countries.

Part of the difference in the market values of firms headquartered in various countries reflects idiosyncratic national differences in economic and financial structure, and part may reflect differences among countries in the rates of return on their equity portfolios. Thus, countries differ in economic size as reflected in their national incomes; other things being equal, the market value of the equities of the countries with larger national incomes should be higher than those of smaller countries. Countries also differ in the scope or extent of the private economic sector; the firms in some industries, such as railroads, electric utilities, and telephone systems, are government owned in France and Italy and in some other countries. The private sector is smaller in these countries, and so the market value of equities is lower.[1] Moreover, the scope of private or family firms relative to publicly owned firms differs by country; German industry is characterized by many family firms, thus the number of publicly traded firms is smaller. And the number and scope of multinational firms headquartered in various countries differ; a relatively large number of multinational firms are headquartered in the Netherlands, Switzerland, and Great Britain, and so the market value of the equities listed on the security exchanges of these countries is higher. In contrast, the market value of firms listed in Canada and Spain and Belgium is lower because a large share of industrial production within these countries is undertaken by foreign-based multinational firms.

While the adjustments for these structural factors might reduce differences among countries in the ratio of market values to national income, large differences in market values by countries would remain. The national income of Japan is twice the national income of Germany, and yet the market value of Japanese firms is 10 to 15 times higher than the market value of German firms. Japanese national income is 50 percent of U.S. national income, yet at the end of 1989 the market value of Japanese equities was 50 percent higher than the market value of U.S. equities—or four times as large per unit of national income. In part, the higher market value of Japanese equities reflects the extensive cross-holdings of shares in individual Japanese firms by other Japanese firms.[2] When an adjustment is made to reduce double-counting, the market valuation of Japanese equities declines by about 35 percent; nevertheless, the investor's return on the portfolio of diversified Japanese equities is not affected significantly, because the scope of cross-holdings has not changed significantly over time.

The excess of the U.S. dollar equivalent of the rates of return on equities of firms headquartered in each of these foreign countries over the rate of return on equities of U.S. firms can be decomposed into three components. One already noted is the change in the price of the U.S. dollar in terms of each of these foreign currencies, which partly—but only partly—reflects national differences in inflation rates; the currency of a country with an inflation rate significantly higher than the U.S. inflation rate is likely to depreciate. The difference between the U.S. dollar rate of return on U.S. equities and the U.S. dollar equivalent of the rate of return on the equities of firms headquartered in each of these foreign countries reflects two factors: one is the difference among countries in the rates of growth of national income, and the second is the difference amoung countries in changes in the ratio of market value of their domestic equities to their national income. Thus, the more rapid the growth rate of a country's economy and its national income, the higher the rate of return on its equities is likely to be. Differences among countries in rates of growth of national income are rarely larger than 2 or 3 percent a year after adjustments for differences in inflation rates.

The change in the valuation of the equities of firms headquartered in individual countries, evident in the changes in the ratio of the market value of equities to national income, is the single most important factor in explaining differences among countries in the rates of return on their equities. And these changes in valuation appear more significant for Japan than for the United States and the five other countries with high national market valuations.

The high rate of return on Japanese equities is the single most important factor in explaining the excess return on the diversified portfolio of international equities. Two questions are raised by the exceptionally high rate of return. The first is whether the rate of return on the diversfied portfolio of international equities in the future will be higher than the rate of return on U.S. equities, because equity prices in some other countries in the 1990s will increase at rates comparable to those of Japan in the 1970s and 1980s. And the second is whether any unique factors associated with the Japanese experience in the 1980s might not be considered representative.

The uniqueness of the Japanese contribution to the rate of return on the diversified international portfolio of equities is the combination of high rate of return on equities and a large country. The rates of return on equities have been high in Hong Kong and Singapore and Ireland, but these countries are small; as a result, the inclusion of equities of firms headquartered in these countries in the portfolio of international equities has a trivial impact on its returns. But because Japan is a large country, the share of Japanese equities in the diversified portfolio of international equities is large—regardless of weights—and hence the inclusion of Japanese equities has had a significant impact on the returns on the portfolio of international equities.

The likelihood that the returns on the Japanese equities in the 1990s could be anywhere near as high as in the 1980s, and espeically in the late 1980s, is extremely low. The increase in the price of Japanese equities in the late 1980s seems inconsistent with the developments in the Japanese economy; some observers have argued that a financial bubble was operating.

The 50-State Equity and Bond Portfolio

Most U.S. investors and virtually all foreign investors who buy U.S. dollar bonds and U.S. equities ignore the states where individual firms are headquartered, produce, and are incorporated. There are a few exceptions; a few investors are concerned about where firms are incorporated, primarily because of state income taxes. And some investors may buy the shares of local banks or other local firms, perhaps because they know the local managers; they want to be able to "kick the tires" on their investments.

Consider the comparison of the risk and return of a portfolio of shares of firms headquartered in each of the 50 U.S. states and the risk and return of the portfolio of firms headquartered in all of these states (the 50-state portfolio), and the risk and return of the U.S. national equity portfolio (or that of any other country) and the risk and return of the diversified international portfolio of equities (the 20-country portfolio). The risk of the 50-state portfolio is lower than the risk of the portfolio of equities of firms headquartered in Alabama or in Wyoming—or in any other state. Moreover, the rate of return on the 50-state equity portfolio would be higher than the rate of return on the equity portfolios of firms headquartered in many individual states; by construction, the rates of return on the equity portfolios of firms headquartered in 25 of the individual states would be above the median average rate of return for the 50-state portfolio.

Similarly, the rates of return on the portfolio of bonds of firms headquartered in each of the 50 states could be compared with the rate of return on the 50-state bond portfolio. The rate of return on the bonds of the 50-state bond portfolio would be higher than the returns on the portfolios of bonds of 25 of the individual states—by construction. And the risk of the 50-state bond portfolio would be lower than the risk of the bond portfolios of each of the 50 states.

The portfolios of bonds and of equities of firms headquartered in each of the 50 states could be ranked by rates of return. The most plausible explanation for differences in the rates of return on the bond portfolios and on the equity portfolios of firms headquartered in each of the 50 states is that the rates of economic growth of individual states differ, perhaps because of the particular demographics of their residents—their age distribution and the rates of growth of their labor forces—or because of differences in the types of goods produced in each state. Firms headquartered in states that were most recently settled may have achieved higher rates of economic growth in recent years than firms headquartered in states settled in earlier years; the populations and the labor forces in the younger states would be increasing more rapidly. Similarly, the number of firms in the younger states would be increasing more rapidly, and the established firms would be growing more rapidly. And the states that produce newer types of industrial products (electronics, jet aircraft, and pharmaceuticals) would be experiencing more rapid growth than the states that produce agricultural products or older industrial products (iron and steel, autos, and machine tools). The implication is that the rates of return on both the bonds and the equities of firms headquartered in the younger states would on average be higher; the rationale is that the investment demand for funds in the younger states would be higher, and so firms headquartered in these states would pay somewhat higher interest rates and dividends to attract funds from investors based in the states experiencing lower rates of economic growth. The rate of return on the portfolio of bonds and of equities of any one state is likely to reflect the rate of growth of the sales and earnings of the firms headquartered in that state; the more rapid the growth of their sales and profits, the higher the rate of return on the portfolio.

The prices of equities of firms headquartered in each of these 50 states—and, hence, the return on the equities of each of these groups of firms—would change in response to news about changing economic conditions in their states, to industry-specific news, and to firm-specific news. Moreover, the prices of the equities of the firms headquartered in virtually every state would change in response to changes in U.S. economic conditions and especially to changes in U.S. monetary policy and the interest rates on U.S. government bonds. Unanticipated news about an increase in the rate of economic growth of a particular firm, industry, or region would be associated with an increase in prices of equities of the firm or firms in the relevant group. An increase in interest rates on U.S. dollar bonds would be associated with a decline in the price of the equities of U.S. firms—and thereafter a higher rate of return on these equities.

The differences among countries in the rates of return and risks of each national equity and bond portfolio are significantly larger than the differences among states in the rates of return and the risks of each state equity and bond portfolio. The 20-country portfolio is similar to the 50-state portfolio in that the returns on the bonds denominated in some currencies and on the equities of firms headquartered in some of these countries might be higher because they are headquartered in countries that are growing more rapidly, because of either more rapid demographic growth or industrial growth. The impacts of more rapid demograpic growth in the gobal context are conceptually identical with the impacts in the 50-state context, although the difference among countries in the rates of economic growth are somewhat larger than the comparable differences among states, partly because the barriers to the movement of factors among countries traditionally have been so much more extensive than the barriers among states.

The major difference between the 50-state portfolio and the 20-country portfolio is associated with the multiplicity of national currencies and, hence, with the implications of changes in the monetary policies in individual countries on both the rate of return and in the price of one national currency in terms of another, on the rates of return to the investor concerned with foreign bonds and with foreign equities. Both the risks and the returns on the portfolios of firms headquartered in particular countries may differ sharply on a year-to-year basis because of the changes in national monetary policies, changes in anticipated inflation rates, and changes in exchange rates.

THE SCOPE OF INTERNATIONAL DIVERSIFICATION

Even though the rate of return on the diversified portfolio of international equities is higher than the rate of return on the portfolio of U.S. equities, the share of foreign equities in portfolios of U.S. investors is small, probably less than 10 percent.[3] Economic intuition suggests that the smaller the scope to diversify among domestic equities, the greater the incentive to buy foreign equities. The share of foreign equities in the portfolios of investors resident in some other countries, such as Canada and Great Britain and the Netherlands, is larger than the share in the portfolios of U.S. investors; still, even then these foreign investors hold a much smaller share of foreign equities in their portfolios than the world index fund would suggest.

In the last several years, U.S. investors have become large buyers of country mutual funds; these funds specialize in holding the equities of firms headquartered in one country or in a geographic region such as Europe or Asia. And there are some global mutual funds. Still, the aggregate value of these funds is less than 1 percent of U.S. equities. And many of the shares of these country mutual funds are held by non-U.S. residents.

Ownership of the equities of U.S. multinational firms for U.S. residents is a modest substitute for the ownership of foreign equities, even though some of these multinational firms extensively participate in foreign economies. To the extent that these firms produce and sell in countries that are experiencing rapid growth, their profits—or this component of their profits—may increase rapidly.

Many factors might explain why investors resident in most countries hold such a small part of their wealth in foreign equities—although this argument seems dubious for residents of most foreign countries. Transactions costs may be higher. Information on foreign equities may be less readily available than information on domestic equities. Concern about unique cross-border risks, especially the risk associated with changes in exchange rates, is extensive.

DEVELOPING AN INTERNATIONAL PORTFOLIO

Once investors accept the proposition that they can achieve a higher rate of return and lower risk on diversified international portfolios of bonds and of equities than on domestic portfolios, the operational problem becomes how to develop or organize the portfolio. Six basic questions must be answered. The first is the weights of bonds or fixed-price assets, real estate, and equities in the international portfolio (the asset allocation decision). The second is the weights of bonds denominated in each currency in the international portfolio, and the third is the weights of equities of firms headquartered in each country in this portfolio; these are the country weight decisions. The fourth is the weight to be given to the individual firms headquartered in each country in the portfolio for all firms headquartered in that country (the firm weight decision). The fifth question is whether the exchange risk associated with the ownership of foreign bonds and foreign equities should be hedged (the foreign exchange exposure decision). The sixth question is whether the portfolio should be actively managed with respect to asset allocation between bonds and equities, the country weights, firm weights, and foreign exchange exposure as new news and insights become available.

The benchmark approach to the development of the portfolio follows the index fund approach; the asset allocation, country weights, and the weights of each individual firm in the portfolio would reflect the national market values. This portfolio would be passively managed; the weights of individual components in the portfolio would be changed only as their shares of total world market value would change. The implication is that the manager should not hedge the foreign exchange exposure associated with ownership of bonds and of equities denominated in a foreign currency.

This benchmark approach still leaves unresolved a number of questions—how would the weight of each country's bonds and equities in the global portfolio be determined? The weights might be economic or financial; economic weights include the national income, exports, and exports of manufacturers, while the financial weights include market value of traded securities. If the market values are used as weights, would short-term money market instruments and demand deposits be included along with corporate bonds?

In part, the answers to these questions depend on the objectives of the managers of the international portfolio. The managers might seek to achieve average performance at lowest possible cost; then they might mimic weights most often used to measure the return on the international portfolio. Or, the managers might seek to enhance the return of their portfolio relative to that of the index fund; return enhancement involves some combination of selective weighting, active management, and active foreign exchange exposure management.

The Asset Allocation Decision

The investor first must choose the weights of bonds, real estate, and equities in the portfolio. For some managers this decision is straightforward since they have chosen to specialize in a bond portfolio or in an equity portfolio. Other managers, however, may have both bonds and equities in their portfolios, just as managers of some domestic portfolios hold both bonds and equities in their portfolios. The managers of these domestic portfolios would alter the bonds and equities in their portfolios as the anticipated return on equities changes relative to the anticipated return on bonds—as the equity risk premium or the *anticipated* equity risk premium changes.

The relationship between the return on bonds and the return on equities by country may differ because of institutional factors, such as tax and a variety of financial regulations. Capital gains income is more heavily taxed in some countries than in others. Interest rates are more extensively regulated in some countries than in others (usually to provide a subsidy to borrowers, including the government). Investors in individual countries differ in their attitude toward risk; if investors in some countries are more risk averse than investors in other countries, then the rate of return on equities in these countries may be exceptionally high relative to the rate of return on bonds. Thus, there may be significant differences amoung countries in the equity risk premium.

The chapter by Gary Brinson and Denis Karnosky groups non-U.S. bonds and non-U.S. equities into individual asset classes. Robert Arnott and Roy Henriksson's chapter considers the global extension of domestic asset allocation procedures. Lee Thomas evaluates a foreign exchange–based strategy as the basis for asset allocation. Eric Sorensen and Joseph Mezrich evaluate one method of developing forecasts useful for this decision. Ed Barksdale and Will Green suggest that a designated asset allocation decision can be implemented by hiring effective managers.

The Optimal Bond Portfolio Decision

The central decision in developing the international bond portfolio is the weights of bonds denominated in each national currency in this portfolio. The basic choice is between economic performance weights and market value weights, which may be different because bond markets, especially for corporate bonds, are not developed in many countries. Moreover, the markets for both government securities and corporate securities lack liquidity, and so the investor must be concerned about the ease with which these bonds might be sold.

Philippe Jorion's chapter considers how bonds denominated in different currencies should be grouped. Gifford Fong and Eric Tang discuss how to establish and measure benchmark portfolios. Chris Orndorff suggests how an actively managed global bond portfolio outperforms a passively managed portfolio. Peter Vann indicates how futures and options contracts can be used to reduce risk for global portfolios.

The Optimal Equity Portfolio Decision

The basic decision is whether the weights of equities of firms headquartered in different countries should reflect some measure of economic performance or market value. The differences in the choice of weights is significant, as indicated by the sharp differences in the ratios of market values to national income by country.

Roger Ibbotson, Larry Siegel, and Paul Kaplan extrapolate from data on performance in national equity markets to suggest future rates of return. Brian Bruce, Heydon Traub, and Larry Martin discuss some of the alternatives to passive equity-weighting strategies. Hans Erickson considers an optimization technique to development of the portfolio. Robert Aliber suggests that portfolios based on economic performance have significantly higher rates of return than those based on market value weights. Gary Bergstrom, Ron Frashure, and John Chisholm evaluate a methodology for selection of equities. Rex Sinquefield considers the potential gains from adding equities of small capitalization firms to the portfolio. Andrew Rudd provides a quantitative approach to the equity markets of the developing countries. Dean LeBaron and Larry Speidell provide a forward-looking universal method of valuing securities in the global portfolio.

The Foreign Exchange Exposure Decision

The unique international aspect of the international bond and equity portfolios is that the value of the currencies of the firms headquartered in various foreign countries may change in terms of the domestic currency, in part because countries follow different monetary policies and have different inflation rates. Differences in the period-to-period returns of foreign components of the global equity portfolio may reflect changes in their own currency price of the national equities. If changes in exchange rates reflected only differences in national inflation rates, then the investor might be able to reduce the risk of the global equity portfolio by fully and continuously hedging the foreign exchange exposure of the foreign bonds and foreign equities in the portfolio; in this way, the 20-country portfolio would become a geographic extension of the 50-state portfolio. There is substantial evidence that changes in exchange rates tend to offset changes in inflation rates in the long run—this, after all, is what purchasing power parity is all about.[4] The implication is that shares of firms headquartered in countries with higher inflation rates might be higher, but the U.S. dollar equivalent would not be higher because of changes in exchange rates. In the short run, however, there are very large deviations from purchasing power parity. And one of the key issues is whether there is a systematic relationship between changes in the local currency value of equities and bonds and changes in the price of the U.S. dollar in terms of these other currencies.

In the long run, interest rates on similar bonds denominated in different currencies tend to correspond to changes in exchange rates. In the short run—periods of three or four years—the difference between changes in exchange rates and interest rate differentials is large on similar securities denominated in different currencies. And even in the long run, the differences in interest rates may not fully reflect the changes in exchange rates—and if so, hedging the foreign exchange exposure incurs a cost.

Alternatively, the investor might not hedge the foreign exchange exposure for one of several reasons—the investor may believe that hedging is too costly, or that changes in exchange rates are more or less reversed in the long run, or that the currency component adds to the rate of return of the global portfolio or reduces the risk.

Fischer Black provides a universal hedging concept. Lee Thomas examines hedging the exposure of foreign equities. David DeRosa describes his currency insurance model, and Remi Browne considers the case for not hedging the foreign exchange exposure.

ENDNOTES

1. The market value of regulated public utilities is 30 percent of the total market value of U.S. firms.
2. Perhaps two thirds of the outstanding shares of the typical Japanese firm is held by other Japanese firms, usually by firms in the same Keiretsu. Each firm in a Keiretsu holds shares in many other firms in the same Keiretsu. So each Japanese firm is partly a producer, and partly a mutual fund.
3. For estimates of the holdings of foreign equities of U.S. residents and of residents of 13 other countries, see Ian Cooper and Evi Kaplanis, ''Costs to

Crossborder Investment and International Equity Market Equilibrium,'' in *Recent Developments in Corporate Finance*, eds. Jeremy Edwards, Julian Franks, Colin Mayer, and Stephen Schaefer (London: Cambridge University Press, 1986).

4. Purchasing power parity states that changes in exchange rates are proportional to changes in inflation rate differentials.

PART 1

ASSET ALLOCATION

CHAPTER 2

GLOBAL ASSET ALLOCATION POLICY

Gary P. Brinson
Denis S. Karnosky

Over the 20 years from 1969 to 1989, the dollar value of global equity and fixed-income securities available to U.S. investors increased tenfold to more than $22 trillion. This increase can be seen in Figure 2–1. Much of the expansion occurred outside the United States, as its portion of the global securities market decreased from 68 percent to 46 percent over the period. As these external markets have expanded, they have also become more accessible, implying that the market portfolio is becoming increasingly global. Thus, portfolios that are not managed within a global asset allocation policy framework are becoming increasingly inefficient, within the context of reducing nonsystematic risk.

One incentive for U.S. investors to add or expand holdings of international securities has been the historically attractive dollar returns that these assets have generated, often surpassing the performance of U.S. assets. The gap was dramatic in the last half of the 1980s, aided by a persistent and rapid depreciation in the value of the dollar in foreign exchange markets from early in 1985 through 1987. The Morgan Stanley Capital International (MSCI) non-U.S. equity index, for example, exceeded the performance of the broad U.S. equity market by almost 1,600 basis points annually from 1984 to 1989. Nondollar bonds outperformed the U.S. bond market by more than 700 basis points per year over the same period.

This performance added materially to the returns of U.S. portfolios that had exposure to international securities. Based on these index returns

FIGURE 2-1
Global Securities Market

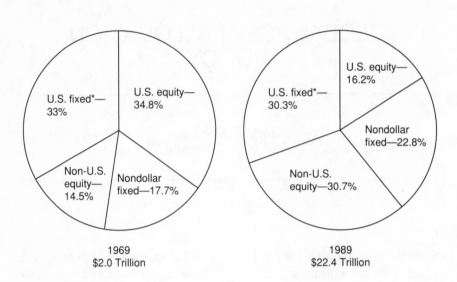

1969
$2.0 Trillion

1989
$22.4 Trillion

*Includes U.S. bonds, international dollar bonds, and cash equivalents.

only, for example, reallocation of 10 percent of a portfolio from U.S. to non-U.S. equities over this period would have been worth an extra 160 basis points per year to the performance of the total portfolio. Shifting an additional 5 percent from dollar to nondollar bonds in 1984 was worth an additional 35 basis points. That is almost 200 basis points of extra return from a modest shift of 15 percent of the portfolio into international assets.

While these extraordinary returns probably accelerated the movement toward global portfolios, they also have changed the fundamental relationships among global assets. In particular, this episode encourages an inconsistent treatment of U.S. versus non-U.S. assets in setting global asset allocation policy.

It is conventional practice to treat the assets of non-U.S. countries as aggregate international indices, with country weights that reflect relative market capitalizations. However, when these indices are inserted into a U.S. portfolio, the normal weights assigned to the associated U.S. assets are typically larger than their global capitalization size. That is, one portion (non-U.S.) of the portfolio is capitalization-weighted while the other (U.S.)

is not. This treatment can easily result in an inefficient portfolio. There are two facets of the problem:

1. The normal allocation to U.S. assets, especially equities, is often much larger than their market capitalization. Yet capitalization weights are assigned to the countries within the non-U.S. component.
2. Alternatively, and more important, the index weights within the non-U.S. component of global portfolios are suboptimal, given the normal weights that are typically assigned to U.S. securities.

Simply stated, if the normal weights of U.S. securities do not reflect their relative capitalizations, it is inconsistent to assign normal weights to non-U.S. securities that are proportional to their relative capitalizations.

The purpose of our discussion is to demonstrate that this inconsistent treatment leads to suboptimal global allocation policies. The focus is on global assets in a portfolio context, examining how their interactions affect total long-term performance. This is the most fundamental of portfolio management issues, the policy decisions that dictate which global assets to include in the normal portfolio and their normal weights. The policy decision sets the standard, defining the expected secular performance of the portfolio in terms of return and risk.

SETTING ALLOCATION POLICY

The three general approaches to formulating global asset allocation policy involve different views on the relationships between U.S. and other assets:

Global indices. The normal (or policy) weights for each country, *including the United States*, reflect some uniform standard such as market capitalization, relative size of the economies, or even equal proportions. All markets—domestic and foreign—are subject to the same criteria. This approach is completely passive, making no effort to account explicitly for the portfolio implications of the interaction among the assets of the various countries.

Partial optimization. Non-U.S. assets are pre-aggregated according to some standard, and global allocation policy is set for U.S.

assets relative to this index of international assets. This ethnocentric approach is less passive, allowing for the performance of U.S. assets relative to a *group* of foreign assets. However, the interactions among the individual components of the foreign group are ignored.

Full optimization. Each country, domestic and foreign, is treated as a distinct asset class, and policy weights reflect the perceived contribution of each country's asset to the performance of the total portfolio.

The nature of these alternative approaches is illustrated in Figures 2–2 and 2–3, which show efficient frontiers for global equities and bonds based on historical dollar returns, volatilities, and correlations. Throughout this discussion, the analysis is focused on global equities and bonds as separate portfolios, rather than a comprehensive portfolio of stocks and bonds.

Our intent is to highlight the effects of alternative allocation methods, and this is best accomplished by restricting the scope of the presenta-

FIGURE 2–2
Global Equities

(Historical Data 1969.4–1989.4)

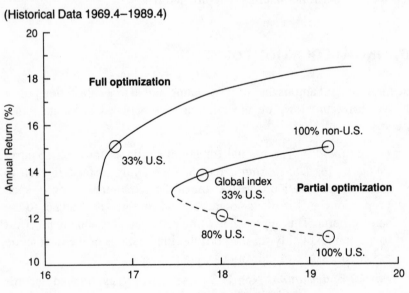

Annualized Standard Deviation (%)

FIGURE 2–3
Global Bonds

(Historical Data 1974.4–1989.4)

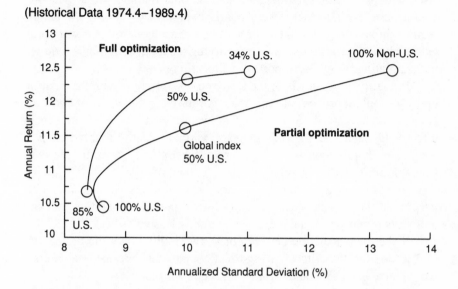

tion. The conclusions, which are derived for these narrow portfolios, apply even more critically in the construction of normal weights for the total portfolio.

The equity data are based on quarterly returns for the period from December 31, 1969, to December 31, 1989. The sample of global bond data is smaller, with an array of individual country data available on a quarterly basis only since December 31, 1974. The Wilshire 5000 index is used to measure the performance of the broad U.S. equity market, the MSCI non-U.S. equity index is used to measure non-U.S. equities, the Salomon Broad Investment Grade bond index represents U.S. bonds, and the Salomon nondollar government bond index is used to measure non-U.S. bonds.

The historical record is applied ex post only for illustration and does not reflect our views of the global relationships that are appropriate for evaluating global equity policy on an ex ante basis. In considering asset allocation policy, our perspective is secular and forward looking.

The focus is on isolating the fundamental relationships among the various classes of assets, which can then provide a basis for adopting consistent forecasts of basic market characteristics. History is an important guide, but care must be taken to evaluate the data within the specific environment in which it was generated. Global markets are a dynamic, simultaneous system that is very poorly explained by adding the simple relationships between each pair of variables. Extrapolation of history is an extremely dangerous method for identifying the long-term trends required in formulating basic global portfolio allocations.

In Figures 2–2 and 2–3, the lower curve is derived with the "partial optimization" approach, plotting the risk/return combinations of two variables: U.S. and non-U.S. indices. The weight of the U.S. component is effectively treated as the only decision variable, as the relative country weights *within* the non-U.S. segment are set passively according to market capitalizations.

In Figure 2–2, the index of non-U.S. equities significantly outperformed the U.S. index over the historical period, generating an extra 380 basis points of annual return with slightly less volatility.

Since the correlation between these two indices over the period was only 0.66, the benefits of diversification into the international market would have been substantial for a U.S. equity investor.

These partial optimization curves illustrate both the superficial attractiveness and the danger of treating U.S. and non-U.S. assets differently in the normal portfolio. Based solely on historical performance, for example, global equity portfolios that consist of more than 50 percent U.S. equities fall on the dashed portion of the curve and would obviously be inefficient. Over that range, expected long-term returns could be enhanced, and volatility reduced, by increasing the normal exposure to international equities. This suggests that while a small allocation to a market-cap weighted index of international stocks would enhance the long-term performance of an equity portfolio for a U.S. investor, only a portion of the potential benefit would be captured.

These results suggest that if the individual countries within the non-U.S. portion of the normal portfolio are allocated on an index-weight basis, the U.S. market should be treated similarly.

At the end of 1989, for example, U.S. equities had a market-cap weight of approximately one third in the MSCI world equity index. As indicated in Figure 2–2, this allocation lies on the efficient portion of the partial optimization curve. At that point, all country weights are equal to market capitalizations, that is, this is the "global index."

Similar results are shown for global bonds in Figure 2–3. Based on historical performance, allocations to U.S. bonds of more than 85 percent of a global bond portfolio are inefficient under the partial optimization approach. The market capitalization of U.S. bonds in the global market was close to 50 percent at the end of 1989. As was true with global equities, the "global index" for bonds is also on the efficient frontier under the partial optimization. The historical record, at least, suggests that U.S. investors committed to using index weights to allocate among non-U.S. assets should be prepared to give similar treatment to their U.S. assets.

There is more to consider, however. Specifically, the appropriateness of using market capitalization weights is questionable in setting global asset allocation policy. First, pre-aggregation of non-U.S. assets into indices presumes there is no useful information about the nature of the fundamental relationships among the individual global markets. More important, it requires considerable confidence that markets are fully integrated on a worldwide basis, with no restrictions on cross-border investing between any countries. While capital mobility has certainly increased, markets remain materially segmented. Normal market pressures and governmental initiatives, like Europe 1992, are weakening these barriers, but segmentation remains, based on official guidelines and de facto practice within many countries. Thus, the capitalization-weighted array of global assets is an imperfect representation of "the market" for investors in any particular country.

There are now over 20 years of monthly performance data for a large segment of international equity markets and more than 15 years of comparable data for a smaller sample of nondollar bonds. Together with a large base of international economic data, these performance data provides a wealth of information for serious global investors. A look at the historical record indicates, in fact, that failure to understand the nature of the global interrelationships severely hinders long-term global investment results.

The full optimization curves in Figures 2–2 and 2–3 treat each country within the respective non-U.S. equity and bond indices as a separate asset class, in addition to the United States. Full use is made of individual country performances and the correlations among the countries in setting portfolio weights. For the sake of illustration, the figures plot constrained optimizations, where the maximum weight for Japan is set at 150 percent of its respective index weights, and the weights for all other countries are restricted to no more than double their relative market capitalizations as of December 1989. The unconstrained frontiers for both global equity and bonds are significantly higher but involve ranges of country allocations that a typical investor would probably reject as "unreasonable." Minimum weights of zero were allowed for all countries.

For both global equities and bonds, the disaggregated treatment of non-U.S. markets results in efficient portfolios that dominate those derived using aggregated indices of non-U.S. equities based on capitalization size. In both figures, the optimal portfolio that has a U.S. weight equal to its global market weight, approximately 33 percent for global equities and 50 percent for global bonds, is indicated.

In the case of equities, this portfolio shows an annual return that is 150 basis points higher than the global index, with an annual volatility more than a full percent less. In global bonds, the volatility of an optimized portfolio that has 50 percent U.S. bonds is equal to that of the global bond index, but it has a return about 100 basis points higher.

The difference between these portfolios and their respective global indices is in the distribution of weights among the non-U.S. markets. The U.S. weights are the same. In the case of global equities with a U.S. weight of 33 percent, for example, Japanese equities would account for 30 percent of the disaggregated portfolio, compared to a market weight of 40 percent. The optimal weight for Canada would be 8.5 percent, compared to an index weight of less than 3 percent. The rest of the portfolio would be held in a variety of continental European equities. However, the mix within Europe bears little resemblance to the relative index weights.

This historical exercise raises several interesting considerations. First, all three approaches for setting asset allocation policy indicate that the potential benefits of diversification into foreign assets are substantial. From our perspective, two results are particularly interesting. First, the approach of treating non-U.S. equities as a capitalization-weighted index indicated that the appropriate weight for the United States in a global equity portfolio would also be close to its global cap weight. This suggests that those investors who use index weights in setting asset allocation policy for international (i.e., non-U.S.) portfolios should also adopt a market weight for the United States in global portfolios.

However, reliance on capitalization-weighted indices to evaluate non-U.S. assets seems very inefficient in terms of the potential gain in long-term performance that might be achieved through treating these markets as distinct and separate asset classes. In other words, for any given level of risk tolerance, restricting international exposure arbitrarily to reflect index weights could involve considerable sacrifice of long-term investment performance.

While the historical record offers some provocative challenges, it does not offer practical solutions. The issue is whether the equilibrium relationships that underlie the historical record can be adequately identified. This involves filtering the available record to isolate the effects of such factors as the rise and fall of OPEC and the diversity of inflation experience, risk tolerance, market integration, economic productivity, and capital formation within the macro-consistent global economy.

To reduce the impact of a specific historical episode on this analysis, we have developed risk premiums for the individual country equity and bond markets, which are based on more fundamental relationships. The associated variance/covariance matrix was also specified. While these estimates of equilibrium performance characteristics are subject to further refinement, they have proven to provide practical insights for evaluating the range of interactions among the global markets. These long-term estimates for global equities and bonds are presented in Table 2–1 for the major global markets. These long-term performance characteristics were

TABLE 2–1
Adjusted Performance Characteristics

	Risk Premium	Risk	Correlations					
			1	2	3	4	5	6
A. Global equities								
1. Canada	5.1%	18.5%	1.00					
2. Germany	5.4	19.5	.30	1.00				
3. Japan	4.6	20.0	.30	.35	1.00			
4. United Kingdom	5.6	21.0	.50	.40	.30	1.00		
5. Other non-U.S.*	5.8	18.5	.60	.80	.70	.70	1.00	
6. United States	5.6	17.0	.80	.40	.30	.60	.70	1.00
B. Global bonds								
1. Australia	2.4%	15.0%	1.00					
2. Canada	2.6	14.0	.35	1.00				
3. Continental	1.6	14.8	.35	.25	1.00			
4. Japan	1.2	16.0	.45	.35	.80	1.00		
5. United Kingdom	2.6	18.0	.45	.35	.60	.55	1.00	
6. United States	1.9	8.0	.35	.85	.40	.35	.30	1.00

*Equally weighted.

FIGURE 2–4
Global Equities

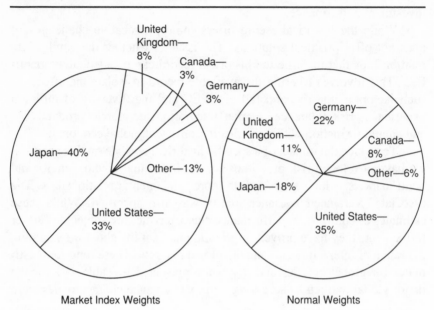

Market Index Weights   Normal Weights

used to derive normal asset allocations for global equity and bond portfolios that imply risk tolerance levels in line with those of the respective
global indices. The results are presented in Figures 2–4 and 2–5.

Notice that for both optimal portfolios the weight for the United
States is relatively close to the current index weight. The weights of the
other countries change considerably from their relative market capitalizations, however. In both cases, the normal weight for Japanese securities is
significantly smaller than the index weight. These differences reflect the
abnormally and unsustainably strong performance of the Japanese markets
in the 1980s, which greatly increased the Japanese weight in both the
global equity and bond indices. Our inputs are reflective of the *sustainable*
potential of the Japanese markets and, thus, include relatively low risk
premiums that these markets offer to non-Japanese investors.

Japanese investors apparently have been content to build wealth on
expectations of persistent capital appreciation independent of earnings
potential and, thus, offer other investors an inferior compensation for risk.

FIGURE 2–5
Global Bonds

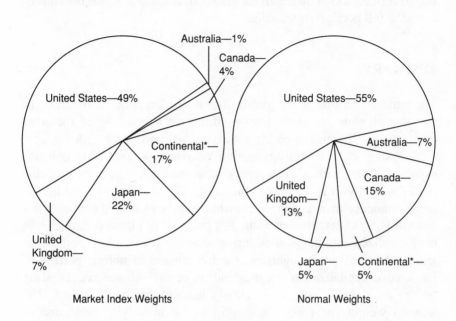

*Continental includes Germany, the Netherlands, France, Switzerland, and Denmark.

The German markets, on the other hand, consistently generate performance that implies high domestic risk premiums relative to other countries. That disparity continues to exist, offering a relative premium to non-German investors. The collapse of communist rule in Eastern Europe and increased ties between East and West Germany have provided an additional reason to expect relatively high risk premiums for German markets. The result is that the implied normal exposure to both German equity and bonds is greater than current index weights.

Notice also that the normal weights for both Canadian equity and bonds are substantially larger than the respective index weights, despite the relatively high correlations with the United States. The key considerations leading to these results are the structure of correlations among all the countries, not just between any one country and the United States.

Those U.S. investors who seek international exposure but dismiss Canadian securities as being too closely tied to the United States are making the mistake of not taking an integrated view of markets and not considering the full portfolio interactions.

SUMMARY

The critical factor in setting global asset allocation policy is the recognition that all elements in the total portfolio are affected by all the other components. The aim of building a diversified portfolio is risk management, using the relationships among various asset classes to enhance expected returns without sacrificing control over risk. The move to global portfolios is a shift in that direction, recognizing that international investments cannot be managed in isolation but must be evaluated explicitly relative to U.S. assets. However, the full potential of global portfolios will not be realized until the relationships among the asset markets of the individual countries are brought into the formulation of normal portfolios. Reliance on capitalization-weighted indices of international assets that are treated as a single asset class clearly hinders this development. The implied weights bear no relationship to the underlying relationships among the markets.

The practice of almost all U.S.-based investors is to set a level of normal exposure to U.S. markets that is significantly higher than the global market-cap weights for the United States. If these U.S. weights are deemed optimal, then assigning all non-U.S. weights according to their market capitalizations leads to suboptimal normal portfolios.

In the future, global portfolio management and asset allocation will move toward treating each major market in the world as a distinct asset class just as we do now for the United States. The notion of bringing together all non-U.S. equities into one "asset class" and all non-U.S. bonds into another "asset class" will become increasingly unpopular as the inefficiency of this superaggregation becomes better known and experience falls short of expectations.

CHAPTER 3

A DISCIPLINED APPROACH TO GLOBAL ASSET ALLOCATION[1]

Robert D. Arnott
Roy D. Henriksson

Does a disciplined approach to active asset allocation lend itself to export? Can the methods developed for the allocation of U.S. assets be applied in overseas markets? Yes. Our preliminary empirical results suggest that the same tools that have proved to be so profitable in the United States have value in the international arena.

The development of a global strategy for tactical asset allocation is a challenging task, if only because the most profitable strategy is to focus on the least comfortable asset class. With an objective measure of prospective market returns, one can determine the relative market outlook for various asset classes, and that outlook can provide valuable guidance on asset allocation. The markets provide objective measure of these returns. We *know* the yield for cash equivalents. We *know* yield-to-maturity for bonds. We can estimate the approximate earnings yield or dividend discount model return for equities. These measures have been used with great success to profit from the relative performance of stocks, bonds, and cash in the United States.[2] The use of a disciplined approach for including other information, such as recent inflation or the economic environment, may provide additional insight into the return prospects for each asset class.[3]

This chapter is an adaption of Robert D. Arnott and Roy D. Henriksson, "A Disciplined Approach to Global Asset Allocation," *Financial Analysts Journal*, March/April 1989. Copyright 1989 by the Financial Analysts Federation.

Past efforts to "globalize" the asset allocation decision have fallen prey to several kinds of error. One common misconception about global markets is that something is fundamentally "wrong" when one market trades at several times the price/earnings ratio of another. Such differences cannot be attributed merely to differences in accounting. Even after these are factored out, the residual differences in the ratio can still be very large. Nevertheless, there is nothing in investment theory to suggest that price/earnings differences between markets represent disequilibrium opportunities. Such differences are no more symptomatic of disequilibrium than are differences in bond yields.

This observation leads to a rather simple conclusion for evaluating equity markets in global asset allocation: The appropriate comparison is not between the earnings yields in one country and their counterpart in another. Rather, one should compare the earnings yield (or some other equity return measure) in one country with the cash or bond yields in the same country, thereby providing a measure of the equity risk premium in that country. These equity risk premiums can then be readily compared across national boundaries.

Such comparisons can provide direct and objective measures of relative opportunities both within and between countries. There is no reason that the equity risk premiums should be the same across countries. The economic risks of each country may be different. However, changes in the relative risk premium between two equity markets can provide a measure of changes in relative valuation and potentially of changes in the relative attractiveness of the two markets. In so doing, these risk premium changes can suggest abnormal relative opportunities within a country and can provide a framework for asset allocation with a truly global perspective. In essence, such a framework would enable comparisons among Japanese stocks, German bonds, and U.S. cash.

WHAT ARE GLOBAL MANAGERS DOING WRONG?

Global markets have been wonderful to U.S. investors. Morgan Stanley Capital International's Europe Asia Far East (EAFE) Index returns for the five years ended June 1989 were 33.4 percent on an annual basis. Over the same period, returns for U.S. stocks and 20-year Treasury bonds have been 20.1 percent and 18.1 percent, respectively.

So, what's the problem? Just this: global managers have routinely underperformed this simple passive index by margins that are truly vast. A recent report by Intersec showed that, despite strong results in the opening months of 1989, the median international manager tracked by Intersec underperformed this passive index by nearly 6 percent per annum for the five years ended June 1989! Even more startling, it found that not a single active manager that it tracks was able to outpace the index in the three years ended 1988. Frank Russell of Tacoma, Washington, and WM Company of Edinburgh, Scotland, independently did studies on the attribution of this underperformance. The finding was that the common scapegoat, an underweight stance in Japan, was *significantly less than* half of this underperformance. It was *primarily* driven by generally dismal issue selection, particularly *outside* the "home market" of the manager.

The major institutional investors of the United States have wisely captured 1,300 basis points of excess return by diversifying overseas and have forfeited half of this gain due to dismal manager results. So, what good have they achieved? With the typical non-U.S. allocation of perhaps 5 percent of plan assets, aggregate plan assets were boosted by 35 percent in just five years. *But the benefit should have been twice this figure!*

An Array of Errors

This vast shortfall cannot be attributed to a single error. Obviously, so large a shortfall must be attributable to many sources.

Global Comparisons in Domestic Markets
Twenty years from now, global investors may drive each of the major markets around the world. Today this does not hold true. Global comparisons are routinely made by global managers. Ironically, these managers seem blind to the self-evident fact that domestic investors will dominate in any market. Their buying or selling will happen (and has happened) almost independently of value comparisons with other world markets. This was the principle source for the spectacular Japanese bull market of the 1980s. We have heard some investors glibly dismiss the domestic comparisons issue as insignificant. This could not be further from the truth. Global investors are ironically blinded by their very global perspectives, because they typically ignore the domestic comparisons that dominate short-term market movements.

Subjective Judgment

In the domestic arena, quantitative practitioners have become important players in the marketplace. This is not yet true in the global arena. Virtually all global managers rely heavily on subjective judgment. Subjective judgment carries with it the excess baggage of emotion. Emotion will always encourage us toward comfortable investment. *But the capital markets do not reward comfort.* Among those who rely on subjective decisions, only those who can set aside emotion can add value relative to a passive portfolio. In short, the heavy reliance on subjectivity virtually guarantees an unsuccessful and unprofitable investment process.

Reckless Conservatism

We are indebted to Evan Schulman for this wonderful oxymoron. If an investment manager incurs a greater cost in the quest for safety than a client would ever have tolerated, that manager is guilty of reckless conservatism. Most global managers diversify in a multitude of markets worldwide. This is done despite the fact that selecting a handful of attractive markets would typically achieve virtually the same risk reduction.

Broad market diversification introduces another problem. If we want to hold 60 stocks, and we want to invest in 20 markets, then we will hold an average of 3 stocks in each market. Which stocks will we hold? The temptation is to hold the bluest of the blue chips, the recognized names, the largest and most comfortable companies. We know that these companies dramatically underperform broader indexes in the United States over the long haul. The same seems to hold true in every market around the world.

Naïveté about Currency

Suppose an investment in an overseas market rises 50 percent due to a plunging dollar or a rising foreign currency. The temptation is to "take our gains." But this rise in the foreign currency does *nothing* to change the fundamental underpinnings of value. The book value, the dividend yield, the earnings, and other measures of financial strength all rise by a like amount. In short, the market has not become one iota more expensive! The global investor will often see the relative performance and be tempted to sell, while domestic investors patiently wait for a valuation rise, rather than a currency rise, to sell.

Lessons to Be Learned

Global investments, intelligently managed, offer extraordinary opportunity. But, "those who fail to learn from the errors of the past are doomed to repeat them." An intelligent global process will focus in large measure on domestic comparisons. The plunge in cash earnings yield (the reciprocal of the price/cash earnings ratio) in Japan during the 1980s has been paralleled by an almost identical plunge in bond and cash yields. In other words, the Japanese market was *not* expensive relative to domestic alternatives. Arguably, it might be today, due to higher interest rates.

Focus on Domestic Comparisons
If we focus on domestic comparisons, then the most attractive market is the one that today offers the highest risk premium relative to *its own normal risk premium*. This can be directly and objectively measured. And, the answers can often be surprising and counterintuitive to those trapped by conventional global comparisons. Global differences in simple value measures (e.g., dividend yields or price/earnings ratios) are often deceptive. Differences in profit margins, accounting standards, real growth rates, competitive positioning in world markets, and other factors can *justly* lead to valuation differences that are *truly vast*. These simple comparisons are seductive but wrong.

Make No Bets Wherever We Have No Skill
Subjective judgment should be applied where *and only where* it may be expected to add value. Subjective judgment *may* have a role to play, but most assuredly *not* if it is used to encourage the comfortable and unprofitable investment. Discipline should be used, *without judgmental overrides,* in any area where our subjective judgment leads us astray. In other words, in areas where we have no skill, we should make no bets.

Make Bets Wherever We Do Have Skill
We should guard against reckless conservatism. Efforts to reduce risk through diversification and through prudent issue selection are usually appropriate. Such efforts should never be pursued to a point where it is likely to cost more than the client will tolerate. The best example of this is found is issue selection. Most global investors are demonstrably disastrous at choosing individual issues outside of their home market. A WM

Company study suggested underperformance outside of the home market of 3 percent to 6 percent *per annum!* If that is the cost of "safety," why not index within the foreign markets? It is less risky, by any objective standard, and assures an "alpha" of zero, which is far better than most global managers do.

Understand the Impact of Currency

Measure valuation relative to fundamental underpinnings of value. Don't mistake a currency gain for a valuation gain.

Obviously, many of the problems in global management are "fixable." Only the client community (the sponsor community) can demand that their global managers manage more intelligently. If vast underperformance is tolerated year after year after year, then something is very wrong.

FUNDAMENTALS OF ASSET ALLOCATION

Pricing in any market reflects the collective judgments of all the participants in that market. By basing a measure of future asset class returns on current indications of relative opportunity, one capitalizes on this information. The assumption underlying such a model is that financial markets demand differential return premiums on different asset classes.

The sophisticated investor must continually ask a critical asset allocation question: In the prevailing market environment, which assets merit emphasis? The natural tendency is to choose the comfortable answer, the answer that minimizes anxiety. The comfortable answer, however, is rarely the profitable answer. Few managers were aggressively cutting U.S. equity holdings in early 1973 or mid-1987. Few managers were doing the opposite in late 1974 or mid-1982. While these may not have been comfortable strategies, they certainly would have been profitable.

A discipline for asset allocation can provide a reasoned basis from which to confidently resist the comfortable answers when pursuit of a contrarian strategy would be most rewarding. This chapter describes such a discipline. In essence, it allows the market to indicate what future returns will be. The asset allocation decision can then be based, as it should be, primarily on the relative attractiveness of returns from the various asset classes. The allocations will change only with changing prospects for the relative return of the assets.

UNLOCKING MARKET OUTLOOK

This disciplined approach to asset allocation rests on four assumptions.

1. Prospective long-term returns for various asset classes are directly observable in the markets. We know the yield on cash; we know the yield-to-maturity on long bonds; and the capital markets provide some crude but objective measures of long-term prospects on equities, in the form of earnings yield, dividend yield, or consensus-based dividend discount models.
2. These returns reflect the consensus view of all market participants on the relative attractiveness of asset classes. For example, if calculated equity returns are high relative to bond returns, then the market is implicitly demanding a substantial equity risk premium. Such a premium suggests that investors are uneasy about equities.
3. These relative returns tend to exhibit a normal or "equilibrium" level.
4. As future returns stray from this normal equilibrium, when measured against investment alternatives, market forces pull them back into line. Such adjustments create an asset allocation profit mechanism.

Even if one disregards the third and fourth assumptions and assumes no equilibrating mechanism in the markets, an objective approach to asset allocation can still work. If long-term equity return prospects rise by 100 basis points relative to other asset classes, the investor will expect to earn 100 basis points of excess return per year, even if there is no tendency to return to equilibrium. On the other hand, this equilibrating mechanism has been the source of impressive profits achieved by many tactical asset allocation practitioners.

For example, suppose the equity risk premium is 100 basis points too high relative to long bonds. Then, either long-bond yields should rise 100 basis points or stock earnings yield should fall 100 basis points to restore equilibrium. These adjustments require a price move in either stocks or bonds amounting to *many times* the 100-basis-point disequilibrium. While this equilibrating mechanism is not essential for successful active asset allocation, it plays a key role in providing the substantial profits that such strategies have delivered.

WHY DO CONVENTIONAL GLOBAL
COMPARISONS FAIL?

As we noted earlier, one of the most obvious errors in global asset allocation is that measures of value, such as dividend yields or price/earnings
ratios, can be fairly compared across national boundaries. Such comparisons are the equivalent of blindly comparing yield differentials between
countries for bonds or cash! Hence, it may be useful to analyze why such
comparisons fail in the bond markets to understand why they also fail for
equity valuations.

Differences in bond yield are explained by equilibrium theory by cit-
ing long-term inflation rate differences and currency shifts. If 10-year
government bonds yield 10 percent in one country and only 5 percent in
another country, there can still be yield parity if the currency in the high-
yield country erodes 5 percent per year vis-à-vis the currency in the low-
yield country. Such a differential would result in a 40 percent currency
depreciation over the course of a decade. Currency moves of this magnitude are so commonplace as to be routine. No serious economist would
suggest that international interest rate differences run contrary to equilibrium theory.

The same point holds for rates of return in the dividend discount
model. If the dividend discount model rate of return is 15 percent for one
country and 10 percent for another, this difference in *nominal* returns can
be fully justified by the long-term expectation of a 5 percent annual currency divergence. The investor from the low-return country seeking to
capture the superior performance offered by the high-return country
would expect to forfeit the differential performance through currency
depreciation. Similarly, if the investor were to seek protection against this
currency erosion by hedging in the foreign exchange markets, the foreign
exchange forward markets would be priced to take away much, if not all,
of the differential rate of return.

Price/earnings ratios historically have tended to be rather closely correlated with dividend discount model rates of return. Hence, the same
argument can be applied to price/earnings comparisons. If $100 buys $5
per year of earnings in one country and $10 per year of earnings in
another, nothing in equilibrium theory suggests that this price/earnings
difference should be inappropriate. Suppose the currency of the high-
price/earnings country appreciates relative to the currency of the low-
price/earnings country. Then the book value, the sales, and the currency-

adjusted earnings of companies in the low-price/earnings country would all diminish when measured in the currency of the high-price/earnings country.

For price/earnings ratios, several factors other than currency risk cloud the comparison of one country with another:

- Accounting principles differ across countries.
- Growth opportunities differ across countries.
- Different countries face different economic risks.
- Differences in political environments will influence investors' perceptions of future cash flows.

All of these considerations, and lesser ones, could justify substantive differences in earnings yields, *even in the absence of currency considerations.*

In general, there is no theoretical support for the common argument suggesting that countries with low price/earnings ratios, low price/cash flow ratios, or low price/book value ratios are inherently more attractive investment opportunities than their high multiple counterparts. The appropriate comparison will be much more complex, so many factors will impact the equilibrium relations of prices and earnings.

RETURNS AND P/E RATIOS

It is true, however, that the empirical evidence shows a weak tendency for countries with low price/earnings ratios to offer higher return prospects than countries with high ratios. There is nothing wrong with this. However, in addition to currency and interest rate considerations, differences in price/earnings ratios can also result from greater growth prospects or higher risks for one country than the other. Differences in equilibrium expected returns, in the absence of market barriers, should result from differences in risks. A riskier market will require a higher expected return, which will be accompanied by a lower price/earnings ratio.

Because P/E ratios should differ across countries, the best way to compare equity markets in different countries is to measure the equity risk premium in each country. The equity risk premiums in different countries can then be compared. Regardless of any price/earnings ratio differences, if the *equity risk premium* in one country is higher than in another, we might argue that the higher risk premium implies a better investment opportunity. Even here, however, there is a potential pitfall. In one country, the *equilibrium* relation between earnings yield and bond or cash yields (hence the normal equity risk premium) might be higher or lower than it is in another country. Thus, since different growth rates, accounting standards, or political and economic climates can justify different price/earnings ratios, even these equity risk premiums cannot be directly compared with one another.

This observation leads to the final step in the comparative analysis. If the equity risk premium is measured in any one country and compared with the "normal" equity risk premium for that country, an *abnormal equity risk premium* can be determined. This abnormal equity risk premium is an indication of how far the equity markets of a given country have strayed from equilibrium, either above or below the normal reward opportunities. The abnormal risk premiums *can* be directly compared across country boundaries.

GLOBAL ASSET ALLOCATION VERSUS CURRENCY SELECTION: TWO SEPARATE DECISIONS

The kind of framework we have described makes no naive assumptions about the normal relations between price/earnings ratios across national boundaries, and it makes no assumptions inconsistent with equilibrium theory. The important thing is such a framework separates the currency forecast from the forecast for asset class returns. In so doing, the investor is presented with an array of fully hedged investment alternatives. Forecasts of hedged asset class returns can be developed directly from measurement of risk premiums. These can then be supplemented with independent forecasts of currency returns.

Distinguishing asset class expectations from currency expectations is important because it achieves two often contradictory objectives: it broadens the set of investment alternatives, and it simplifies the evaluation of those alternatives at the same time. If asset class decisions are made based on fully hedged (local currency) return expectations, the resulting structure gives approximate equivalency among cash equivalents around the globe, since the forward markets are largely driven by this arbitrage. This is graphically illustrated in Figure 3–1.

FIGURE 3–1
Return Expectations

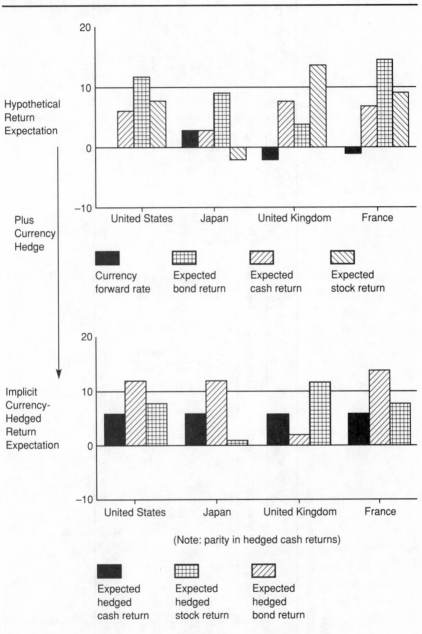

(Note: parity in hedged cash returns)

TABLE 3–1
Total Return of International Equities

	1-Year*		3-Year		5-Year		10-Year	
	Unhedged	Hedged	Unhedged	Hedged	Unhedged	Hedged	Unhedged	Hedged
France	32.9%	13.5%	51.9%	33.3%	40.6%	33.4%	24.4%	20.3%
Germany	16.6	–1.1	46.5	30.7	35.4	31.4	18.3	19.2
Italy	22.4	na	68.3	na	43.0	na	27.6	na
Japan	76.3	59.5	64.2	42.7	48.6	36.5	29.2	24.9
United Kingdom	52.4	40.5	46.2	34.8	32.6	32.9	24.3	23.4
United States	23.8	23.8	30.3	30.3	27.2	27.2	16.2	16.2
World	43.4	35.0	42.2	34.0	34.1	31.1	20.5	19.9

Note: na = Not available.
* All periods ending 6/87; data from Frank Russell International.

TABLE 3–2
Volatility of International Equities

	3-Year*		5-Year		10-Year	
	Unhedged	Hedged	Unhedged	Hedged	Unhedged	Hedged
France	30.2%	24.8%	24.9%	20.6%	28.1%	21.9%
Germany	24.9	20.5	22.7	18.2	21.7	15.7
Italy	41.4	35.7	37.8	32.6	36.4	33.4
Japan	23.9	15.3	26.5	16.2	24.2	15.0
United Kingdom	21.0	15.8	20.8	15.0	21.7	16.4
United States	15.6	15.6	15.3	15.3	14.8	14.8
World	13.2	10.9	13.9	11.3	14.7	11.8

*All periods ending 6/87; data from Frank Russell International.

This structure leads to direct comparability of the asset classes and to variance and covariance measures that are independent of the "home currency." The currency decision can then be made separately, based on whether the incremental return associated with an attractice currency would justify the incremental risk associated with lifting the hedge. In fact, the appropriate "no-forecast" allocation for investors will be fully hedged since the two-sided nature of the currency market makes it unlikely that the normal expected return from being unhedged is sufficiently positive to justify bearing the additional risk.

THE DECOUPLING OF ASSET ALLOCATION AND CURRENCY SELECTION

This view of the global capital markets clearly suggests that the currency decision and the asset allocation decision can and should be made independently. It is worth asking whether history supports this view. Tables 3–1 and 3–2 summarize the historic return and volatility of international equities. In examining historic data, we should note that historic returns tend to be poor indicators of future returns and that historic volatility tends to be a better, but still imprecise (witness October 1987), indicator of future volatility. Therefore, it is not appropriate to scrutinize the individual numbers, but the general pattern of the results is quite important.

During the three-year period ending June 1987, a hedged strategy sharply impaired the performance of a global portfolio. The reason is clear: the dollar fell relative to other world currencies far more than the forward rates used for hedging would have suggested. On the other hand, the results over a longer horizon are somewhat more encouraging. It would seem that the dollar outpaced forward-rate expectations early in the past decade by nearly as much as it underperformed in the past three years.

Without hedging, the volatilities of individual equity markets around the world, denominated in U.S. dollars, all exceed the volatility in the United States. The correlations among the world markets, however, are low enough that the volatility of the world market, even on an unhedged basis, was slightly lower than that of the United States. This has been equally true over spans of 3, 5, or 10 years.

By hedging, the investor is exposed only to the volatility of each market in local currency terms and the currency risk of the unknown change in asset value over the hedging interval. The empirical evidence supports the assertion that this second source of risk is quite small, therefore making it possible to effectively decouple market and currency risk. Here the results are striking. Over any historic time span, most individual world equity markets still exhibit somewhat more volatility than the U.S. market. With the exception of Italy, however, their volatility has only been moderately above that in the United States.

The hedged world portfolio consistently exhibits about 20 percent lower volatility than the unhedged world portfolio. Even though the historical correlations are slightly higher among hedged equity returns than unhedged equity returns, the lower volatilities of the hedged returns more than offset the diminished ability for risk reduction from diversification. This result holds true even though the U.S. market represents a large portion (between 35 percent and 60 percent, depending on the year) of the world market! In other words, hedging reduces risk even more sharply than this data might suggest. When compared with a simple U.S. equity investment, the risk reduction ranges from 20 percent to 30 percent, again despite the fact that the United States is a large part of the index.

What is the cost and reward of hedging? Table 3–3 gives some insight into the penalty that risk extracts from returns. Suppose one believed that all world markets offered an expected return of 12 percent. Then, an investment solely in the U.S. market, with its average volatility of 15 percent, might be expected to deliver a compounded geometric return of 10.9 percent. If that risk can be reduced by a fifth (from 15 per-

TABLE 3–3
The Penalty of Risk

Average Return	Standard Deviation	Geometric Return
12%	10%	11.5%
12	12	11.3
12	15	10.9
12	20	10.0
12	25	8.9

cent to 12 percent) through the use of a global hedged portfolio, then the geometric return rises by 40 basis points to 11.3 percent.

In the wake of October 1987, if a higher standard deviation is assumed, the penalty of risk is greater still. This result follows without making any assumptions at all about active management or the ability to select countries or markets. Currency hedging on the forward markets is quite inexpensive, costing far less than this very real penalty of risk. If the disciplines described in this chapter can be effectively used to select the better performing world markets, then the reward of hedged international investing is greatly enhanced, because the penalty of currency risk is avoided. If a high currency standard deviation is assumed, the penalty of risk is greater still.

We would not advocate the automatic use of a currency hedge. If the investor believes a certain foreign currency will perform much better than its forward rates, then a hedge is not necessarily desirable. Clearly, over the past three years, a currency hedge for U.S. investments overseas would have been costly due to the plunging dollar. In the absence of a confident view on foreign currency strength, however, a currency hedge not only significantly reduces the risk of global investing, but in so doing it also actually improves the long-term expectations.

STAGE I: DO OBJECTIVE MEASURES OF FUTURE RETURNS MATTER?

The expected return on bonds can be represented by their yield-to-maturity; the expected return on cash is cash yield. Equity valuation presents a more difficult problem. Ideally, it calls for a measure of the net present value of future cash flows. In a practical international context, however, normalized earnings yields prove to be the most manageable and consistent indicator of stock performance.[4] To fully calculate total returns for equity, it is necessary to add a measure of sustainable growth. The addition of economic variables to the regressions indirectly but effectively introduces such a measure.

None of these measures differ conceptually from those now widely employed in similar models in the United States. In general, remarkably few changes were required to adapt a U.S. model to the markets of other countries.

In a Stage I asset allocation model, one assumes that objective measures of prospective relative return are positively correlated with subsequent actual relative returns. Is the equity risk premium versus bonds (stock earnings yield minus bond yield) positively correlated with the subsequent relative performance of stocks versus bonds? Is the equity risk premimum versus cash (stock earnings yield minus cash yield) positively correlated with the subsequent relative performance of stocks versus cash? Is the bond maturity premium (bond yield minus cash yield) positively correlated with the subsequent relative performance of bonds versus cash? If the answers to all these questions are affirmative, then a Stage I model will be profitable. In essence, a Stage I model assumes that there is an equilibrating mechanism between asset classes, whereby unusual market conditions give rise to unusual subsequent relative performance.

Tables 3–4, 3–5, and 3–6 give univariate regression coefficients of 15 different countries for Stage I asset allocation. In each instance, we are testing the relation between objective measures of the prospective return differences and the subsequent realized return differences over a one-month horizon.

To better understand the information in the tables, consider the regression coefficient for Japan in the Stock/Bond column of Table 3–4. In this table, the equity risk premium is measured against bonds (stock earnings yield minus bond yield). In the Stock/Bond column, this risk premium measure is regressed against the subsequent excess returns of stocks minus bonds. The resulting regression coefficient is 1.39. In other words, for every 100-basis-point change in the Japanese stock/bond risk premium (stock market earnings yield minus 10-year bond yield), there is an average difference of 139 basis points in the relative performance of stocks versus bonds over the subsequent month.

TABLE 3–4
Stock Earnings Yield minus Bond Yield

| | Coefficient of Regression with Subsequent Asset Class Relative Performance | | |
	Stock/Bond	Stock/Cash	Bond/Cash
Australia	−0.23	−0.76	−0.53
Austria	1.09	0.98	−0.11
Belgium	0.24	0.19	−0.05
Canada	0.33	0.28	−0.05
Denmark	0.05	−0.18	−0.23*
France	0.16	−0.05	−0.21†
Germany	0.46	0.29	−0.16
Italy	0.04	−0.05	−0.10†
Japan	1.39	1.36	−0.03
Netherlands	1.64†	0.97†	−0.67*
Spain	2.90†	2.79†	−0.11
Sweden	0.79	0.44	−0.34
Switzerland	0.86*	0.88*	0.02
United Kingdom	1.36†	0.80	−0.54
United States	0.36	0.10	−0.26
Average	0.76	0.54	−0.22†

Note: The data cover various time periods. For most countries, data are included from December 1972 through February 1987; for Australia, Austria, Japan, Spain, Sweden, and the United Kingdom, however, data beginning in September 1979 or July 1981 were included.
*Significant at 5% level.
†Significant at 1% level.

At first glance this number might seem extraordinary. How can a 100-basis-point change in the risk premium translate into more than 100 basis points for the subsequent month's performance? The answer is found in the leverage inherent in the capital markets. Suppose the earnings yield were 4 percent, at a time when the 10-year bond yield was 6 percent. A 100-basis-point rally in stocks would depress the earnings yield by only 4 basis points (from 4.00 percent to 3.96 percent). A 100-basis-point rise in bonds would depress 10-year bond yields by only about 13.5 basis points (from 6.00 percent to about 5.865 percent). A relative performance difference of 139 basis points in a single month, stemming from a 100-basis-point stock/bond disequilibrium, could result from either a 5.5-basis-point

TABLE 3–5
Stock Earnings Yield minus Cash Yield

	Coefficient of Regression with Subsequent Asset Class Relative Performance		
	Stock/Bond	*Stock/Cash*	*Bond/Cash*
Australia	−0.30	−0.32	−0.03
Austria	0.25	0.42	0.16*
Belgium	0.11	0.18*	0.07*
Canada	0.17	0.22	0.05
Denmark	0.03	0.01	−0.03
France	0.56*	0.95†	0.40†
Germany	0.27	0.35*	0.08
Italy	0.12	0.32	0.20†
Japan	1.77	1.64	−0.13
Netherlands	0.60†	0.61†	0.01
Spain	0.68	0.72	0.04
Sweden	0.43	0.24	−0.18
Switzerland	0.16	0.28	0.12†
United Kingdom	0.34	0.14	−0.18
United States	0.30*	0.37†	0.07
Average	0.36	0.41†	0.04

*Significant at 5% level.
†Significant at 1% level.

change in the stock earnings yield or an 18.6-basis-point change in bond yields.

The striking finding in Table 3–4 is that the equity risk premium versus bonds serves as a predictor for the subsequent relative returns of stocks versus bonds in 14 of the 15 countries tested—4 of them with statistical significance. The average link between the stock/bond disequilibrium and subsequent stock/bond relative performance is a strong one: every 100 basis points of measured disequilibrium translates into 76 basis points of relative performance in the subsequent month! Intriguingly, this variable is also quite powerful in suggesting future bond behavior, as can be seen in the Bond/Cash column. In 14 of the 15 countries tested, if the equity risk premium is abnormally high, the subsequent bond market performance is adversely affected relative to cash.

TABLE 3–6
Bond Yield minus Cash Yield

	Coefficient of Regression with Subsequent Asset Class Relative Performance		
	Stock/Bond	Stock/Cash	Bond/Cash
Australia	−0.47	−0.44	0.03
Austria	0.08	0.43	0.36†
Belgium	0.12	0.23*	0.12†
Canada	−0.02	0.25	0.28†
Denmark	−0.16	0.24	+0.26*
France	0.20	0.54†	0.34†
Germany	0.19	0.42†	0.22†
Italy	0.04	0.28*	0.24†
Japan	−0.72	−0.81	−0.09
Netherlands	0.26	0.53†	0.27
Spain	−0.48	−0.34	0.14
Sweden	−0.01	0.00	0.01
Switzerland	−0.02	0.14	0.16†
United Kingdom	−0.04	−0.12	−0.06
United States	0.22†	0.52†	0.30†
Average	−0.05	0.12	0.17†

*Significant at 5% level.
†Significant at 1% level.

Table 3–5 suggests that the equity risk premium versus cash (stock earnings yield minus cash yield) is a good indicator of stock excess returns versus cash in 14 of the 15 countries tested. The stock/cash risk premium is also indicative of the relative performance of stocks versus bonds in 14 of the 15 countries tested.

Finally, Table 3–6 suggests that the slope of the bond market yield curve is a powerful indicator of subsequent bond performance relative to cash. If the yield curve is unusually steep (that is, if bond yields are high relative to cash yields), the outlook is good for fixed-income returns. This relationship is statistically significant for over half of the countries tested.

This finding for the slope of the bond market yield curve flies in the face of conventional wisdom. The conventional wisdom is that a steep yield curve suggests a likelihood of rising yields. If this were true, then a steep yield curve would correspond to *weak* bond results relative to cash. The empirical evidence is quite persuasive in refuting this conventional wisdom. While the relationship is not invulnerable to error, a steep yield curve tends to correspond to stronger returns on bonds than on cash.

The implications of these three tests are relatively straightforward: market-implicit rate of return matters. If the equity risk premium is unusually high, it follows that most investors are averse to equities. The investor with the courage to bear that risk will tend to be rewarded. If the bond market maturity premium is high, most investors are evidently averse to interest rate risk. The investor willing to bear that risk reaps reward.

STAGE II MODELING: A CHANGING EQUILIBRIUM

Recent studies of capital markets behavior suggest that the *equilibrium relationships between asset classes can change.*[5] An obvious question is whether it makes sense to employ a process in which current market conditions are measured against recent, rather than long-term, equilibriums.

To test the effects of a changing equilibrium, Tables 3–7, 3–8, and 3–9 adopt a short-term definition of equilibrium. These tables, rather than comparing the current risk premium with a long-term equilibrium relation, compare the current risk premium with the average value over the most recent 24-month period. For example, to measure the U.S. stock/bond disequilibrium for January 1987, the average stock versus bond risk premium (stock earnings yield minus bond yield) is calculated for January 1985 through December 1986. The risk premium that existed at the beginning of January 1987 is compared with this 24-month average. Any difference is then viewed as a disequilibrium suggesting relative opportunities between stocks and bonds.

As Tables 3–7, 3–8, and 3–9 show, this approach actually worked better than the Stage I approach for most countries. The improvement is especially noticeable for the stock/bond and stock/cash relations as the regression coefficient increases in 11 of the 15 countries. A Stage I approach, based on the naive assumption of static equilibrium relation, has merit and can add value. But an approach that recognizes the potential for changes in equilibrium may lead to better predictive power.

TABLE 3–7

24-Month Trend in Stock Earnings Yield minus Bond Yield

	Coefficient of Regression with Subsequent Asset Class Relative Performance		
	Stock/Bond	Stock/Cash	Bond/Cash
Australia	−0.48	−0.70	−0.22
Austria	0.11	0.24	0.13
Belgium	0.36	0.28	−0.09
Canada	0.44	0.75*	0.31*
Denmark	0.08	0.13	0.05
France	1.18*	1.57†	0.38*
Germany	0.66	0.92†	0.26
Italy	0.14	0.47	0.33†
Japan	4.16*	3.16	−0.99
Netherlands	1.32†	1.00†	−0.33
Spain	2.58†	2.42*	−0.16
Sweden	1.00	0.78	−0.23
Switzerland	0.96	1.39†	0.43†
United Kingdom	1.22*	0.82	−0.34
United States	0.49	0.84†	0.35
Average	0.95†	0.94†	−0.01

*Significant at 5% level.
†Significant at 1% level.

Real Interest Rates

In a study published in 1983[6], the trend in real interest rates [defined as Treasury bill yields minus 12-month consumer price index (CPI) inflation] was found to be a powerful factor in the performance of the U.S. capital markets. The results in Table 3–10 reaffirm that relation. These results suggest that a rise in real interest rates in the United States leads to a substantial flight of money out of stocks. The result is significant at the 1 percent level, and every 100-basis-point rise in real interest rates translates into a one-month performance penalty of 50 basis points for stocks versus bonds!

As we seek to broaden this research, however, we find that the relations between real interest rates and the markets are not consistent around

TABLE 3–8
24-Month Trend in Stock Earnings Yield minus Cash Yield

	Coefficient of Regression with Subsequent Asset Class Relative Performance		
	Stock/Bond	*Stock/Cash*	*Bond/Cash*
Australia	−0.26	−0.26	0.00
Austria	−0.20	0.00	0.19†
Belgium	0.08	0.14	0.05
Canada	0.11	0.30	0.20*
Denmark	0.04	0.33*	0.29*
France	1.28	1.61*	0.34†
Germany	0.32*	0.50†	0.18*
Italy	−0.04	0.18	0.22†
Japan	2.11	1.90	−0.22
Netherlands	0.55†	0.62†	0.07
Spain	3.07*	2.97*	−0.10
Sweden	0.22	0.16	−0.08
Switzerland	0.24	0.41*	0.17†
United Kingdom	0.16	0.06	−0.07
United States	0.39*	0.61†	0.22
Average	0.47*	0.57†	0.10

*Significant at 5% level.
†Significant at 1% level.

the globe. We find statistical significance for only three countries (albeit highly significant for each): namely, the United States, West Germany, and the Netherlands. Elsewhere, the relation is spotty and inconsistent at best. In short, CPI inflation appears to have only limited merit for active asset allocation decisions in the global arena.

Does this mean the results for the United States, West Germany, and the Netherlands are spurious, stemming from random noise in the data? Or does it mean that in these countries the relations between markets and real interest rates are especially powerful? Statistical tools cannot answer these questions. Nevertheless, we are skeptical about such inconsistent relations, which do not stand up to a global evaluation. We are inclined to ignore models, such as the trend in real yields, that show only intermittent statistical significance.

TABLE 3–9
24-Month Trend in Bond Yield minus Cash Yield

	Coefficient of Regression with Subsequent Asset Class Relative Performance		
	Stock/Bond	*Stock/Cash*	*Bond/Cash*
Australia	−0.38	−0.34	0.05
Austria	−0.54	−0.14	0.40†
Belgium	0.01	0.10	0.08†
Canada	−0.05	0.19	0.24
Denmark	−0.02	0.24	0.26*
France	−0.04	0.28	0.32†
Germany	0.27	0.45*	0.19*
Italy	−0.12	−0.04	0.08
Japan	0.30	0.64	0.34
Netherlands	0.37	0.60†	0.23
Spain	−0.60	−0.50	0.10
Sweden	0.63	0.69	0.06
Switzerland	0.21	0.41	0.20†
United Kingdom	−0.10	−0.11	−0.01
United States	0.40*	0.60†	0.20*
Average	0.02	0.20	0.18†

*Significant at 5% level.
†Significant at 1% level.

STAGE III MODELING: THE INFLUENCE OF THE MACROECONOMY

Capital markets do not exist in a vacuum. Asset values do not rise and fall of their own accord. Rather, they embody the views of the investment community about future macroeconomic prospects. In a world where the judgments of millions of investors shape market pricing patterns, it might seem reasonable to assume market efficiency, to assume the macroeconomy cannot provide useful guides to future capital market performance. If the consensus views of investors fairly reflect macroeconomic factors, then the markets should be fairly priced to reflect this kind of objective information. The empirical evidence shows this may not be the case.

TABLE 3–10
24-Month Trend in Real Cash Yield

	Coefficient of Regression with Subsequent Asset Class Relative Performance		
	Stock/Bond	*Stock/Cash*	*Bond/Cash*
Australia	−0.21	−0.11	0.10
Austria	0.69	0.47	−0.22
Belgium	0.00	−0.03	−0.03
Canada	−0.18	−0.16	0.01
Denmark	0.08	−0.01	−0.09
France	0.03	−0.08	−0.11
Germany	−0.40*	−0.54†	−0.14
Italy	−0.03	0.02	0.04
Japan	−0.76	−0.35	0.40
Netherlands	−0.42†	−0.46†	−0.04
Spain	−0.88	−0.86	0.02
Sweden	−0.29	−0.01	0.28
Switzerland	0.01	0.00	−0.01
United Kingdom	−0.16	0.16	0.35
United States	−0.50†	−0.43†	0.07
Average	−0.20	−0.16	0.04

*Significant at 5% level.
†Significant at 1% level.

Several macroeconomic factors appear somewhat predictive of the subsequent performance of various assets. We studied the following variables:

1. Stock return variance.
2. Rate of change in retail sales.
3. Rate of change in producer prices.
4. Levels of employment.
5. Rate of change in unit labor costs.

Each of these variables was tested by regression analysis, in which the data were appropriately lagged to reflect reporting delays that differ from country to country. The results were surprisingly significant.

Stock return variance simply represents the volatility of stock market performance over the preceding six months. A Salomon Brothers study in

TABLE 3–11
Stock Return Variance

	Coefficient of Regression with Subsequent Asset Class Relative Performance		
	Stock/Bond	*Stock/Cash*	*Bond/Cash*
Australia	−0.33	0.77	1.01
Belgium	0.65*	0.88†	0.23†
Canada	2.00*	2.48†	0.47
Denmark	0.14	0.60	0.46
France	−0.47	−0.84	−0.37
Germany	0.22	0.44	0.22
Italy	0.36	0.37	0.02
Japan	1.00	1.13	0.13
Netherlands	0.73	1.04	0.32
Sweden	2.40	2.88*	0.48
Switzerland	0.25	0.28	0.04
United Kingdom	−0.18	−0.25	−0.11
United States	1.27*	1.83†	0.56
Average	0.62*	0.89†	0.27†

*Significant at 5% level.
†Significant at 1% level.

April 1987 found this variable to be a powerful indicator of future stock market performance in the United States. As a predictor for relative stock market returns, past volatility and subsequent reward are positively correlated relative to bonds in 10 of the 13 countries tested and relative to cash in 11 of 13 countries. See Table 3–11. This consistency suggests that stock market volatility has global relevance.

One might think that the rate of change in retail sales is a useful indicator of economic activity and hence an indicator of equity prospects. Unfortunately, the evidence in Table 3–12 suggests that retail sales are fully discounted in securities prices, as the regression coefficients display no consistent directional patterns. In fact, retail sales are significantly positively correlated with West German stock performance and significantly negatively correlated with British equity performance. These results would not earn the confidence of any sensible investor.

TABLE 3–12
Percentage Change Retail Sales

	Coefficient of Regression with Subsequent Asset Class Relative Performance		
	Stock/Bond	*Stock/Cash*	*Bond/Cash*
Australia	0.00	0.02	0.01
Belgium	0.02	0.02	0.00
Canada	0.14	−0.09	−0.23
Denmark	0.04	0.07	0.03
France	0.04	−0.05	−0.09
Germany	0.34*	0.37†	0.03
Italy	0.00	0.00	0.00
Japan	0.34	0.12	−0.23
Netherlands	0.02	0.05	0.03
Sweden	−0.01	−0.05	−0.03
Switzerland	0.07†	0.07*	0.00
United Kingdom	−0.62	−0.77*	0.14
United States	0.31	−0.09	−0.39*
Average	0.05*	−0.03	−0.08

*Significant at 5% level.
†Significant at 1% level.

On the other hand, the rates of change for producer prices give more promising results. Whereas the results in Table 3–10 suggested that real yields, based on CPI inflation, are of limited value, inflation as measured in producer prices, as shown in Table 3–13, turns out to be consistently useful. In every single country tested, an acceleration in producer price index (PPI) inflation translates into a subsequent erosion of bond performance. In 6 of the 13 countries, the relation was statistically significant, and in 5 of the 13 countries, it was significant at the 1 percent level.

Acceleration in PPI inflation also has a bearing on stock market performance. Accelerating PPI inflation depresses subsequent stock market performance versus cash in 9 of 13 countries. Five of 13 coefficients are statistically significant, and each of the significant coefficients is negative. In short, although CPI inflation appears nearly irrelevant, PPI inflation acted as a depressant on both stocks and bonds.

TABLE 3–13
Percentage Change Producer Price Index

| | Coefficient of Regression with Subsequent Asset Class Relative Performance | | |
	Stock/Bond	Stock/Cash	Bond/Cash
Australia	0.13	0.08	−0.06
Belgium	−0.43	−0.55*	−0.12*
Canada	2.34	1.43	−0.91
Denmark	0.60	0.13	−0.47
France	−0.14	−0.34	−0.20†
Germany	−0.98	−1.91†	−0.92†
Italy	−0.02	−0.75	−0.73†
Japan	0.46	0.45	−0.01
Netherlands	−0.62	−0.87*	−0.25
Sweden	−0.90	−1.36	−0.46
Switzerland	−1.45†	−1.81†	−0.35†
United Kingdom	0.17	−0.60	−0.78
United States	−0.18	−1.08†	−0.90†
Average	−0.08	−0.55	−0.47†

*Significant at 5% level.
†Significant at 1% level.

The final two tests gave consistent and interesting results. The first of them, Table 3–14, is a test of unemployment. If unemployment is above average, both stocks and bonds achieve better subsequent rewards. The relation is slightly more consistent for bonds than it is for stocks: for bonds the relation holds in every country except Canada, whereas in stocks it fails to hold in three countries. However, the average impact on stocks was greater than the average impact on bonds. All of the statistically significant results point to stronger capital markets performance when unemployment is above average than it is when unemployment is below average.

Finally, if people are working and are well paid, unit labor costs can rise rapidly (Table 3–15). Here we find a relation even more consistent than the one with unemployment rates. Rising unit labor costs hurt stock market performance in each country where this statistic is available. Bonds are hurt by rising unit labor costs in all but one country (Canada) in which this data is available.

TABLE 3–14
Unemployment

	Coefficient of Regression with Subsequent Asset Class Relative Performance		
	Stock/Bond	Stock/Cash	Bond/Cash
Australia	−0.96	−0.16	0.80
Belgium	0.15*	0.23†	0.08†
Canada	−0.11	−0.24	−0.13
Denmark	−0.42*	−0.07	0.36
France	0.46	0.96	0.49*
Germany	0.26†	0.39†	0.12*
Japan	0.05	0.06	0.02
Netherlands	0.12	0.21	0.09
Switzerland	1.82	20.9	0.16
United Kingdom	0.02	0.23	0.22
United States	0.33	0.69†	0.35
Average	0.17	0.40	0.23†

*Significant at 5% level.
†Significant at 1% level.

Evidently, the capital markets and the work force operate at cross-purposes. Crudely stated, if the work force is happy, the investors will be sad, and vice versa.

CONCLUSION

The most telling conclusion of this research is that the relationships successfully applied to asset allocation strategies in the United States also have promise for other countries around the globe. Although statistical significance was sometimes elusive, the consistency of the results from one country to another is ample grounds for encouragement about the merit of these investment tools.

What about the investor who wants to take a disciplined approach to asset allocation on a global basis? The evidence would suggest that such a disciplined approach is not only intuitively appealing, but that it also can add value.

TABLE 3–15
Percentage Change Unit Labor Costs

	Coefficient of Regression with Subsequent Asset Class Relative Performance		
	Stock/Bond	Stock/Cash	Bond/Cash
Belgium	−0.40	−0.51	−0.11
Canada	−0.08	−0.06	0.02
Denmark	0.37	−0.30	−0.67
France	−1.18	−2.03	−0.84
Germany	−0.31†	−0.30	0.01
Italy	−0.23	−0.40	−0.17*
Netherlands	−0.46	−1.16	−0.70
Sweden	0.09	−0.04	−0.13
United Kingdom	0.47	−0.02	−0.54
United States	0.06	−0.44	−0.50
Average	−0.17	−0.53†	−0.36*

*Significant at 5% level.
†Significant at 1% level.

ENDNOTES

1. Reprinted and updated from R. D. Arnott and F. J. Fabozzi, eds., *Asset Allocation* (Chicago: Probus Press, 1988).
2. See Jeremy Evnine and Roy Henriksson, "Asset Allocation and Options," *The Journal of Portfolio Management,* Fall 1987, pp 3–9.
3. This approach to asset allocation was detailed, for the U.S. investor, by Robert D. Arnott and James N. von Germeten, "Systematic Asset Allocation," *Financial Analysts Journal,* November/December 1983, pp 3–9.
4. See also "The Equity Risk Premium and Stock Market Performance," Salomon Brothers, Inc., July 1987.
5. See "Equity Risk Premium Review; Reflections on the Risk Premium," Salomon Brothers, Inc., February 16, 1988.
6. Robert D. Arnott and James N. von Germeten, "Systematic Asset Allocations," *Financial Analysts Journal,* November/December 1983, pp 3–9.

CHAPTER 4

GLOBAL ASSET ALLOCATION

Lee R. Thomas

This Chapter describes a strategy for global asset allocation—selecting an internationally diversified investment portfolio that reflects your forecasts of security prices and exchange rates, your investing objectives, and your willingness to bear risk.

The blueprint for global asset allocation that we will propose has a number of advantages. First, it is highly structured and disciplined, but it is also flexible. It can accommodate whatever approach to security analysis and market forecasting you prefer. Second, it is easy to implement in practice. Third, our allocation rules isolate different sources of investment risk and compare each risk to its corresponding promised return. Fourth, the approach we describe fosters an efficient division of labor between portfolio managers, economic forecasters, and security analysts. It is suitable for investors who rely on one group of professionals to forecast security prices and on another to forecast exchange rates. Fifth, it explicitly recognizes the opportunity you have to use hedging instruments. In fact, forward foreign exchange contracts are central to our approach—even for investors who decide not to hedge.

This chapter is an adaptation of Lee R. Thomas, "Bringing Discipline to Global Asset Allocation," *Investing*, Spring 1990. Copyright 1990 by DMA Communications, Inc.

THREE INVESTING PITFALLS

Before we describe our rules for portfolio selection, let's consider three common approaches to global asset allocation. In each case, we will show how the strategy in question deals with currency risk and explain why it can produce inferior results.

Bottom-Up Investing

We may term the first approach *bottom-up* international investing. "I'm an equity and bond investor," a proponent of this approach might say. "My expertise is in evaluating securities, not currencies. Anyway, I understand that, in the long run, the currency effect pretty much washes out. So, I just ignore currencies and pick stocks and bonds I find intrinsically attractive, regardless of where I find them. Sometimes the foreign currency adds to my profit. Sometimes the currency reduces my return or, unluckily, even eliminates it altogether. But I just wait the currency cycles out."

There is some merit to this approach. First, if your expertise is in picking stocks, you should pick stocks. If your expertise is in picking bonds, pick bonds. Don't try to pretend you are an expert currency forecaster if you are not, or fool yourself into thinking that you can successfully pick currencies without first doing your homework. Currency forecasting requires its own set of skills.

Second, it is true that currency cycles wash out in the long run.[1] Sometimes foreign currencies outperform the dollar, and sometimes they underperform it. After a long series of rolls of the dice, foreign currency bets just seem to break even.

But the conclusion—don't bother to manage the currency exposures in your foreign investments—is wrong. If you leave your foreign currency exposures unhedged, you bear exchange rate risks. Since you could have hedged, the risks are unnecessary. And in this case, since you believe the foreign currency exposure does not usually add to your foreign investments' profitability, you are bearing exchange rate risks gratuitously. Bearing risk for free doesn't make sense.

Currency-Driven Investing

International investing approach number two takes the opposite tack. Instead of ignoring currency decisions, it makes them central. ''I start by choosing good currencies,'' a typical proponent might explain. ''Then I look for securities denominated in those currencies. After all, if you get the currency right, you're more than halfway home. If I can find *undervalued* assets denominated in the currencies I like, so much the better.''

The currency-driven approach also contains a grain of truth. Getting the currency right is important, especially for bond investors. But in a way, the currency-driven approach is too sophisticated. It misses the obvious point that nobody needs to buy offshore assets in order to take foreign exchange positions. The world is much simpler than that. If you want to go long of a currency, you can choose a pure currency play such as a foreign currency Eurodeposit. Or, you can use swaps, foreign exchange futures, or forward contracts to synthetically redenominate some of your existing security holdings into the currency of your choice.[2]

If you use foreign stocks and bonds to implement what are basically currency choices, you will probably end up bearing equity and interest rate risks that have nothing to do with your exchange rate views. That is, if you take the currency-first approach, you are likely to bear some equity or interest rate risks thoughtlessly or gratuitously. That is the same mistake the bottom-up international investor makes.

The Selective Investor

The selective investor is aware of both of these pitfalls. In avoiding them, he deftly falls into another: ''I'm a careful investor. Before I buy a foreign security, I make sure I like *both* the security and the currency it is denominated in. I won't touch an undervalued asset if it is denominated in a weak currency, or an unattractive asset just because it is in a strong currency. If I have doubts on either score, I pass.''

If the world were awash in great investment opportunities, this approach wouldn't be too bad. But it's not, and being too selective means you will pass up some potentially profitable opportunities. Why should you eschew an attractive investment just because you don't like the currency in which it is denominated? After all, you can buy the asset, then hedge away its currency risk. If, after taking the costs of hedging into account, you still think a foreign security offers good value, you should buy it. If you do not, your return will suffer, compared with your more aggressive rivals who currency hedge when it is appropriate.

All three of these approaches are flawed because they violate one of two international investing principles:

1. Never buy a foreign security only as a currency play. When you like the currency, buy the currency.
2. Never avoid a foreign security just because it is denominated in an unattractive currency. Instead, invest where you find value, then currency hedge if necessary.

Taking these two principles together, they imply that you should keep your asset decisions and your currency decisions separate.[3] One way to impose this discipline on your international investing decisions is to adopt the three-step approach to global asset allocation that we will describe in the following section.

RULES FOR GLOBAL ASSET ALLOCATION

To keep our asset decisions and our currency decisions independent, we will choose our international portfolio in three steps. In the first step, we will choose which securities to hold. At this step, it is important that we choose from the menu of domestic and foreign investments in a currency-agnostic way. Then, in step two, we will select a currency overlay for the portfolio that reflects our exchange rate expectations and the riskiness of foreign currency exposures. The final step is to reconcile our asset and currency selections.

Step One: The Asset Allocation Committee (AAC)

Imagine your organization has established a committee that has the responsibility for selecting the securities you will hold—but *not* the currency exposures you will bear. That is, the asset allocation committee (AAC) will choose stocks and bonds independently of the currencies in which they are denominated. (Later, the currency allocation committee will decide which foreign exchange risks are worth bearing.)

To choose securities to own independently of exchange rate considerations, the AAC must compare the securities' prospective returns and risks in a currency-neutral way. So, it needs to construct a list of the expected *currency-hedged* returns and risks to each possible investment.

To calculate the return to a foreign investment held currency-hedged, we start by estimating its prospective profitability measured in its own currency. You can make these forecasts in any way that suits you—they may be based on historical returns, fundamental analysis, economic modeling, technical analysis, or seat-of-the-pants intuition. That is, our global allocation plan is compatible with any approach you choose to take to evaluating stocks and bonds.

The next task is to notionally currency hedge each prospective foreign investment. The AAC must estimate what each foreign investment will return if it is combined with a forward currency contract that will substantially eliminate its exchange rate risk. This involves adjusting each investment's predicted return to reflect the appropriate forward foreign exchange discount or premium. Later we will show how easy it is to calculate an investment's currency-hedged return, given your forecast of its likely return measured in its own currency.

You should *notionally* currency hedge at this stage whether or not you, in the end, actually decide to hedge away your exchange rate risks. By comparing all investments in a currency-neutral way, you will avoid confusing currency selection with security selection.

Notice that the AAC only needs two pieces of information to construct its menu of prospective currency-hedged investments. The first is its forecasts of the local currency return to each investment. The second is the relevant forward currency discounts or premiums, which are readily observable in the foreign exchange markets. The committee's exchange rate forecasts don't ordinarily matter.[4]

Of course, the AAC will want to consider risks as well as prospective returns. Again, it is the riskiness of *currency-hedged* foreign investments that matter at this step.[5]

After comparing all of the prospective investments' currency-hedged expected returns, and factoring in risk, the AAC will compile a list of the securities it wants to own. This list is the output from the first step of our global asset allocation strategy. Notice that the approach we have taken means we will never select a security at step one just because we expect its currency to appreciate. Nor will we ever reject a potential investment just because it is denominated in an unattractive currency.

Unfortunately, our work is not yet completed. If we stopped here, we might pass up attractive opportunities to take positions in foreign currencies. Our global asset allocation strategy certainly does not say that you should never take a currency bet, or that you should always currency hedge all of your foreign investments.

Step Two: The Currency Allocation Committee (CAC)

To hedge or not to hedge? An unhedged foreign investment will outdistance a hedged one if the relevant foreign currency turns out to be stronger than the forward foreign exchange rate that was quoted when you contemplated putting on the hedge. On the other hand, if the U.S. dollar ends up stronger than its forward rate, after the fact, you will wish that you had hedged.

The CAC's primary job is to forecast whether each foreign currency will outperform or underperform its forward foreign exchange rate against the U.S. dollar. Then it factors in the riskiness of unhedged foreign currency positions.[6] Based on these, it selects the portfolio's currency overlay—a list of preferred currency exposures. The currency overlay is the output from the second step of our three-step procedure.

Initially—after the asset allocation committee has met, but before the currency allocation committee has had its say—the portfolio's currency overlay is simple: all U.S. dollars. Taking on foreign currency exposures is an active decision that involves adding risk to your portfolio. So, the CAC should only consider adding exchange rate risk to the portfolio—that is, it should only decide to lift some of the hedges notionally imposed by the AAC—if it expects foreign currencies to outperform the U.S. dollar.[7] Your base case is to hedge.

Notice that the CAC might want an exposure to a particular currency, even though the AAC did not choose to own any securities denominated in that currency. And, just because the asset allocation committee happened to choose a particular security, there is no reason to assume the currency allocation committee will like the corresponding currency. This is the sense in which our asset choices and our currency choices are independent.[8]

Currency hedge/no hedge decisions can have a major impact on your portfolio's performance. So, who should be included on the currency committee?

It may have the same membership as the asset association committee—but, then again, it may not. A dual structure with separate membership invites matching talent to task—assigning your most accomplished security analysts to the job they do best, and letting your most experienced currency forecasters exploit their own comparative advantage. Sometimes an analyst may be good at both jobs, but many times you will want to encourage each of your managers to specialize in what he or she does best.

If you are a fund sponsor, the role of the asset allocation committee may be played by a group of international money managers who you think are particularly good at picking foreign stocks and bonds. Their mandates will direct them to currency hedge all their foreign security holdings. The currency allocation committee's role may be played by another international manager, one who is particularly good at calling exchange rates. His or her job is to choose your fund's currency exposures, not to select securities. And his or her performance should be compared to the passive investment alternative on the currency side of your portfolio—hedging all your exposures back into U.S. dollars. That is, whoever runs the currency overlay should have to beat an all-dollar bogey.

Step Three: Implementing Your Security and Currency Choices

Step one produced your list of preferred assets, and step two produced your list of preferred currencies. In step three, we will use forward foreign exchange contracts to reconcile those choices. Sometimes—when your preferred currency exposure exceeds your preferred asset exposure—you may be buying foreign currencies forward. Other times—when you like a country's securities more than its currency—you will be selling foreign exchange for forward delivery.

The result is the best of both worlds: you will own the securities you expect to perform the best, effectively denominated in the currencies you expect to perform the best.

AN EXAMPLE

A simple example will show how the three-step approach to global asset allocation might work in practice.

Recall that step one involves selecting investments based on their prospective total return, after they have been currency hedged into U.S. dollars. We will begin by showing how to calculate the prospective dollar return on a currency-hedged foreign security.

Suppose you expect an investment in Japanese equities to return 10 percent, measured in yen, over the coming year. Further suppose the current spot and (one-year) forward rates are 128.30 and 122.43, respectively, representing a yen forward premium of 4.6 percent.

Evaluated at the spot rate, an initial $100 investment in Japan represents ¥12,830. According to your forecast, this will grow by 10 percent to ¥14,113 during the year. Sold forward, ¥14,113 is worth $115.27. So, the expected currency-hedged return to an investment in Japanese equities is 15.27 percent.

Based on (1) your predictions of total return, measured in the local currency, for each asset or asset class and (2) the observed forward discount or premium of each foreign currency against the U.S. dollar, we can forecast the total dollar return to a currency-hedged investment in any foreign security. The next step is to estimate the risks of currency-hedged foreign investments. Usually, you will rely on historical volatility. Alternately, you may use the volatilities implied by observed stock and bond option prices to furnish these risk estimates.

You can construct a menu of hedged risk and return opportunities by listing the forecasted return and volatility of each possible foreign investment. It is often useful to graph the information, as we have done (for a hypothetical forecast) in Figure 4–1. The most attractive investments are found in the northwest of this diagram: they have the highest expected returns and the lowest risks.

Now you allocate your investable funds to various security markets based on this menu of hedged returns and risks. You might, for example, start with Figure 4–1 and then select hedged investments using modern portfolio theory. In this case, you will attempt to maximize your portfolio's expected return per unit of risk borne.[9] However, most practicing portfolio managers do not use a formal optimizing approach to select their investment portfolios, and this is not crucial to the three-step procedure we are advocating.[10] What matters is that you start with the risk/return menu shown in Figure 4–1 and use some reasonable procedure to choose a list of securities to buy. For example, using the menu illustrated in Figure 4–1, we might select the securities shown in Table 4–1.

One way to look at this allocation is by asset class: 60 percent equity, 40 percent bonds. Or, it can be organized by country: United States, 55 percent; Japan, 20 percent; Germany, 10 percent; United Kingdom, 10 percent; France, 5 percent.

FIGURE 4–1
Hypothetical Security "Menu"

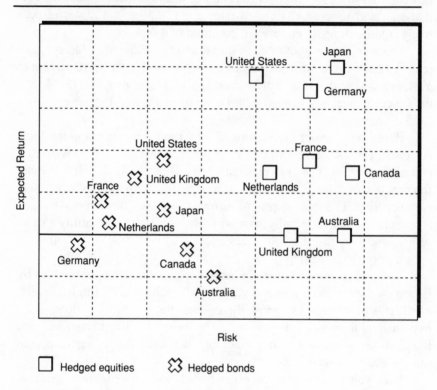

Hedged equities   Hedged bonds

Next, we proceed to step two, selecting the currency overlay. As before, we wish to start with a list of risk and return forecasts, this time for foreign currency exposures. The promised incremental return to foreign currency positions can be found by talculating the percentage difference between your forecast of the future spot exchange rate and the forward rate.[11] The volatility estimates you need could come from historical exchange rate data or by calculating the volatilities implied by observed currency option prices. A hypothetical menu of currency opportunities is illustrated in Figure 4–2.

Now, suppose that after considering the menu of currency risk and return opportunities shown in Figure 4–2, the CAC proposes the currency overlay shown in Table 4–2.

Notice that the CAC has chosen one country that the AAC may not have even considered—Finland. And, the CAC chose to avoid yen altogether, even though the AAC took a significant position in the Japanese

TABLE 4–1
The Asset Allocation Committee's Choices

Investment	Portfolio Share (Percent)
U.S. equities	30%
U.S. bonds	25
Japanese equities	20
German equities	10
U.K. bonds	10
French bonds	5
Total	100%

stock market. Our three-step global asset allocation strategy is flexible enough to target opportunities that arise only in a foreign security market, only in a foreign currency market, or in both of these markets simultaneously.

FIGURE 4–2
Hypothetical Currency "Menu"

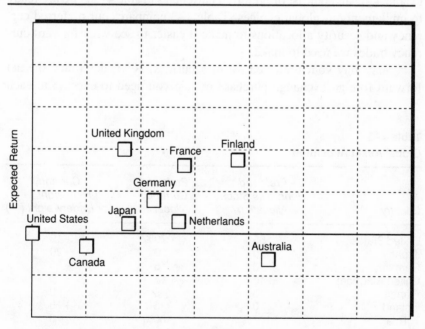

TABLE 4–2
The Currency Allocation Committee's Choices

Currency	Share (Percent)
U.S. dollar	70%
Japanese yen	0
German mark	5
U.K. pound	15
French franc	5
Finnish markka*	5
Total	100%

*The choice of the markka may surprise you. However, you should know that as a consequence of making this allocation, due diligence will require the chairman of the currency allocation committee to visit Finland occasionally to evaluate local economic conditions. Also, his girlfriend lives in Helsinki.

Now that we have selected our list of preferred stocks and bonds (Table 4–1) and our list of preferred currencies (Table 4–2), we are ready to implement our global choices. Table 4–3 compares our preferred currency and security allocations to make it easier to see what forward currency trades we need to make.

First, buy your preferred list of securities. Next, determine the net forward foreign exchange purchase or sale you need to execute in each

Table 4–3
Global Asset Allocation

Country	Preferred Bond plus Stock Allocation	Preferred Currency Allocation	Currency Overweight (+) or Underweight (−)
United States	55%	70%	+15
Japan	20	0	−20
Germany	10	5	− 5
United Kingdom	10	15	+ 5
France	5	5	0
Finland	0	5	+ 5
Total	100%	100%	0

currency. The key to the forward trades you must execute is found in the last column of Table 4–3. If a currency must be underweighted compared to its corresponding security allocation, then we will sell it forward. If a currency must be overweighted, then we buy it forward.

The following trades, based on a portfolio of $100MM, implement our preferred security and currency allocations:

1. Buy $30MM of U.S. equities and $25MM of U.S. bonds.
2. Buy $20MM of Japanese equities. Sell $15MM of yen forward for dollars and $5MM of yen forward for pounds. This eliminates your yen exposure and raises your dollar and pound currency allocations to the preferred level.
3. Buy $10MM of German bonds and sell $5MM of German marks forward for Finnish markkas. This reduces your German mark exposure and raises your Finnish markka exposure, as desired.
4. Buy $5MM of French bonds. Since your preferred French franc currency exposure happens to conform to your preferred French security exposure, you do not need to execute a forward French franc transaction.

CONCLUSIONS

You can own foreign stocks or bonds without bearing exchange rate risks, and you can make currency bets without buying foreign stocks and bonds. So, as a portfolio manager you can "mix and match" your preferred international asset allocation with your preferred currency allocation. The key is to use forward foreign exchange contracts to unbundle a foreign security's own prospective return from the return offered by the associated foreign currency.

We have described a three-step approach to selecting an international portfolio. Our rules explicitly recognize the role that forward exchange contracts can play in constructing a portfolio, without neglecting the opportunities offered by foreign currencies. We do not advocate currency hedging all the time, but we do treat currency hedging as the base case for all foreign exchange rate exposed investments.

The key is to choose the securities you hold in a currency-neutral way, while choosing your foreign exchange exposures based only on the currencies' own prospective returns and risks. Forward contracts are used to reconcile your security and currency selections.

Our strategy for global asset allocation has five major attractions: (1) it is easy to implement; (2) it is flexible; (3) it routinely integrates hedging opportunities into the portfolio selection process, rather than adding them on as an afterthought; (4) it compares prospective security returns to security risks, and prospective currency returns to currency risks; and (5) it encourages an efficient division of labor between security analysts and currency analysts.

ENDNOTES

1. That is, the long-run total return to holding foreign deposits, translated back into your domestic currency, is about the same as total return to domestic deposits. So, the long-run return to foreign investments is about the same whether or not you currency hedge them.
2. Of course, you must obey any legal, regulatory, or contractual restrictions that apply to using derivative securities. For a description of the mechanics of constructing synthetic assets, see Lee R. Thomas, "Foreign Bonds: Stripping away Currency Risk," *Investment Management Review*, March/April 1988, pp. 31–38.
3. Even a good idea can be taken too far. If exchange rates and security prices are correlated, your portfolio should reflect that correlation. And, your exchange rate views may be relevant to your asset decisions indirectly, in ways we will describe below. On this point see Blu Putnam, "False Bottom to the Holy Grail," *Risk*, December 1988.
4. The AAC will consider exchange rate prospects only if they are relevant to predicting the future course of stock prices or interest rates—and then only to formulate its stock and bond market forecasts. Otherwise, exchange rates should be firmly excluded from its agenda.
5. Currency-hedged foreign investments are ordinarily much less risky than their unhedged counterparts. See, for example, Lee R. Thomas, "The Performance of Currency-Hedged Foreign Bonds," *Financial Analysts Journal*, May-June 1989, pp. 25–31.
6. In particular, the currency committee should be sensitive to how much risk each foreign currency exposure *adds* to your portfolio. This is best measured using a concept analogous to a stock's "beta." See Philippe Jorion, "International Asset Allocation," *Investment Management Review*, January/February 1989, pp. 41–49.
7. You may also hold a currency you expect to underperform its forward rate, if its return is negatively correlated with the rest of your investment portfolio. In this unusual case, the foreign currency is held because it reduces the overall riskiness of your holdings.

8. The CAC may want to consider prospects for stock prices or interest rates in each country—but only if they are relevant to formulating an exchange rate forecast. That is the sense in which asset and currency choices are interdependent.

9. In this case, you will need to estimate the correlation coefficients relating all the currency-hedged investment classes.

10. For a discussion of the pros and cons applying mean-variance analysis to international portfolio selection, see Michael Adler, "Global Asset Allocation: Some Uneasy Questions," *Investment Management Review*, September/October 1987, pp. 13–18.

11. Notice that the *incremental* return to U.S. dollars is, by definition, zero. Since we are doing our analysis in nominal rather than inflation-adjusted terms, U.S. dollar positions are riskless.

CHAPTER 5

QUANTITATIVE ASSET ALLOCATION FORECASTING: UNCOVERING THE "EFFICIENT FRONTIER"

Eric H. Sorensen
Joseph J. Mezrich

INTRODUCTION

Quantitative investment applications have made major advances in recent years. For example, investors desiring to index their portfolios have used quantitative optimization algorithms. In addition, many active investors who seek to outperform benchmarks have used quantitative models to rank assets and to construct portfolios. Figure 5–1 presents a dual-axis schematic of investment strategy approaches. The horizontal axis represents the investment objective in its broadest interpretation: active or passive. The vertical axis represents the investment method in its broadest sense: quantitative or traditional.

Based on modern portfolio theory, academicians and broad-minded practitioners have argued for more abundant use of international asset diversification. At the heart of their argument for holding global assets is the fact that securities across world markets historically have been less correlated than those within a specific market.

FIGURE 5–1
Investment Strategy Approaches

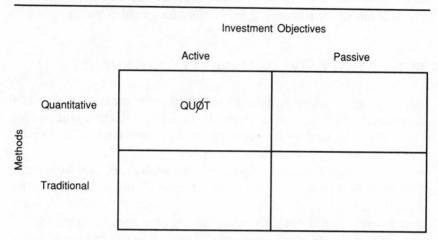

In this chapter, we discuss the quantitative techniques required to manage global asset allocation. These techniques are necessary to manage money in accordance with the upper half of Figure 5–1.[1]

THE GLOBAL APPROACH: ACTIVE OR PASSIVE

At least two major issues must be decided in an active quantitative portfolio strategy. First, the valuation model must have sufficient predictive ability to lead to enhanced performance, that is, to eke out an alpha. Second, the predictive results must be married successfully to a compatible portfolio construction approach.

By comparison, passive strategies that are largely quantitative tend to reduce or to remove the need for both requirements: by definition, a passive strategy has no alpha. In addition, the object of a passive strategy typically is to minimize benchmark tracking error, so the standard mean/variance framework that highlights covariance is the most obvious choice for portfolio construction.

If the objective is to track a global index such as the Salomon-Russell primary market index (PMI) or the Salomon-Russell extended market index (EMI), one approach that minimizes tracking error requires estimates of cross-crountry correlations. The benefits of exploiting the covariance structure across countries is well known; indeed, risk minimization is one of the compelling motivations for global investing.

BETTER ESTIMATES OF MARKET COMOVEMENTS

Recently, however, some have questioned whether the benefits of global diversification remain intact. After all, they note, all the world markets have moved in tandem in recent years—down substantially in October 1987, followed by a two-year upward march.[2]

Are the global markets moving synchronously and, therefore, disadvantageously correlated in an investment sense? Nothing could be further from the truth. Indeed, the world is getting larger, not smaller. Correlations between world stock markets generally have been heading lower. In fact, global equity markets currently have average comovements of approximately 0.30, far lower than many investors believe.

In Figure 5–2, we present two visual representations of the underlying comovements in price behavior across world equity markets.

The charts map the correlations between various pairs of equity markets. The higher the correlation, the closer the two countries appear on the map.

The top panel—comprising standard analyses of all the monthly returns over the past three years, including October 1987—answers the question What are the mathematical correlations across countries using *all* the recent data points? In other words, it provides "an exact answer to the wrong question." World stock markets are not as closely linked as the map indicates. Hence, a simple correlation calculation between two assets can produce a misleading and potentially erroneous input to investment decisions.

A more appropriate question is What are the diversification benefits of investing between pairs or groups of countries? Using all the data in computing correlations will not yield a correct answer to this question. In this instance, an approximate answer, technically speaking, is preferable. The best approach is to use a data base that omits "outliers"—returns of such extreme high or low values that they clearly are not representative of normal conditions—because the inclusion of outliers greatly distorts the picture. In addition, the best answer will be a forecast, rather than a static look at historical data.

The cross-country comovements in the bottom panel of Figure 5–2 provide an "approximate answer" that is far superior for portfolio

FIGURE 5–2
Global Stock Market Comovement Maps, 1989

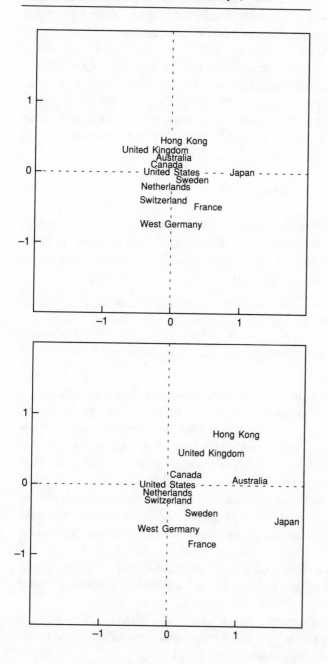

management. The correlations in this figure were calculated using a scientifically proven means of omitting misleading observations. For example, extraordinary (and sometimes inexplicable) data such as those for October 1987 were eliminated, resulting in a far different picture.

Researchers often use this technique, "trimming" the data, to evaluate true relationships. The correlations based on trimmed data differ dramatically from those that used all the data because all the markets dropped drastically on October 19 and 20, 1987, and this one observation greatly skewed results. While comovements across countries unquestionably were very high in October 1987, that was a highly atypical month.[3]

THE HISTORY OF CORRELATIONS

Professional statisticians have long been concerned with the issues of nonrepresentative data and the misapplication of statistical analyses. In 1805, the French mathematician Adrien Marie Legendre commented on the misuse of data in estimating relationships:

> If among these errors [statistical deviations] are some which appear too large to be admissible, then those observations which produced these errors will be rejected, as coming from too faulty experiments, and the unknowns will be determined by means of the other observations, which will then give much smaller errors.[4]

To understand the impact of outliers, consider the following hypothetical example. In the postdiluvian tribe of Nimrod in ancient Mesopotamia, suppose a mathematician set out to determine the proper region where the tribe should locate to have the ideal rainfall for hunting, as well as general living conditions. Suppose further that his analysis involved correlating and forecasting the historical rainfall levels between many geographical subregions.

Imagine the impact on his results if the mathematician included the period of the great flood—during which it rained continuously over consecutive data points in all the subregions at precisely the same time and in precisely the same amounts—in his analysis. The inclusion of such irreproducible and unlikely data elements would produce a totally misguided view of future correlations. The flood experience would definitely bias the forecasts.

Many global managers rely on correlation calculations to arrive at optimal asset allocations. By using traditional correlation calculations, they subject their analysis to a type of "flood bias."

THE DOWNWARD DRIFT IN GLOBAL EQUITY COMOVEMENTS

Recent outliers in global market returns can similarly blur true relationships, albeit to a much smaller degree than in our great flood example. As shown in Figure 5–2, the removal of outliers (bottom panel) provides a significantly different set of correlations.

The use of appropriately trimmed correlations gives a clearer representation of comovements in asset prices over time. Figure 5–3 shows the median value of stock market comovements across 11 world equity markets. The trend line—a rolling three-year window of monthly data—comprises the median value of stock markets in 11 countries (55 paired comparisons).

The level of comovements today is much lower than it was from 1984 to 1987. Comovements among world markets peaked at an average of 0.43 in late 1984 and then fell to 0.23 in the third quarter of 1987. In 1988 and 1989, the median of global equity market comovements has ranged from 0.25 to 0.30, well below pre-1987 levels. This range is lower and, in our view, more accurate than those produced by other analyses.

FIGURE 5–3
Comovement Trends among Global Stock Markets, 1983–1989

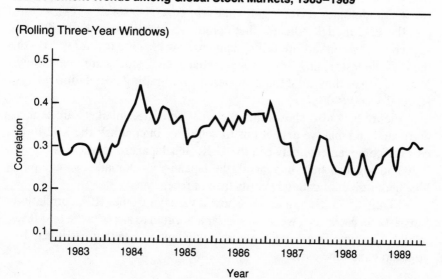

(Rolling Three-Year Windows)

THE FUTURE OF FORECASTS

To make our work on market comovements of practical use for the active global manager, we must make two important modifications. First, the above-mentioned figures are comprehensive averages and, therefore, too gross to apply to an investment decision between any two countries. Second, active applications require forecasts that have predictive value.

Our technique is a two-step process that combines optimization with robust time series analyses; we have named this process RS2 (robust series, two stage). Our forecasts are based on the optimal algorithms for trimming the historical return series. The trimmed series are then subjected to historical analyses, using robust regression techniques.

The RS2 models cover a large universe of global stock, bond, and currency markets. The approach is designed to produce estimates and historical graphs of the comovement trends that are superior forecasts of future price relationships.

The RS2 models forecast the relationship between any pair of markets up to six months into the future. These projected comovements often differ substantially from those suggested by simple historical correlations.

In Figure 5–4, we compare the traditional measure of trailing correlation with our RS2 model forecasts of U.K. stock market trends relative to other global equity markets. The projections produced by these two methodologies differ significantly in several instances. For example, the RS2 model indicates that comovements between the U.K. and French equity markets are falling and are now heading toward 0.20. For the U.K. investor, this would suggest that French stocks are much more attractive than they might appear based on a trailing correlation analysis, and vice versa.

Figure 5–4 also shows that the U.S. and U.K. markets are highly correlated and that we expect this to continue. In contrast, the RS2 forecast for comovements between the U.K. and Japanese markets is below 0.20 and suggests that, in general, the Japanese stock market should provide better diversification benefits than in recent years.

Figures 5–5, 5–6, and 5–7 show a variety of other RS2 correlation forecasts. In each case, we use a similar algorithm to arrive at the best RS2 model. The time frame is a three-year window of data that easily can be adjusted to suit the user.

FIGURE 5–4

RS2 and Trailing-Correlation U.K. Stock Market Forecasts: Comovements between the FT All-Shares Index and Stock Market Indexes of Other Countries, 1983–1989

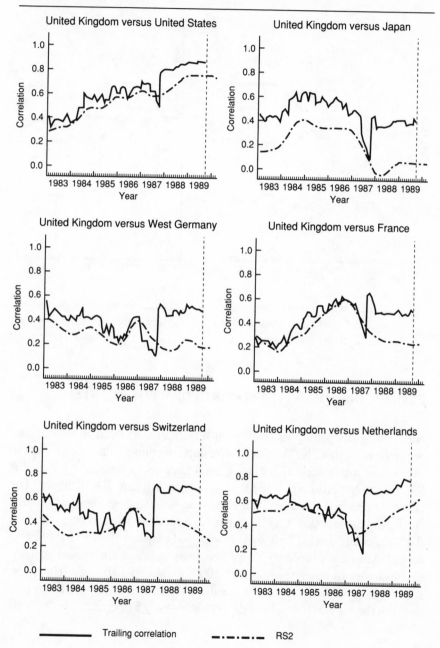

FIGURE 5–5
**RS2 U.S. Stock Market Forecasts: Comovements between the S&P 500
Index and Stock Market Indexes of Other Countries, 1986–1989**

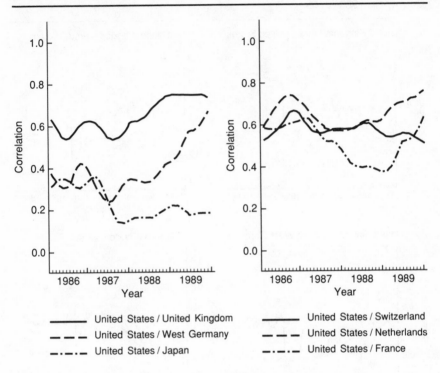

United States / United Kingdom
United States / West Germany
United States / Japan

United States / Switzerland
United States / Netherlands
United States / France

PRODUCING QUANTITATIVE RETURN FORECASTS

An equally compelling motivation of quantitative analysis is to construct return forecast models. The portfolio results, of course, depend on the accuracy of the predictions of country asset and currency returns. And what is the "shooting percentage" needed for an approach like QUØT to win? The accuracy required to outperform a buy-and-hold strategy depends on how frequently the investor is willing to trade. Recent research indicates that, in the U.S. equity market for the 40-year period between 1946 and 1986, predictive accuracy exceeding 72 percent was required for annual market-timing trades to outperform a S&P 500 buy-and-hold strategy. However, the required predictive accuracy for monthly market-timing trades to outperform the S&P 500 was considerably less—only 51 percent.[5]

FIGURE 5–6

RS2 Currency Forecasts: Selected Comovements between Nondollar Currencies, 1986–1989 (relative to the U.S. dollar)

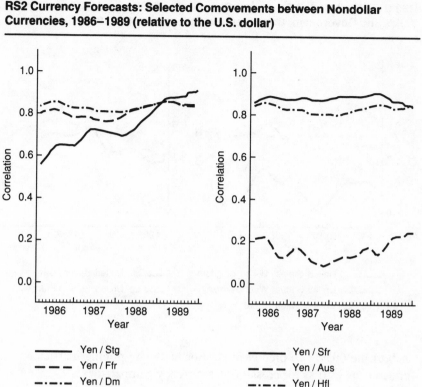

Because a high degree of forecast accuracy is central to any asset allocation strategy, we must evaluate and determine the best method to value and rank worldwide asset and currency choices. The primary consideration is the approach's universality: As in a soccer match, it must put the relative contenders on a level playing field with equal footing. It must be legitimately comparative—it is not sufficient merely to compare price/earnings ratios across countries, nor is it sufficient simply to compare fundamentals across countries. Growth in Hong Kong may be priced differently than growth in the Netherlands.

The QUØT model uses a series of statistical arbitrage pricing models to value the relative attractiveness of stocks, bonds, and cash within each country. The analysis is executed so as to detect undervalued and overvalued asset classes across borders. Historical statistical analysis

FIGURE 5–7

RS2 U.S. Bond Market Forecasts: Comovements between U.S. Treasury Yields and Government Bond Yields in Other Countries, 1986–1989

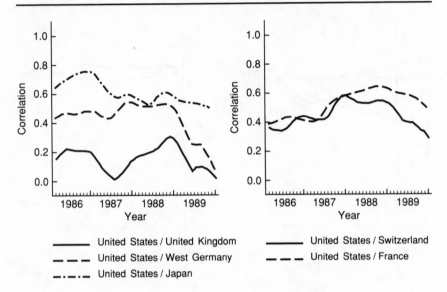

```
           United States / United Kingdom          United States / Switzerland
    - - -  United States / West Germany      - - - United States / France
    -·-·-  United States / Japan
```

enables the QUØT to predict modest or moderate pricing inefficiencies, for assets as well as for cross-border currency comparisons.

Our approach to forecasting returns assumes systematic factors determine the patterns of relative returns over time. In other words, within a local market, say, Japan, the month-to-month variations in differential returns between stocks and bonds, stocks and cash, and bonds and cash behave in a rational fashion. We used advanced statistical techniques to model the relative return pattern of asset classes to identify the factors that most indicate future returns.

A major ingredient of the QUØT is a large set of return predictors across multiple country stock and bond markets. In addition, QUØT produces a set of relative currency forecasts derived purely from quantitative factor modeling. In each case, the forecasts are determined by econometric modeling of the historical risk and return of each asset class over the most recent 5- to 10-year period.

Three classes of variables are used in each predictive model: macroeconomic series that determine the business cycle and liquidity of the country; financial market price/value variables that serve as barometers for assets that are expensive or "cheap"; and technical variables that capture market sentiment. For example, the QUØT predictor for Japanese Treasury bonds incorporates leading indicators such as cross-country interest rate spreads, trends in inflation, trends in economic growth, and the bond price relative to stock market prices.

In Figure 5–8, we show the recent history of the predictor for several major stock markets. Figure 5–9 describes an example of the Japanese market in more detail. In particular, we depict the predictors of future return. The return indicator is based on multiple regression, using the risk-adjusted return as the dependent variable, with a set of multifactor macroeconomic and market inputs as the independent variables. The regressions span a history of between 5 and 10 years and are updated monthly.

Each asset model adapts slowly to structural change over time. The estimates are made using historical (out-of-sample) data to forecast the future direction and magnitude of return continuously.

In Figure 5–9, we illustrate some of the inputs into the Japanese model. Through econometric techniques, we have determined these factors that have predictive content, and we then identified the appropriate lead relationship. For example, the graph entitled Fixed-Income Returns depicts lagged monthly bond market returns. Movements in interest rates have been found to have a significant impact on subsequent equity prices. Beneath this graph, we plot the sensitivity (as measured by a correlation coefficient) that indicates the importance of the variable in our model.

In the case of fixed-income returns, we see that the sensitivity line is rising, suggesting that interest rates have had an increasing impact on stock market moves. The relative value variable is defined as the dividend yield of the stock market less the yield of the 10-year Government. Typically, as this yield differential becomes more positive (that is, stock yields become more attractive relative to bond yields), the stock market is more likely to move higher. Not surprisingly, inflation, as measured by the wholesale price index, has proven to be a significant negative for the stock market.

The return indicator for the Japanese market adapts over time to structural change in financial markets. Typically, there are four to seven variables in the model at any time. The importance of the variables relative to each other will slowly evolve, as demonstrated by the sensitivity by graphs.

FIGURE 5–8
QUØT Forecasts: World Equity Market

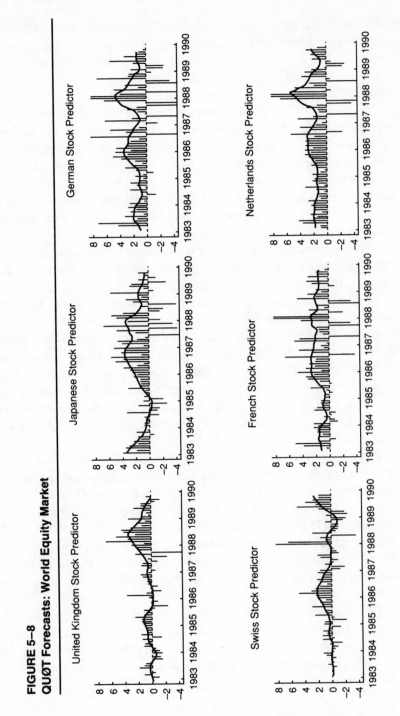

FIGURE 5–9
Japanese Stock Model

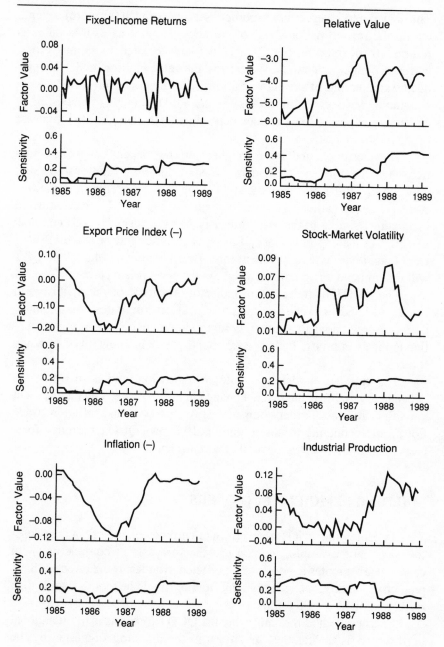

PRODUCING UNIVERSAL CURRENCY PREDICTORS

The decision to invest in cross-border assets is as much (or more) dependent on the reward/risk analysis of currency movements as it is on asset returns. In developing the QUØT, we have created numerous cross-currency predicting models. We can test the value of these models by producing simulations of currency positions according to the predictors. As in simulating the asset return models, we use a tilt technique of increasing or decreasing exposure to a currency depending on the relative attractiveness of the return indicator.

The decision to under/overweight a currency depends on two calculations: (1) the forecast change in the spot currency relationship, say, between the dollar and the yen; and (2) the forward premium in the forward exchange markets. The currency relationship models are constructed in a manner similar to the asset forecasts. We use financial and economic variables as leading indicators. If the spot currency forecasts are of sufficient magnitude, after adjustment for forward premiums, then the QUØT will recommend an under/overweight in the appropriate currency.

The QUØT includes return indicators for most of the major world stock and bond markets. In addition, QUØT incorporates cross-country currency predictions by estimating regression models similar in construction to the asset return models. Each month, there is a new set of currency forecasts.

The currency models are multiple regression models in which the dependent variable is the percent change in the spot rate. The independent variables are cross-border comparisons of interest rates, inflation, trade flows, and economic trends. Figure 5–10 shows QUØT currency forecasts for the dollar versus several other currencies.

BUILDING EFFICIENT FRONTIERS

We can deploy the QUØT asset return or currency predictors in many useful ways. For example, we can use the forecasts in conjunction with covariance estimates to construct an efficient frontier. If the forecasts have predictive validity, then the efficient frontier should be more valuable than merely using historical returns.

Another method for employing the QUØT forecasts is to tilt a global portfolio so as to bias the weightings in the direction suggested by the

FIGURE 5–10
QUØT Currency Forecasts

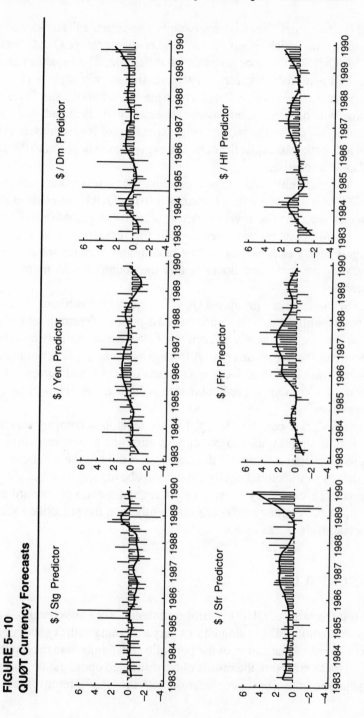

QUØT indicators. That is, overweight the countries' stocks and bonds depending on which (if any) have a higher-than-average QUØT predictor.

A QUØT tilt can be adaptable and flexible. The investor can set the level of aggressiveness from very aggressive to only slightly more assertive than a pure passive index approach. In addition, the investor can choose which countries and asset classes are to be included. The investor can also decide on the normal or passive weight for each asset class, as well as whether to adjust the currency exposures in addition to the country and asset allocations.

There are numerous ways to combine the currency components of the QUØT with the asset return forecasts. First, a QUØT investment strategy can be made for the investor who places more emphasis on currency movements than on asset returns. In this case, we would adjust the weights of the asset classes by first ranking the currency models and then allocating to stocks and bonds within the countries with more attractive currencies.

Second, we can produce a QUØT strategy by combining the currency forecasts with each asset return forecast prior to determining the allocations. That is, we can assess each asset class across borders from the perspective of the home currency. A foreign asset class will be attractive only if some combination of local asset return indicator and currency forecast produces a combined prediction that is higher, on average, than other alternatives.

Third, we can use the QUØT to develop a comprehensive asset allocation strategy and to combine a currency exposure overlay. This approach would allocate all the assets according to the asset class return model, as in the global equity simulation above, and then add a currency overlay. This currency overlay would require the use of forward markets to adjust the currency exposure differently than the prescribed allocation to a country's stocks or bonds.

TEST RESULTS

To test the value of QUØT portfolio strategies, we have conducted numerous simulations. These simulations vary according to the type of optimization alogrithm, the nature of the portfolio constraints, and the inputs used.

Here we present the results of a constrained optimization, which uses a quadratic optimizer in conjunction with the QUØT return forecasts and

RS2 correlations.[6] The simulation begins in 1983 and constructs a new optimization each month through November 1989.

Suppose a hypothetical investment strategy is to invest in several world equity and world bond markets. Suppose further that the asset classes and normal weights are set as follows: U.S. stock, 25 percent; U.K. stock, 6 percent; Japanese stock, 32 percent; German stock, 1 percent; Swiss stock, 1 percent; French stock, 1 percent; Netherlands stock, 1 percent; Swedish stock, less than 1 percent; Australian stock, 1 percent; Canadian stock, 1 percent; Hong Kong stock, less than 1 percent; U.S. bonds, 15 percent; U.K. bonds, 2 percent; Japanese bonds, 7 percent; German bonds, 2 percent; Swiss bonds, less than 1 percent; French bonds, 2 percent; Canadian bonds, 1 percent.

In this simulation, we allow the relative attractiveness of the asset indicators to tilt toward favorable assets and away from the less favorable assets. Hypothetically, if all the asset relative return indicators have the same reading, such as zero, then the portfolio would never be adjusted or tilted away from the normal weights, unless the asset correlations induced it.

In reality, the QUØT return indicators often diverge when predicting that the reward/risk ratio is much higher in one stock (bond) market than in another. We therefore set limits for how much to overweight or underweight each asset. Table 5–1 shows the monthly allocations in the QUØT simulation conducted for the six years from February 1983 to November 1989. Each month's weighting is based only on data that would have been known at the time. That is, the weights in February 1983 are constructed with multifactor return models using data and estimates only up to February 1983.

This simulation is a somewhat conservative use of the QUØT. Table 5–1 shows the preset normal weights and maximum or minimum constraints. The next three rows of the weighting report show the maximum, minimum, and seven-year average for each country's stock or bond market according to the simulation.

It is important to note that often the actual average weight in a country is typically above or below the preset normal weight for two reasons: (1) the normal weight is considered a "long-term" goal and (2) over the seven-year simulation, one country's return and correlation predictors may have been above or below average relative to other countries. For example, the QUØT weighted the U.S. stock market from 15 percent to 35 percent of the total, with the monthly average being 22 percent.

TABLE 5–1

QUØT Optimized Simulation—Global Stocks, Bonds, and Cash

Stock Allocations: QUØT General Global Portfolio

	U.S. Stocks	U.K. Stocks	Japanese Stocks	German Stocks	Swiss Stocks	French Stocks	Nether- lands Stocks	Swedish Stocks	Australian Stocks	Canadian Stocks	Hong Kong Stocks
Constraints											
Maximum	35.2%	7.9%	45.3%	2.0%	0.9%	1.8%	0.9%	0.3%	1.0%	2.0%	0.6%
Minimum	15.1	3.4	19.4	0.9	0.4	0.8	0.4	0.1	0.4	0.9	0.3
Normal	25.2	5.7	32.3	1.4	0.6	1.3	0.7	0.2	0.7	1.4	0.5
Results											
Maximum	35.2%	7.9%	45.3%	2.0%	0.8%	1.8%	0.9%	0.3%	1.0%	2.0%	0.6%
Minimum	15.1	3.4	19.4	0.8	0.4	0.8	0.4	0.1	0.4	0.8	0.3
Average	21.6	5.4	36.3	1.6	0.6	1.6	0.8	0.2	0.8	1.3	0.5
8302	35.2%	3.4%	38.3%	0.8%	0.4%	0.8%	0.4%	0.1%	0.4%	0.8%	0.3%
8303	35.2	3.4	34.2	2.0	0.8	0.8	0.4	0.1	0.4	2.0	0.6
8304	18.7	3.4	45.3	2.0	0.4	1.8	0.9	0.1	0.4	0.8	0.6
8305	15.1	3.4	45.3	2.0	0.4	1.8	0.9	0.1	0.4	0.8	0.6
8306	15.1	7.9	45.3	2.0	0.4	1.8	0.9	0.1	1.0	0.8	0.6
8307	15.1	7.5	45.3	2.0	0.8	0.8	0.9	0.1	1.0	0.8	0.6
8308	15.1	7.9	45.3	2.0	0.8	1.8	0.9	0.3	1.0	0.8	0.6
8309	22.8	3.4	45.3	2.0	0.4	1.8	0.4	0.1	0.4	0.8	0.3
8310	35.2	3.4	19.4	2.0	0.4	1.8	0.9	0.3	1.0	1.6	0.6
8311	15.1	3.4	45.3	2.0	0.8	1.8	0.9	0.3	1.0	0.8	0.6
8312	15.1	3.4	34.1	2.0	0.8	1.8	0.9	0.3	1.0	0.8	0.6
8401	15.1	3.4	32.6	2.0	0.8	1.8	0.9	0.3	1.0	0.8	0.6
8402	15.1	3.4	45.3	2.0	0.8	1.8	0.9	0.1	0.4	0.8	0.6
8403	15.1	3.4	45.3	2.0	0.4	1.8	0.9	0.3	0.4	0.8	0.3
8404	15.1	7.9	33.4	2.0	0.8	1.8	0.9	0.3	1.0	0.8	0.6
8405	15.1	3.4	45.3	2.0	0.4	1.8	0.9	0.3	0.4	0.8	0.6
8406	15.1	7.9	35.9	0.8	0.8	1.8	0.9	0.3	0.4	0.8	0.6
8407	30.0	7.9	19.4	2.0	0.8	1.8	0.9	0.3	1.0	0.8	0.6
8408	15.1	3.4	45.3	2.0	0.8	1.8	0.9	0.1	0.4	0.8	0.6
8409	15.1	7.9	29.8	0.8	0.8	1.8	0.9	0.3	1.0	0.8	0.6
8410	35.2	7.9	19.4	2.0	0.8	1.8	0.9	0.3	1.0	2.0	0.6
8411	35.2	3.4	36.8	0.8	0.4	1.8	0.4	0.1	0.4	0.8	0.3
8412	25.6	7.9	19.4	2.0	0.8	1.8	0.9	0.3	1.0	0.8	0.6
8501	35.2	3.4	39.3	0.8	0.4	0.8	0.4	0.1	0.4	0.8	0.3
8502	35.2	3.4	19.4	2.0	0.4	0.8	0.9	0.3	1.0	2.0	0.6
8503	15.1	7.9	45.3	0.8	0.4	0.8	0.4	0.1	0.4	0.8	0.6
8504	33.3	7.9	19.4	0.8	0.4	1.8	0.9	0.1	0.4	0.8	0.6
8505	15.1	7.9	44.2	0.8	0.8	0.8	0.9	0.1	1.0	0.8	0.6
8506	35.2	7.9	19.4	2.0	0.8	1.8	0.9	0.3	1.0	2.0	0.6
8507	15.3	7.9	45.3	2.0	0.4	0.8	0.4	0.1	1.0	0.8	0.3
8508	15.1	3.4	45.3	0.8	0.8	0.8	0.9	0.1	1.0	0.8	0.6
8509	15.1	3.4	45.3	2.0	0.8	1.8	0.9	0.1	0.4	0.8	0.3
8510	35.2	3.4	19.9	2.0	0.8	1.8	0.9	0.3	0.4	2.0	0.6
8511	24.7	3.4	45.3	2.0	0.8	1.8	0.9	0.1	0.4	0.8	0.6
8512	15.1	3.4	45.3	0.8	0.4	1.8	0.4	0.1	0.4	0.8	0.3
8601	15.1	3.4	43.3	2.0	0.4	1.8	0.9	0.1	0.4	0.8	0.3
8602	15.1	3.4	45.3	2.0	0.4	1.8	0.4	0.1	0.4	0.8	0.3
8603	15.1	3.4	42.3	2.0	0.8	1.8	0.4	0.1	0.4	0.8	0.3
8604	15.1	3.4	45.3	0.9	0.8	0.8	0.4	0.3	0.4	0.8	0.3
8605	35.2	3.4	21.3	2.0	0.8	1.8	0.9	0.3	0.4	2.0	0.3
8606	35.2	3.4	19.4	2.0	0.8	1.8	0.9	0.3	0.4	2.0	0.6

TABLE 5–1—*Continued*

Bond Allocations: QUØT General Global Portfolio

	U.S. Bonds	U.K. Bonds	Japanese Bonds	German Bonds	Swiss Bonds	French Bonds	Australian Bonds	Canadian Bonds
Constraints								
Maximum	21.1%	3.2%	9.8%	3.3%	0.1%	2.4%	0.4%	1.7%
Minimum	9.0	1.4	4.2	1.4	0.0	1.0	0.2	0.7
Normal	15.1	2.3	7.0	2.3	0.1	1.7	0.3	1.2
Results								
Maximum	21.1%	3.2%	9.8%	3.3%	0.1%	2.4%	0.4%	1.7%
Minimum	9.0	1.4	4.2	1.4	0.0	1.0	0.2	0.7
Average	14.9	2.1	6.3	2.3	0.0	2.1	0.3	1.1
8302	9.0%	1.4%	4.2%	1.4%	0.0%	1.0%	0.2%	1.7%
8303	9.0	1.4	4.2	3.3	0.1	1.0	0.2	0.7
8304	9.0	3.2	9.8	1.4	0.0	1.0	0.2	0.7
8305	16.9	3.2	4.2	1.4	0.0	2.4	0.2	0.7
8306	9.0	1.4	8.8	1.4	0.1	2.4	0.2	0.7
8307	9.0	1.4	9.8	1.4	0.0	2.4	0.2	0.7
8308	11.1	3.2	4.2	1.4	0.0	2.4	0.2	0.7
8309	9.0	1.4	4.2	3.3	0.0	2.4	0.2	1.7
8310	21.1	3.2	4.2	1.4	0.1	2.4	0.2	0.7
8311	9.0	3.2	9.8	1.4	0.1	2.4	0.2	1.7
8312	21.1	1.4	9.8	3.3	0.1	2.4	0.2	0.7
8401	21.1	3.2	9.8	1.9	0.1	2.4	0.2	1.7
8402	10.7	1.4	9.8	3.3	0.1	2.4	0.2	0.7
8403	11.4	1.4	9.8	3.3	0.1	2.4	0.2	0.7
8404	21.1	3.2	4.2	3.3	0.1	2.4	0.2	0.7
8405	11.1	1.4	9.8	3.3	0.0	2.4	0.2	0.7
8406	21.1	1.4	4.2	3.3	0.1	2.4	0.2	1.7
8407	21.1	3.2	4.2	1.4	0.0	2.4	0.2	1.7
8408	13.5	3.2	4.2	3.3	0.1	2.4	0.2	1.7
8409	21.1	3.2	9.8	1.4	0.1	2.4	0.2	1.7
8410	12.8	3.2	4.2	3.3	0.1	2.4	0.2	1.7
8411	9.0	1.4	4.2	1.4	0.0	2.4	0.2	0.7
8412	21.1	2.7	9.8	1.4	0.1	2.4	0.4	0.7
8501	9.0	1.4	4.2	1.4	0.0	1.0	0.2	0.7
8502	21.1	1.4	6.7	1.4	0.0	2.4	0.2	0.7
8503	9.8	3.2	9.8	1.4	0.0	1.0	0.2	1.7
8504	21.1	3.2	4.2	1.4	0.1	2.4	0.2	0.7
8505	9.0	3.2	9.8	1.4	0.0	1.0	0.4	1.7
8506	12.6	3.2	4.2	3.3	0.0	2.4	0.4	1.7
8507	9.0	3.2	9.8	1.4	0.0	1.0	0.4	0.7
8508	16.7	1.4	7.1	1.4	0.1	2.4	0.4	0.7
8509	11.1	1.4	9.8	3.3	0.0	2.4	0.2	0.7
8510	21.1	1.4	4.2	1.4	0.1	2.4	0.2	1.7
8511	9.0	1.4	4.2	1.4	0.0	1.0	0.2	1.7
8512	21.1	1.4	4.2	1.4	0.0	1.0	0.2	1.7
8601	21.1	1.4	4.2	1.4	0.0	2.4	0.2	0.7
8602	16.8	1.4	4.2	3.3	0.0	2.4	0.2	1.7
8603	21.1	1.4	4.2	1.4	0.0	2.4	0.2	1.7
8604	21.1	1.4	4.2	1.4	0.0	2.4	0.2	0.7
8605	21.1	1.4	4.2	1.4	0.0	2.4	0.2	0.7
8606	21.1	1.4	4.2	2.0	0.0	2.4	0.2	1.7

TABLE 5–1—*Continued*

Stock Allocations: QUØT General Global Portfolio

	U.S. Stocks	U.K. Stocks	Japanese Stocks	German Stocks	Swiss Stocks	French Stocks	Netherlands Stocks	Swedish Stocks	Australian Stocks	Canadian Stocks	Hong Kong Stocks
Constraints											
Maximum	35.2%	7.9%	45.3%	2.0%	0.9%	1.8%	0.9%	0.3%	1.0%	2.0%	0.6%
Minimum	15.1	3.4	19.4	0.9	0.4	0.8	0.4	0.1	0.4	0.9	0.3
Normal	25.2	5.7	32.3	1.4	0.6	1.3	0.7	0.2	0.7	1.4	0.5
Results											
Maximum	35.2%	7.9%	45.3%	2.0%	0.8%	1.8%	0.9%	0.3%	1.0%	2.0%	0.6%
Minimum	15.1	3.4	19.4	0.8	0.4	0.8	0.4	0.1	0.4	0.8	0.3
Average	21.6	5.4	36.3	1.6	0.6	1.6	0.8	0.2	0.8	1.3	0.5
8607	17.2%	3.4%	45.3%	0.8%	0.4%	0.8%	0.4%	0.1%	0.4%	0.8%	0.3%
8608	26.3	3.4	45.3	2.0	0.4	1.8	0.9	0.3	0.4	0.8	0.3
8609	27.4	3.4	45.3	0.8	0.8	0.8	0.4	0.1	0.4	0.8	0.3
8610	15.1	3.4	38.4	2.0	0.8	1.8	0.9	0.3	1.0	2.0	0.6
8611	15.1	3.4	45.3	2.0	0.4	1.8	0.9	0.1	1.0	0.8	0.6
8612	15.1	3.4	45.3	0.8	0.8	0.8	0.9	0.1	1.0	0.8	0.3
8701	24.4	3.4	45.3	0.8	0.8	1.8	0.4	0.1	1.0	2.0	0.3
8702	34.6	3.4	19.4	0.8	0.4	1.8	0.9	0.3	1.0	0.8	0.3
8703	15.1	3.4	45.3	2.0	0.4	1.8	0.9	0.3	1.0	0.8	0.6
8704	15.1	7.9	45.3	2.0	0.8	1.8	0.9	0.3	1.0	0.8	0.6
8705	15.1	3.4	45.3	0.8	0.4	0.8	0.4	0.1	0.4	0.8	0.3
8706	35.2	3.4	19.4	0.8	0.8	1.8	0.9	0.3	1.0	2.0	0.6
8707	34.3	3.4	19.4	2.0	0.8	1.8	0.9	0.3	1.0	2.0	0.6
8708	15.1	3.4	45.3	2.0	0.8	1.8	0.9	0.3	0.4	2.0	0.6
8709	15.1	7.9	45.3	2.0	0.4	1.8	0.9	0.3	1.0	0.8	0.6
8710	15.1	3.4	32.2	0.8	0.8	1.8	0.9	0.1	0.4	2.0	0.3
8711	15.1	7.9	45.3	0.8	0.4	0.8	0.4	0.1	0.7	0.8	0.3
8712	22.9	7.9	19.4	2.0	0.8	1.8	0.9	0.3	1.0	2.0	0.6
8801	15.1	3.4	45.3	2.0	0.8	1.8	0.9	0.3	1.0	2.0	0.6
8802	35.0	7.9	19.4	2.0	0.8	1.8	0.9	0.3	1.0	2.0	0.6
8803	17.8	7.9	45.3	2.0	0.8	1.8	0.9	0.3	1.0	2.0	0.6
8804	21.4	7.9	45.3	0.8	0.4	0.8	0.4	0.1	1.0	2.0	0.3
8805	20.9	7.9	45.3	2.0	0.4	1.8	0.9	0.3	1.0	0.8	0.6
8806	35.2	3.4	19.4	2.0	0.8	1.8	0.9	0.3	1.0	2.0	0.6
8807	31.9	7.9	19.4	2.0	0.4	1.8	0.9	0.3	1.0	2.0	0.6
8808	15.1	7.9	38.5	0.8	0.8	0.8	0.4	0.1	1.0	2.0	0.3
8809	24.6	7.9	19.4	0.8	0.4	0.8	0.9	0.3	0.4	2.0	0.6
8810	15.1	7.9	45.3	2.0	0.4	1.8	0.9	0.1	1.0	0.8	0.6
8811	15.1	7.9	45.3	2.0	0.4	1.2	0.4	0.1	1.0	0.8	0.3
8812	33.6	3.4	19.4	2.0	0.4	1.8	0.9	0.3	1.0	2.0	0.6
8901	15.1	7.9	34.0	0.8	0.4	1.8	0.9	0.3	1.0	0.8	0.6
8902	15.1	7.9	45.3	2.0	0.8	1.8	0.9	0.3	0.4	2.0	0.6
8903	24.1	7.9	19.4	0.8	0.4	1.8	0.4	0.1	0.4	2.0	0.6
8904	15.1	7.9	29.6	0.8	0.4	1.8	0.4	0.1	1.0	2.0	0.6
8905	15.1	7.9	45.3	2.0	0.4	1.8	0.9	0.1	1.0	2.0	0.6
8906	15.1	7.9	45.1	2.0	0.8	1.8	0.9	0.1	1.0	2.0	0.6
8907	35.2	7.9	19.4	2.0	0.8	1.8	0.9	0.3	1.0	2.0	0.6
8908	15.1	7.9	44.2	2.0	0.8	1.8	0.9	0.1	1.0	2.0	0.6
8909	33.2	7.9	19.4	2.0	0.8	1.8	0.9	0.3	1.0	2.0	0.6
8910	15.1	3.4	31.3	2.0	0.8	1.8	0.9	0.3	1.0	2.0	0.6
8911	15.1	4.7	45.3	2.0	0.8	0.8	0.9	0.3	1.0	2.0	0.3

TABLE 5–1—*Concluded*

Bond Allocations: QUØT General Global Portfolio

	U.S. Bonds	U.K. Bonds	Japanese Bonds	German Bonds	Swiss Bonds	French Bonds	Australian Bonds	Canadian Bonds
Constraints								
Maximum	21.1%	3.2%	9.8%	3.3%	0.1%	2.4%	0.4%	1.7%
Minimum	9.0	1.4	4.2	1.4	0.0	1.0	0.2	0.7
Normal	15.1	2.3	7.0	2.3	0.1	1.7	0.3	1.2
Results								
Maximum	21.1%	3.2%	9.8%	3.3%	0.1%	2.4%	0.4%	1.7%
Minimum	9.0	1.4	4.2	1.4	0.0	1.0	0.2	0.7
Average	14.9	2.1	6.3	2.3	0.0	2.1	0.3	1.1
8607	21.1%	1.4%	4.2%	1.4%	0.0%	1.0%	0.2%	0.7%
8608	9.0	1.4	4.2	1.4	0.0	1.0	0.2	0.7
8609	9.0	1.4	4.2	1.4	0.0	2.4	0.2	0.7
8610	21.1	1.4	4.2	3.3	0.1	2.4	0.4	0.7
8611	12.3	1.4	9.8	1.4	0.0	2.4	0.4	0.7
8612	19.5	3.2	4.2	1.4	0.0	1.0	0.4	0.7
8701	9.0	1.4	4.2	1.4	0.0	2.4	0.4	0.7
8702	21.1	3.2	4.2	3.3	0.1	2.4	0.2	1.7
8703	12.4	1.4	9.8	1.4	0.0	2.4	0.2	0.7
8704	12.9	1.4	4.2	1.4	0.1	2.4	0.2	0.7
8705	21.1	1.4	4.9	1.4	0.1	2.4	0.2	0.7
8706	21.1	1.4	4.2	3.3	0.1	2.4	0.4	0.7
8707	21.1	1.4	4.2	3.3	0.1	2.4	0.2	0.7
8708	9.4	1.4	9.8	3.3	0.1	2.4	0.2	0.7
8709	13.4	1.4	4.2	1.4	0.0	2.4	0.2	0.7
8710	21.1	3.2	9.8	3.3	0.1	2.4	0.4	1.7
8711	9.0	3.2	9.8	3.3	0.0	1.0	0.2	0.7
8712	21.1	1.4	9.8	3.3	0.1	2.4	0.4	1.7
8801	9.0	1.4	9.8	3.2	0.0	1.0	0.4	1.7
8802	9.0	1.4	9.8	3.3	0.0	2.4	0.4	1.7
8803	9.0	1.4	4.2	1.4	0.1	2.4	0.2	0.7
8804	9.0	1.4	4.2	1.4	0.0	2.4	0.4	0.7
8805	9.0	1.4	4.2	1.4	0.0	1.0	0.2	0.7
8806	19.2	1.4	4.2	3.3	0.0	2.4	0.2	1.7
8807	21.1	1.4	4.2	1.4	0.0	2.4	0.4	0.7
8808	21.1	1.4	4.2	3.3	0.1	1.0	0.4	0.7
8809	21.1	3.2	9.8	3.3	0.1	2.4	0.2	1.7
8810	9.0	3.2	6.0	1.4	0.0	2.4	0.2	1.7
8811	9.0	3.2	9.8	1.4	0.0	1.0	0.2	0.7
8812	21.1	1.4	4.2	3.3	0.1	2.4	0.4	1.7
8901	21.1	3.2	4.2	3.3	0.0	2.4	0.2	1.7
8902	10.1	3.2	4.2	3.3	0.0	1.0	0.2	0.7
8903	21.1	3.2	9.8	3.3	0.0	2.4	0.4	1.7
8904	21.1	1.4	9.8	3.3	0.0	2.4	0.4	1.7
8905	9.0	3.2	4.6	1.4	0.0	2.4	0.4	1.7
8906	9.0	1.4	4.2	3.3	0.1	2.4	0.4	1.7
8907	12.6	3.2	4.2	3.3	0.1	2.4	0.4	1.7
8908	9.0	3.2	4.2	3.3	0.1	2.4	0.4	0.7
8909	9.0	3.2	9.8	3.3	0.1	2.4	0.4	1.7
8910	21.1	3.2	9.8	3.3	0.1	1.0	0.4	1.7
8911	9.0	1.4	9.8	3.3	0.1	1.0	0.4	1.7

Note that the QUØT underweighted the U.S. market in general, compared with the normal weight of 25 percent set prior to the simulation. This is because the U.S. stock indicator was, on average, lower than the indicators in some of the other countries. In the same simulation, Japan received an average monthly weight of 36 percent, with a range of 19 percent to 45 percent.

The simulation constructs an optimized portfolio using the forecasting techniques described above. The optimization program solves for the efficient frontier, using a quadratic program and utility maximization. The point on the frontier, in the risk dimension, shown in Table 5–1, is determined by a utility maximization. The investor is assumed to seek the same level of risk as a global passive strategy. The program determines the optimal portfolio each month consistent with this level of risk.

The simulation considers currency exposure as well as local market return forecasts. The optimization is conducted in terms of U.S. dollars. Thus, each correlation and return forecast is translated into dollar estimates, using the QUØT currency models. The country weights are, therefore, incurring currency exposure as well as asset risk.

Figure 5–11 shows the cumulative wealth relative, in U.S. dollar terms. The lower line is the benchmark that has asset weightings similar to a global benchmark (shown as norms at the top of Table 5–1). The benchmark stock-versus-bond mix is assumed to be 70 percent stocks and 30 percent bonds. The benchmark weights do not change from month to month.

The annualized dollar performance of the benchmark was 23.6 percent. The simulated QUØT performance, however, was 28.4 percent. Each month the QUØT portfolio is rebalanced, with the limits being approximately plus or minus 40 percent of the benchmark positions. At the start of the optimized simulation, both the benchmark and the portfolio have the same weights, after which the active portfolio is allowed to vary to within 40 percent of the benchmark weight.

CONCLUSIONS

John Tukey wrote, "Far better an approximate answer to the right question, which is often vague, than an exact answer to the wrong question, which can always be made more precise."[7]

In the world of quantitative investing, Tukey's insight translates into the corollary that without carefully constructed inputs, optimizers revert

FIGURE 5–11
Global Quantitative Simulation, 1983–1989

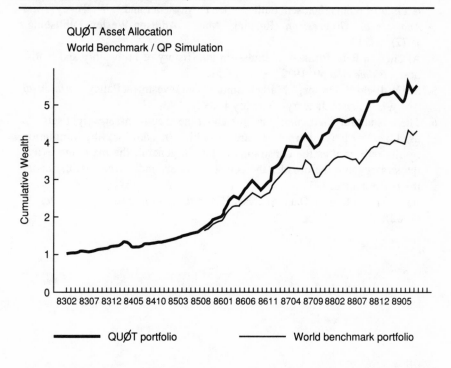

QUØT Asset Allocation
World Benchmark / QP Simulation

————— QUØT portfolio   ————— World benchmark portfolio

to little more than error maximizers. Our work on global optimization demonstrates that using inputs such as QUØT and RS2 forecasts can be very profitable.

ENDNOTES

1. QUØT is a quantitative global asset allocation product used at Salomon Brothers, Inc. QUØT, which stands for quantitative underweight/overweight tilt, utilizes many of the techniques discussed in this chapter.
2. This issue has been raised several times recently. For example, see "Rethinking International Diversification," Margaret A. Elliott, *Corporate Finance*, September 1989, p. 69.
3. Mosteller and Tukey illustrate robust correlation with a simple example. Suppose a series X consists of values .02, .99, 2.01, 2.98, 4.03, 5.01, 6.05, 6.98, 8.07, 9.03, 25.00. Correspondingly, a series Y consists of values .04, 1.03,

1.97, 2.96, 3.97, 4.98, 6.07, 7.03, 8.00, 8.96, −25.00. The standard correlation of X and Y is −0.733. The robust, trimmed correlation is +0.999. The last pair of points represent outliers. See F. Mosteller and J. W. Tukey, *Data Analysis and Regression* (Reading, Mass.: Addison-Wesley Publishing, 1977), p. 213.

4. As cited in R.L. Plackett, "Studies in the History of Probability and Statistics," *Biometrika* 59, 1972, pp. 239-251.
5. See William G. Droms, "Market Timing as an Investment Policy," *Financial Analysts Journal*, January–February 1989, pp. 73–77.
6. There is nothing particularly unique about the specific asset weight settings used here. Many alternatives are possible. In addition, the simulation results will vary as the constraints differ. In general, the more aggressive the strategy and the broader the choice of assets and currencies, the better the performance.
7. See "The Future of Data Analysis," *Annals of Mathematical Statistics* 33 (1962).

CHAPTER 6

IMPLEMENTING THE ASSET ALLOCATION DECISION

Edgar W. Barksdale
William L. Green

The analysis and hiring of a manager, whether predominantly quantitative or qualitative in style, is an inexact science often requiring analysis of a puzzle with misplaced strategic pieces. For this reason, it is critical to the success of the analysis procedure that as many things be done as logically as possible. Unfortunately, through laziness or inexperience, most manager analyses are done backward that is, by screening initially on the basis of historical performance. This approach results in dissatisfaction and ongoing mediocrity, leading eventually to outright termination. The purpose of this chapter is to present the criteria that have proven important in observing money management firms and to describe an organized process of analysis designed to result in more satisfying and long-lasting relationships than often occur in investment programs.

Proper hiring methodology, regardless of the manager's style, involves both qualitative and quantitative criteria, in that order. Performing the qualitative side first involves more work because one cannot rely on the shortcut that is responsible for the failure of most money manager evaluations: historical performance as a predictor of future success. In a recent in-house study, the performance of 189 major investment management firms was examined over a 10-year period. The firms were ranked in performance quintiles based on their results during the first five years of the period, and each quintile was then examined to see how the firms in that quintile performed relative to the universe during the second five years of the period. Of the firms with returns in the first quintile over the initial five years, exactly one half had performance below the 189-manager sample median during the subsequent five-year period. These results strongly suggested that future relative returns of an investment management firm could not be predicted using historical relative returns.

In fact, the use of historical performance rankings is akin to reading the last chapter of a mystery novel first—it is then easy to separate the heroes from the villains. Unfortunately, the mystery of investment performance seldom unfolds the same way twice. Performance rankings may solve the mysteries of the past, but they provide no clues for the future. This is not to say that historical data is not useful. Actually, it is quite useful in ways that will be discussed later in the quantitative portion of this chapter.

THE QUALITATIVE SIDE

To properly evaluate a manager from a qualitative standpoint, one must perform substantial background work. This should include the obvious process of determining asset mix, thereby establishing the general type of manager required, as well as a thorough understanding of the benchmarks available for the type of management to be implemented. This, in turn, leads to a required study of the manager styles available for the investment. Assuming all of this has been done, the most important task is one of ongoing contact with as many investment firms as humanly possible. Questionnaires, designed to help circumvent this process, often become pieces of paper in a file that make sure one is never accused of neglecting fiduciary responsibility. Seldom, if ever, should they take the place of person-to-person contact as they are designed to shorten the list of manager candidates, not to answer the detailed questions of how and why that are so essential to successful manager evaluation.

Many very good investment managers are available. The problem is that they are hidden within the walls of institutions and rightly protected by a vanguard of marketing and client service people whose job it is to make sure they are not bothered on a day-to-day basis by other than the most serious clients or prospects. Most prospective clients interview the investment firm from the top down, accepting the "house" product without adequately questioning from whence it came. To reach these key decision makers within an organization, it is best to deal with the firm from a bottom-up basis. While this is generally judged to be more important advice when looking at qualitative managers, consider the implications from the standpoint of magnitude of a change to a "black box" model versus the qualitative decision to invest in a single security. Even purely passive approaches require critical implementation judgments and ongoing evaluation of potential improvements.

Figure 6–1 shows some of the vital areas that should be covered in interviews, and it should be of no surprise that they overlap somewhat with the information requested on many questionnaires. The difference, of course, is the opportunity to go into detail on important points and to understand the context in which the answers are given. The basic purpose of the first interview with a firm is twofold. First of all, it is to gather basic information and ascertain whether there is any reason why the firm clearly does not fit into current or future needs. Most firms should make it past the first interview.

Second, it is important to obtain as much quantitative data on historical performance as possible and to carefully identify who was the responsible party(ies). Data collection must be incredibly thorough. Obviously, publicly audited and reported information is best because there have been cases of "manufactured" data. Care must be taken to assure that the data provided accurately reflects the record of the firm. For example, are the criteria for selecting the accounts comprising the performance record designed to exclude terminated accounts or portfolios with poor returns? Are returns shown before or after fees? Are the results "real" or "simulated"? Nothing should be assumed in the data collection process. At the

FIGURE 6–1
Sample Topics for Manager Interviews

- Detailed work histories of the principals involved—experience in use of quantitative techniques, investment management industry contacts, etc.
- Dynamics of the organization—who controls the final decision in such matters as a change in model parameters or how quickly decisions are carried out.
- Flexibility of approach to changing market environments.
- Comfort with relevant benchmarks—the manager's idea of his perfect "normal" portfolio.
- Compensation structure—incentives for superior performance.
- Organization size and plans for future growth—reasonableness given firm's style and strategy, plans for new approaches.

very least, backup information should include the benchmark(s) of record, the benchmark the manager was targeting, legal or client constraints, assets managed during each period of performance (both firm and account), range of performance between managed accounts with similar objectives, and special events occurring during the period of record (personal illness, forced liquidations, etc.). In the case of ex post (constructed) data, which is often offered in lieu of actual results as justification for the consideration of a purely quantitative approach, all assumptions and methodology need to be rigorously examined.

Once the data analysis process is complete, the firm should then be judged qualitatively from a preliminary basis with respect to its investment style and what that style should have achieved given the market action during the defined time period. Normal portfolios, discussed in the next section, that segment different styles from overall market action can be very helpful in this exercise. The qualitative conclusions drawn from this analysis can then be compared to the actual results to see if the qualitative impressions match the quantitative results. This process is equally applicable to managers having qualitative or quantitative styles. A primary difference in analyzing quantitative and qualitative relates to the differences from the benchmark, which is tolerated or expected. For quantitative managers that emphasize risk control, only small differences from benchmarks are tolerated—referred to as "tracking error" by indexers. For less quantitative managers, larger differences are expected and analyzed in terms of relative variance and coefficients of correlation.

THE QUANTITATIVE SIDE

As implied early in this chapter, quantitative analysis is extremely helpful in finding and evaluating good managers. The problem is that it is often used in the wrong way; for example, when used as a screening device, historical performance rankings are implicitly assumed to be predictive of the future. Unfortunately, quantitative analysis is sometimes used as justification for a decision that has already been made. For that reason, it is extremely important to understand the implications of any implicit or explicit assumptions in the quantitative analytical process. The focus of quantitative tools should be on the determination of the value that a manager adds to the investment management process. Many of these tools are as much common sense based as they are theory based, and, prior to the quantitative evaluation of a manager, thought should be given to the correct tools to be used in the evaluation process. Expectations with respect to the likely results of the quantitative evaluation process should be formed based on knowledge gained in the qualitative evaluation process.

The first tool to be considered is an appropriate benchmark, usually referred to as a *normal portfolio*. Broadly defined, a normal portfolio represents a "fair" benchmark against which to measure and interpret a manager's performance. It consists of a neutral, nonjudgmental representation of the manager's investment universe. It is intended to capture any permanent style "bias," as reflected in particular portfolio characteristics, but should not reflect information that the manager uniquely incorporates into his investment approach. The normal portfolio should be well diversified, eliminating any undue influence from individual issues. Passive styles, by definition, have already established the index benchmark as the normal portfolio. For active styles, in many cases the normal will differ from the benchmark of record, usually a recognized market index. It is paradoxical that most investors expect a manager to beat the major market benchmark on a consistent basis (i.e., in the short term) with a portfolio that substantially differs from the market and, in fact, terminate managers for running portfolios that track the market too closely ("closet indexers"). The fact is that there usually is an alternative index, a combination of indices or an artificial portfolio that can be more helpful in explaining value added than a major market index.

While a normal portfolio can be constructed in a variety of ways, the preferred methodology depends largely on certain aspects of a manager's approach. Many start out by using the qualitative knowledge gained in discussions with a manager to determine likely existing benchmark indices that might be appropriate as normal portfolios. Often, many levels and combinations of indices are required to accurately describe a style. For example, in the case of an unrestricted top-down global strategy, one of the recognized global indices might be appropriate. However, it may very well be necessary to remove an individual country component of that index and substitute an alternative (for example, replacing the first section of the Tokyo stock exchange with a hybrid combining both the first and second sections) or, in another instance, eliminate some country indices altogether. On the country level, style universes, such as portfolios of "growth" or "value" stocks, are appropriate for managers following those philosophies.

Unfortunately, there are no generally accepted style indices, but good normals can be developed through screening techniques. More complex normals can be tailor-made for individual managers. In cases where a manager's investment process begins with several screens, the resulting universe of securities through which the manager then applies his proprietary selection skills can serve as the normal portfolio. Alternatively, the normal portfolio may be developed by selecting a diversified list of issues having the characteristics of the manager's average exposure over time to various "factors" of return (such as size, yield, or industry weights). Regardless of design, however, the normal must be a viable alternative to the manager's portfolio; that is, the normal must be an investable portfolio of securities. As such, it can be viewed as a lower-cost, passive alternative against which the value added from the active manager's decisions obtained at relatively higher cost can be compared. Correlation results between the manager and the normal indicate the practicality of using the normal as a benchmark. After determining the normal portfolio, further analysis should be related to the study of the variances that exist between the manager and the normal.

The study of the variances can be accomplished statistically through the residual variance (goodness of fit) between the manager and the normal or through less complex methods, such as the one shown in Figure 6–2. Here the benchmark (normal) is portrayed as 1.0, and the manager's performance is shown on a quarterly and smoothed (four-quarter moving average) basis relative to the benchmark. This type of graph has several uses: two obvious ones are the graphic representation of relative volatility in the short term and the ability to observe smoothed performance data over time periods equal to the time horizon (i.e., patience level) of the investor. Time series analysis such as this is particularly helpful in follow-up qualitative conversations with a manager. It also enables one to create a pictorial histogram of relative variance, which is useful when hiring, firing, or rebalancing decisions are required (e.g., giving a manager additional assets when he has just had poor performance on the low end of his personal histogram of relative returns should be considered).

Although this type of analysis is valuable, it is only one tool of many that should be employed. Another that is helpful, shown in Figure 6–3, has the purpose of examining variance in advancing and declining markets. Experience has shown that manager style can be consistent yet not produce the same variance in declining markets as in rising markets. The

FIGURE 6–2
Relative Performance

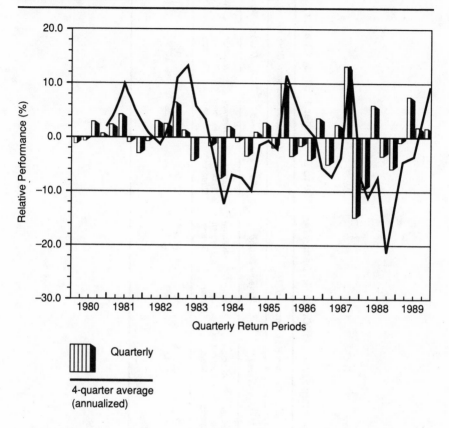

Quarterly

4-quarter average
(annualized)

figure shows that while both managers have outperformed their international benchmarks on an annualized basis over time, they did so with markedly different patterns of volatility. Manager B, for example, tends to have much more of a defensive orientation, particularly in declining markets.

Attribution analysis, which breaks total return into its component parts, is another tool frequently used in understanding performance. Unfortunately, the methodology behind this type of analysis is not standardized across the industry, and popular simplifications—such as analysis of given time horizons using a static portfolio or examination of factors on a segmented basis—can result in misleading results on the bottom line.

FIGURE 6–3
Relative Performance in Up and Down Markets versus MSCI EAFE, December 1980 to December 1989, by Quarter

Manager Name	Full-Period Return		Quarters Benchmark Up (27)				Quarters Benchmark Down (9)			
			Manager Ahead		Manager Behind		Manager Ahead		Manager Behind	
	Manager	Benchmark	Number of Quarters	Average Percent Ahead	Number of Quarters	Average Percent Behind	Number of Quarters	Average Percent Ahead	Number of Quarters	Average Percent Behind
Manager A	24.76	22.59	17	3.39%	10	(4.22)%	5	4.45%	4	(4.26)%
Manager B	23.57	22.59	15	1.42	12	(2.41)	7	2.25	2	(1.44)

* Returns for periods greater than one year are annualized.

Basically, attribution analysis makes the assumption that managers make each decision (currency selection, country selection, industry selection, etc.) in a vacuum. Since this is not the way active managers make decisions, the results are often misleading when reviewed in total. On the other hand, intensive examination of the components of the analysis can provide important insights. Attribution analysis, however, as with any of the tools discussed herein, should not be regarded as anything more than a piece to a puzzle, a basis for asking questions that will eventually result in an overall understanding of manager style.

CONCLUSION

There are certainly many more observational tools and techniques that can be developed using a basic knowledge of common statistical measures of risk along with a feel for the important situation-related factors that need evaluation. The key is to accept no single technique, either quantitative or qualitative, as the answer to an individual evaluation. Manager evaluation is most successful when it is thorough, not only because of the sheer complexity of the business and its products, but also because it can substantially reduce the possibility of negative surprises and the related psychological effects that can damage a long-term relationship.

PART 2

OPTIMAL BOND PORTFOLIOS

CHAPTER 7

INTERNATIONAL BONDS: THE ASSET CLASS

Philippe Jorion

Few investors would consider an investment strategy that systematically excludes the fixed-income market from his or her portfolio. Yet, U.S. investors routinely ignore nondollar bonds, which account for 64 percent of the world bond market. To illustrate this point, Figure 7–1 breaks down the world bond market by country. The sheer size of these markets combined with good liquidity suggests that nondollar bonds belong to diversified portfolios. Nevertheless, less than 1 percent of the total assets of U.S. pension funds are invested in nondollar bonds.

This oversight has serious implications. International bonds have a demonstrated potential for diversifying away the risks of the U.S. bond market. Also, a global bond strategy may provide increased returns without adding risk.

WHY INVEST IN INTERNATIONAL BONDS?

The case for diversification is well known: the volatility of a portfolio can be reduced by investing in securities that do not exactly move together. In fact, an actively managed portfolio that is not fully diversified will have to generate excess returns just to overcome the loss of diversification. The benefits of fixed-income diversification have been widely recognized in the U.S. markets. Witness the creation of the so-called "index" funds,

FIGURE 7–1
World Bond Market

(Market Value: $9.8 Trillion in December 1988)

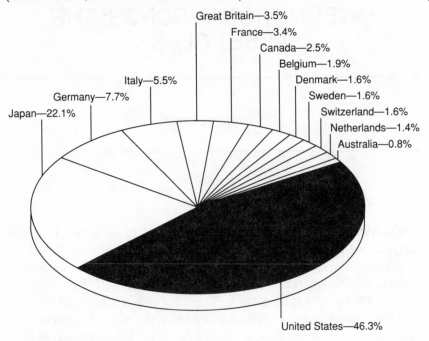

Great Britain—3.5%
France—3.4%
Canada—2.5%
Belgium—1.9%
Italy—5.5%
Denmark—1.6%
Germany—7.7%
Sweden—1.6%
Japan—22.1%
Switzerland—1.6%
Netherlands—1.4%
Australia—0.8%

United States—46.3%

Source: Salomon Brothers.

and the proliferation of bond and equity indices, which usually compete on the basis of breadth of coverage.

The main point of this argument, however, has been overlooked by U.S. investors. The lower the correlation, the greater the diversification benefits. Within the dollar fixed-income market, correlations are relatively high. These high correlations reflect common sources of uncertainty in U.S. monetary and fiscal policies as well as in U.S. economic activity. Therefore, as the number of U.S. fixed-income instruments in the portfolio increases, the reduction in risk soon becomes marginal.

Foreign economies and policies, however, are not synchronized with those of the United States. Because of the lack of comovements across national markets, the risk reduction attained from investing in a given number of global securities is likely to be much greater. Therefore, there

TABLE 7–1

Performance of World Bond Markets, January 1978–September 1989

	Government Bonds Denominated in							
	U.S. Dollar	Canadian Dollar	German Mark	Japanese Yen	British Pound	Swiss Franc	Dutch Guilder	French Franc
Annual average								
Return	10.1	10.4	8.9	13.6	11.3	6.4	9.4	9.5
Risk	11.0	13.6	16.2	17.3	18.3	16.1	15.3	14.2

is no reason to try to ecompass a wide universe of U.S. fixed-income investments and reap minimal diversification benefits. Much better results can be achieved through international diversification, if only in a few securities. Rejecting this path means exposing the portfolio to risks that could be avoided in a global portfolio.

THE HISTORICAL RECORD

Table 7–1 presents the performance of eight major government bond markets: the United States, Canada, Germany, Japan, Great Britain, Switzerland, the Netherlands, and France. These data are based on the "International Bond Indices" computed by Salomon Brothers, which include all bonds with more than five years to expiration, and are weighted by market value. The returns are measured in dollars and cover the period from January 1978 to September 1989. These monthly returns include capital gains, coupon payments, and currency effects and have been annualized for ease of exposition.

Figure 7–2 compares the return and risk of these markets by plotting the average return against the volatility. From 1978 through 1989, a number of nondollar bond markets have significantly outperformed the U.S. government bond market. The Japanese market, for instance, has returned an average of 13.6 percent per annum versus 10.1 percent for the United States.

So, why have U.S. investors shied away from these markets? Probably because of their perceived riskiness. It is true that the volatility of nondollar bonds, ranging from 14 percent to 19 percent per year, has been consistently greater than the 12 percent volatility of U.S. government

FIGURE 7–2
Are International Bonds Too Risky?

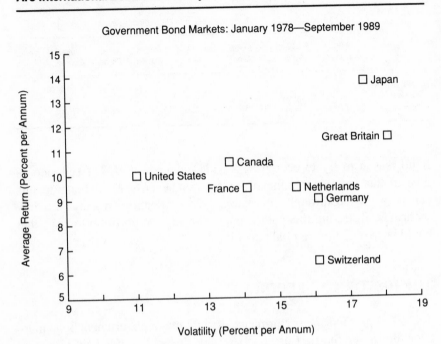

Government Bond Markets: January 1978—September 1989

bonds. This is because exchange rate risk is compounded to local interest rate risk, and exchange rates are quite volatile.

But this perception of risk is fundamentally wrong! The basic premise of modern portfolio theory is that what matters is not the individual risk, but the contribution to total portfolio risk. We know that diversification benefits are driven by low correlations among asset returns. As Table 7–2 shows, most nondollar bond markets are weakly correlated with U.S. government bond returns. Correlations range from 0.3 to 0.7, rather low numbers compared to those in the U.S. bond market. For instance, the correlation between Treasuries and U.S. corporate bonds is of the order of 0.92. Unless one is willing to consider noninvestment-grade bonds, the correlations between different sectors of the U.S. fixed-income markets are generally above 0.90. Therefore, the basic ingredients are in place for substantial benefits to accrue from international diversification in nondollar bonds.

TABLE 7–2

Correlations of World Bond Markets, January 1978–September 1989

	Government Bonds Denominated in							
	U.S. Dollar	*Canadian Dollar*	*German Mark*	*Japanese Yen*	*British Pound*	*Swiss Franc*	*Dutch Guilder*	*French Franc*
Correlation with								
U.S. dollar	1.000							
Canadian dollar	.738	1.000						
German mark	.347	.400	1.000					
Japanese yen	.273	.279	.655	1.000				
British pound	.325	.404	.558	.514	1.000			
Swiss franc	.296	.336	.890	.670	.537	1.000		
Dutch guilder	.359	.384	.965	.663	.555	.882	1.000	
French franc	.301	.360	.886	.691	.514	.813	.896	1.000

THE BENEFITS FROM INTERNATIONAL DIVERSIFICATION

These benefits can be illustrated in a number of ways. First, we can show a simple mean-variance frontier based on our data. This line—called the *efficient frontier*—is the locus of portfolios that minimize risk for a specified level of expected return. These portfolios uniformly dominate investments in single markets.

As can be seen from Figure 7–3, the U.S. index is well below the efficient frontier. This indicates that the benefits from going international can be substantial. For instance, an investor could have maintained the 10.1 percent return on the U.S. index while reducing risk from 11.0 percent to 9.8 percent. Alternatively, keeping the portfolio risk constant, the return could have been increased from 10.1 percent to 11.7 percent. This improvement of 160 basis points could have been achieved by passively investing 51 percent in the dollar, 43 percent in the yen, 4 percent in Canadian dollars, and 2 percent in pounds.

These results, however, should not be taken at face value. The optimal portfolio is based on average returns, risk measures, and correlations measured over the 1978–89 period. In practice, it is not clear that a portfolio manager could have known these parameters in advance and, thus, actually invested in this superior portfolio. A more practical approach is to build portfolios on the basis of past information only, as would a portfolio manager. The out-of-sample

FIGURE 7–3
The Case for International Bonds

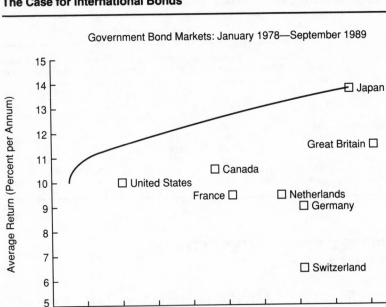

Government Bond Markets: January 1978—September 1989

performance of this strategy reflects more accurately the gains from going international (see Jorion, 1985).

More simply, the performance of the U.S. dollar bond index can be compared to that of various global bond indices. This approach is more conservative and gives a more realistic description of how returns can be affected by the inclusion of nondollar bonds. Table 7–3 shows what happens when the individual currency sectors are brought together into a nondollar index. In Table 7–1, the volatility of nondollar bonds is about 16 percent, on average. By diversifying across foreign markets, this risk is reduced to 13.8 percent. And over this time period, nondollar bonds would have returned 11.3 percent, against 10.1 percent for U.S. bonds. Finally, the value-weighted world index dominates the dollar index. It has a slightly higher return of 10.6 percent and lower risk of 10.2 percent. Clearly, nondollar bonds are not so risky when combined with domestic assets.

TABLE 7–3
Performance of Bond Portfolios, January 1978–September 1989

	U.S. Dollar Value-Weighted Index	Nondollar Value-Weighted Index	World Value-Weighted Index	Global Equal-Weighted Index	Global Hedged Equal-Weighted Index
Annual average					
Return	10.1	11.3	10.6	10.0	10.7
Risk	11.0	13.8	10.2	12.0	5.5

THE IMPACT OF CURRENCY HEDGING

If currency exposure is to be avoided, the risk of nondollar bonds can be dramatically reduced by hedging. Forward or futures contracts can be purchased, then liquidated at chosen intervals. Currency options can also be used to control currency risk while offering a wider range of protection patterns.

For currency hedging, one possible strategy is enter a forward contract every month to sell the value of the investment in the foreign currency. At the end of the month, if the foreign currency has depreciated, the translation loss on the bond will be offset by the gain on the forward contract. Of course, any gain due to a currency appreciation will also be offset by a loss on the forward contract. Overall, this strategy should yield much more stable returns.

Stripping away the currency risk by forward hedging also allows the investor to measure how returns are affected by exchange rates. This method is much more precise than comparing returns in dollars and in the local currency. Local currency returns are completely irrelevant for U.S. investors, whereas hedged foreign returns could have been realized in practice. Thus currency-hedged returns provide the only correct benchmark to measure the impact of exchange rate movements.

The results from currency hedging are reported in Table 7–4. The risk of the individual bond markets is drastically reduced by hedging. For instance, the volatility of the yen bond market drops from 17.3 percent to 6.4 percent per year. This is now much lower than the volatility of the U.S. bond market. At the same time, the average rate of return has been

TABLE 7–4
Performance of Hedged World Bond Markets, January 1978–September 1989

	Government Bonds Denominated in							
	U.S. Dollar	Canadian Dollar	German Mark	Japanese Yen	British Pound	Swiss Franc	Dutch Guilder	French Franc
Annual average								
Return	10.1	9.9	11.3	12.8	10.4	9.9	11.2	9.8
Risk	11.0	11.5	5.8	6.4	10.4	4.1	5.7	5.9

increased for some bonds. For instance, the return on DM bonds would have increased through hedging from 8.9 percent to 11.3 percent.

This can be explained by the fact that the DM has been consistently selling at a forward premium against the dollar, but the average appreciation of the DM has not fully matched the average premium. As a result, currency hedging has captured the forward premium without having to pay a large appreciation and has been profitable on a net basis. Yet, this effect cannot be used as evidence in favor of hedging since it is sample dependent and is even reversed for some currencies.

This point can be further demonstrated by comparing the performance of hedged and unhedged portfolios across various periods. Table 7–5 shows that hedging would have been beneficial during the appreciation of the dollar (1980 to 1984). On the other hand, hedging currency risk would have been disastrous in the following years (1985 to 1987). But, as the saying goes, "Hindsight is 20–20"—particularly with the dollar!

DIVERSIFICATION WITH CURRENCY HEDGING

Figure 7–4 compares two mean-variance frontiers: one with currencies hedged, the other without. Clearly, the portfolios of hedged global bonds have a sharply reduced volatility. The benefits from hedging have also been noted by Madura and Reiff (1985) and Pérold and Schulman (1988).

Over this time period, hedging shifted the efficient frontier not only to the left, but also downward. Should we have expected such a trade-off between risk and return? Unfortunately, the precise risk/return

TABLE 7–5
Impact of Hedging on Performance, by Subperiod

Period	Government Bonds Denominated in							
	U.S. Dollar	Canadian Dollar	German Mark	Japanese Yen	British Pound	Swiss Franc	Dutch Guilder	French Franc
Strong dollar: January 1980– December 1984								
Unhedged	10.4	10.9	−2.0	9.9	4.5	−5.3	−1.3	−4.1
Hedged	10.4	12.6	14.4	15.7	17.2	11.7	15.4	10.1
Weak dollar: January 1985– December 1987								
Unhedged	14.9	14.2	32.9	35.9	31.3	30.9	32.9	32.9
Hedged	14.9	11.9	11.4	12.7	10.7	8.9	10.3	10.5
Overall: January 1978– September 1989								
Unhedged	10.1	10.4	8.9	13.6	11.3	6.4	9.4	9.5
Hedged	10.1	9.9	11.3	12.8	10.4	9.9	11.2	9.8

relationship is difficult to identify. It varies greatly from one period to the next. And, the gains of these optimized portfolios may not be achievable in practice—because the manager could not have chosen such portfolios at the beginning of the sample period.

By focusing on a simple strategy, such as investing in an equally weighted portfolio, more realistic results can be obtained. The last column of Table 7–2 reports the performance of such a portfolio hedged against currency risk. The volatility of this global bond portfolio is reduced from 12.0 percent to 5.5 percent, while improving the performance by 70 basis points! A portfolio of hedged global bonds, therefore, is a much less risky asset than one solely denominated in dollars.

We can assess the benefits of hedging in light of financial theory. Long-term relationships exist between expected return and risk. Assuming risk is priced uniformly in the bond market and in the foreign exchange market, any reduction in risk must be accompanied by a reduction in expected return. In this situation, hedging reduces risk but adds no value to the portfolio on a risk-adjusted basis.

On the other hand, what if segmentations occur in international capital markets? It could very well be that risk is not priced uniformly across markets. In such a case, hedging could add value. This dilemma—still

FIGURE 7–4
Hedging Foreign Currency Bonds

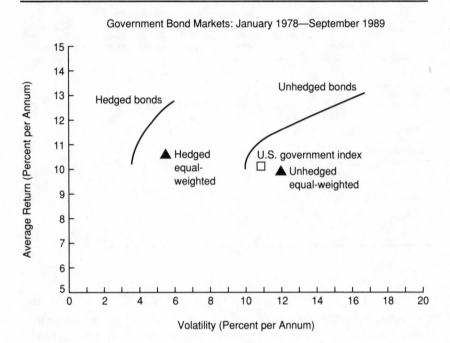

Government Bond Markets: January 1978—September 1989

TABLE 7–6
Correlations of Hedged World Bond Markets, January 1978–September 1989

	Government Bonds Denominated in							
	U.S. Dollar	Canadian Dollar	German Mark	Japanese Yen	British Pound	Swiss Franc	Dutch Guilder	French Franc
Correlation with								
U.S. dollar	1.000							
Canadian dollar	.793	1.000						
German mark	.526	.576	1.000					
Japanese yen	.393	.364	.589	1.000				
British pound	.376	.367	.381	.395	1.000			
Swiss franc	.308	.397	.505	.401	.352	1.000		
Dutch guilder	.488	.504	.698	.442	.282	.399	1.000	
French franc	.320	.418	.436	.365	.309	.266	.510	1.000

unresolved—remains a major challenge to researchers in international investments.

Another point to note from Table 7-6 is that the correlations with the U.S. bond index increase with hedging. This is because movements in exchange rates are only weakly related to movements in U.S. bond prices. Thus, hedging exchange rate risk removes a source of diversification, leaving only exposure to foreign interest rate risk, which is postively correlated across national markets. A direct implication of this observation is that hedging may not matter so much if the amounts invested in the foreign assets are small. As Jorion (1989) shows, if an investor with a 60/40 U.S. asset mix decides to invest only 5 percent in foreign bonds, the overall portfolio volatility is not much affected by hedging. In other words, the mean-variance frontier above is only truly relevant if an investor is willing to invest most of his or her portfolio into hedged foreign currency bonds.

ACTIVELY MANAGING INTERNATIONAL BONDS

The benefits of investing in international bonds can be measured by looking at the performance of naive strategies, such as holding a value-weighted or equal-weighted portfolio. But, can performance be enhanced by active management? Of course it can.

International financial markets are much more complex than domestic markets. Differing tax laws, governmental regulations, accounting standards, and exchange rate uncertainty are all complicating factors. An international portfolio manager must, therefore, demonstrate an unusual breadth of expertise. But he or she might also yield superior performance if he or she can take advantage of market imperfections due to these factors.

Take the growth of the currency swap market, for instance. Currency swaps arise because of different perceptions of credit risk across national borders, which imply different risk premiums. Translating these risk premiums into a common currency through swap agreements can reveal wide discrepancies across markets. As a result, the growth of the swap market has been fueled by corporate borrowers who scan global markets and raise funds where their comparative advantage yields the lowest cost of capital.

CONCLUSIONS

Relatively few U.S. investors know of international bonds. What does this imply? That international bonds may be mispriced relative to a U.S. risk/return trade-off.

Going international will enable investors not only to reap diversification benefits, but also to pick up abnormal returns. But as more and more U.S. investors go international, these abnormal returns are likely to fade away.

BIBLIOGRAPHY

Adler, Michael. "Global Fixed-Income Portfolio Management." *Financial Analysts Journal*, September 1983, pp. 41–48.

Cholerton, Kenneth; Pierre Pieraerts; and Bruno Solnik. "Why Invest in Foreign Currency Bonds?" *Journal of Portfolio Management*, Summer 1986, pp. 4–8.

Grubel, Herbert. "Internationally Diversified Portfolios: Welfare Gains and Capital Flows." *American Economic Review*, December 1968, pp. 1299–1314.

Jorion, Philippe. "International Portfolio Diversification with Estimation Risk." *Journal of Business*, July 1985, pp. 259–78.

————. "Asset Allocation with Unhedged and Hedged Foreign Stocks and Bonds." *Journal of Portfolio Management*, Summer 1989, pp. 49–54.

Levy, Haim, and Zvi Lerman. "The Benefits of International Diversification in Bonds." *Financial Analysts Journal*, September 1988. pp. 56–64.

Madura, Jeff, and Wallace Reiff. "A Hedge Strategy for International Portfolios." *Journal of Portfolio Management*, Fall 1985, pp. 70–74.

Pérold, Andre, and Evan Schulman. "The Free Lunch in Currency Hedging: Implications for Investment Policy and Performance Standards." *Financial Analysts Journal*, May 1988, pp. 45–50.

Solnik, Bruno, and Bernard Noetzlin, "Optimal International Asset Allocation." *Journal of Portfolio Management*, Fall 1982, pp. 11–21.

CHAPTER 8

INTERNATIONAL BOND PORTFOLIO PERFORMANCE: MEASUREMENT AND ATTRIBUTION

H. Gifford Fong
Eric M. P. Tang

It is important for an investor to track the performance of his fixed-income portfolio and to identify the sources of return on that portfolio. For instance, measuring portfolio performance would allow an investor to compare the return on his investment against another portfolio or an established benchmark, that is, a bond market index. Knowing the total return on a portfolio, however, is not sufficient. An investor should also monitor the effectiveness of the manager and identify his strengths and weaknesses by disaggregating the portfolio's total return into various components. This analysis would provide valuable insight to the investor in selecting a manager with the desired skill or management style.

A framework for performance measurement and attribution analysis for a single currency bond portfolio has been proposed by Fong, Pearson, and Vasicek.[1] The model presented in that paper decomposed the return of a portfolio into external and management effect. The management contribution is further broken down into maturity, sector/quality, and individual security selection effect. This chapter extends the Fong-Pearson-Vasicek model to a bond portfolio that includes fixed-income securities denominated in multiple currencies.

Reprinted with permission from *Journal of Portfolio Management*, Spring 1983.

EVALUATING A SINGLE-CURRENCY BOND PORTFOLIO

In evaluating the performance of a single-currency bond portfolio, the first step is the measurement of return on the portfolio over the evaluation period. The next step is an analysis of return. We can think of the analysis of return as the identification and quantification of the factors that contributed to the realized performance. The total portfolio return is partitioned into components, each component representing the effect of the given factor.

The first level of this decomposition aims at distinguishing between the effect of the external interest rate environment and the management contribution. This allows the investor to separate events that are outside the control of the portfolio manager from the effect of the portfolio management process. Denoting the total realized portfolio return by R, such a partition can be written as:

$$R = I + C, \tag{1}$$

where

I = Effect of the external interest rate environment beyond the portfolio manager's control.

C = Contribution of the management process.

If the portfolio contains the entire universe of fixed-income securities, then the return would be I, or the return due to the environment. As a proxy for this management-free portfolio, we can use the total of all default-free securities, best approximated by all outstanding domestic government issues. These are the only available securities that are truly fixed-income securities in the sense that the promised coupons and principle payments can be expected with virtual certainty free of any default risk. Including private or government agency issues constitutes an element of the management process: it involves a decision to accept a degree of default risk in exchange for the higher yields typically expected on lower-quality securities. The standard for identification of the effect of the internal interest rate environment is thus a value-weighted Treasury index.

One might argue that the relevant portfolio bogey should vary according to investor preference. In the determination of the investor's investment objectives, individual preferences are certainly appropriate.

The intent here, however, is to measure the interest rate effect on a universe that involves no other aspect, such as credit risk or spread relationships. That does not mean a comparison of the portfolio return to a broader bond market index is inappropriate. Such comparison is, in fact, an integral part of the performance analysis. It is done by performing the return analysis for the chosen bogey as well, thus allowing a direct comparison of the resulting components of return between the actual portfolio and the specialized bogey.

The effect of the external interest rate environment in each country can be measured as the total return on all outstanding domestic Treasury securities. Total return includes all the interest received during the period plus any capital appreciation or depreciation. In the U.S. market, for instance, this figure would be equivalent to the return on published indices such as the Shearson-Lehman Treasury bond index or the Salomon Brothers treasury index. Once the external interest rate effect is determined, we can attribute the difference between the actual portfolio return and the actual Treasury index return to the management process.

In evaluating the management contribution (C), consider the means by which the management process can affect the portfolio. Three principal management skills that have an effect on performance include maturity management, sector/quality management, and selection of the individual securities. A partitioning of the management contribution is as follows:

$$C = M + S + B \qquad (2)$$

where

M = Return from maturity management.
S = Return from spread/quality management.
B = Return attributable to the selection of specific securities.

We can measure the return components by security repricing. Consider maturity management first. If all securities held during the evaluation period were Treasury issues and if each issue were consistently priced exactly on the term structure of default-free rates (so that there would be no specific returns on any security), the maturity management component (M) of the total return would be equal to the difference between the realized total return (R) and the effect (I) of the external environment. In other words, if the sector/quality effect and the selectivity effect were eliminated, the total management contribution can be attributed to maturity management. This means we can reprice each security as if it were a Treasury issue priced from the term structure, measure the total return under such pricing, and subtract the external effect component (I) to obtain the effect of maturity management.

Practically, this is accomplished by estimating the term structure of default-free rates from the universe of Treasury issues as of each valuation date throughout the evaluation period. The default-free price of each security held on that date is then calculated as the present value of its payments discounted by the spot rates corresponding to the maturity of that payment. The total return over the evaluation period is then calculated using the default-free prices but otherwise maintaining all actual activity in the portfolio, including all transactions, contributions and withdrawals, cash account changes, and the like. Finally, the actual Treasury index return over the evaluation period is subtracted to arrive at the maturity management component (M).

To determine the spread/quality management component (S) of the total return, we price each security as if it were exactly in line with its own sector/quality group (i.e., with no specific returns), calculate the total return under such prices, and subtract the total of the external component (I) and the maturity management component (M).

Here we have to be careful to determine the sector/quality prices correctly. It is not correct to base the sector/quality pricing on sector/quality indexes, since the differences in actual performance among various sector/quality indexes is primarily due to the different maturity composition of the market segments. For instance, the telephone issues in the United States would generally perform poorly during periods of increasing interest rates, not because they are telephones, but because they are longer than the bond market as a whole.

We therefore adopt the following approach. First, we define a meaningful classification of the bond market by sector/quality groups. We then estimate the term structure of default-free rates from Treasury issues. Next, for each valuation date, we calculate the default-free prices for all securities existing in the market on that date. We then calculate the spreads, or yield premiums, for each security as the difference between the actual yield and yield determined from the default-free price. These yield premiums are then averaged over all securities in the given sector/quality group to determine the average yield premium for the sector/quality group as of the given date. After this is done, we can calculate the sector/quality prices of the securities in the given portfolio by determining their default-free prices from the term structure, calculating the yield, adding the appropriate average yield premium depending on the sector/quality of that security, and converting this yield back to price. When all securities in the portfolio have been priced according to their sector/quality group at each of the valuation dates, we calculate the total portfolio return with the sector/quality prices. Again, the portfolio return with these prices is calculated, including all actual purchases, sales, swaps, contributions, and withdrawals. We then obtain the sector/quality component (S) of the portfolio management by subtracting the external effect component and the maturity management component from the return calculated on the sector/quality prices.

Finally, to determine the selectivity component of the management contribution, we use the actual prices, which reflect the specific returns on each security. The selectivity component (B) is thus calculated by subtracting the total of all previously determined components from the actual total portfolio return.

A numerical example of this analysis is provided in Table 8–1. In that example, a portfolio is compared against the Shearson-Lehman government corporate bond index. The total portfolio's return was 97 basis points above the benchmark. All of this superior performance resulted from successful maturity and sector/quality management.

PERFORMANCE MEASUREMENT AND ATTRIBUTION IN A MULTIPLE-CURRENCY BOND PORTFOLIO

Single-currency and multiple-currency bond portfolios differ in several important ways. First, the total return on a multiple-currency bond portfolio, measured in a base currency, is affected by foreign exchange fluctuations in addition to interest rate movements. Consequently, profits or losses from currency positions are likely to play a major role in the portfolio's total return. Second, interest rates in different countries do not always move in the same direction or magnitude. As a result, the manager's contribution is likely to be different across countries. If interest rate forecasting is part of the management process, the manager would have to project future interest rates for every country. Third, the manager may decide to hedge against the currency risk of the portfolio. For instance, a portfolio may contain bonds from several countries. To minimize

TABLE 8–1
Bond Performance Analysis

*Portfolio: Sample
portfolio*

Beginning date: January 1, 1982

Ending date: March 31, 1982

Evaluation Period Returns

	Portfolio	*Lehman Brothers Kuhn Loeb (now Shearson Lehman) Government Corporate Index*
I. Interest rate effect		
1. Expected	2.89%	2.89%
2. Unexpected	0.34	0.34
Subtotal	3.23	3.23
II. Management effect		
3. Maturity	0.48	0.10
4. Sector/quality	1.54	0.23
5. Individual bonds	−0.72	0.00
Subtotal	1.30	0.33
III. Total return	4.53	3.56

exchange rate risk, the manager may use currency swaps or futures contracts to hedge against unexpected movements in foreign currencies or
to lock in the exchange rate in a base currency. This way, the aggregate
portfolio will be exposed to the interest rate changes of foreign countries. But the total return on the portfolio will be mostly protected
against foreign exchange risk. Fourth, the benchmark used in judging
the relative performance of an internationally diversified fixed-income
portfolio would contain bonds from several countries. To construct a
relevant benchmark for such a portfolio, an investor might combine the
bond index for each local market weighted by their respective sizes. For
instance, the return on the international benchmark can be computed as
the weighted-average return on the bond indices of the major fixed-
income securities markets.[2] This capitalization-weighted international
bond index can be used as the reference portfolio in comparing portfolio
return.

    To evaluate the performance of a multiple-currency portfolio, an
investor would first measure the return on the portfolio from each local

market. Within a local market, the return in that country can be disaggregated into external effect and management contribution. External effect is simply the return on the fixed-income security index for that country. Management contribution is the difference between the portfolio's return in that country and the external effect. For example, if the total return on Japanese bonds in a portfolio were 43.99 percent during the evaluation period and the return on the Japanese fixed-income securities index were 43.64 percent, the manager's contribution to the return in that country would be 0.35 percent. Thus, the manager's value added can be measured as the difference between the portfolio's return and the base market return available in that country.

After the management's total contribution in a country is identified, the manager's value can be further disaggregated into local market return and currency return. Local market return is the portfolio's actual return in a country denominated in the local currency. This variable gauges the manager's skill in managing fixed-income securities in that country. For instance, the entire portfolio may be allocated to the various countries in exactly the same weight as the international bond benchmark. In the absence of currency swaps, the internationally diversified portfolio would have the same currency exposure as the index. The manager, however, may try to enhance the portfolio's return by anticipating the movement of interest rates in the local markets. In other words, the manager may be making duration bets locally. Alternatively, the manager may concentrate his portfolio in certain issuing sectors or quality classes that differ from the local index. To the extent that the manager is not attempting to replicate the local index perfectly, the return in each market based in the local currency will differ from the benchmark.

A manager can enhance the return on the portfolio with the currency markets in two ways. First, the manager can simply concentrate his investments in various countries different than the chosen international benchmark. This way, the portfolio would be exposed more to both the local market and the foreign exchange returns in those countries. Second, if the manager is interested only in enhancing the currency return, he may distribute his portfolio in the various countries in exactly the same proportion as the index. Then, the manager may use currency swaps or futures contracts to alter his foreign exchange exposure. For example, if the German mark is expected to appreciate against the U.S. dollar, the manager may take short positions in U.S. dollars and long positions in the mark. In doing so, he is attempting to outperform the international index by anticipating currency movements. When currency swaps or futures contracts are used, a manager can never hedge away all the currency risk because local market and exchange rate returns cannot be completely isolated. For example, if the manager tries to lock in the exchange rate in U.S. dollars for all the different countries, he may take short positions in the non-U.S. currencies and a long position in U.S. dollars. The actual return in each local market, however, is not known in advance. A manager can only guess what the total future value of the fixed-income portfolio denominated in the local currency will be on the horizon date. He can only take a short-currency position based on that projected value. If the realized performance in the local market is better than expected, the portfolio is underhedged because the actual amount of local currency available on the horizon date is greater than expected. This extra amount will be subjected to exchange rate uncertainty despite the initial hedge. Similarly, the portfolio will be overhedged against exchange rates if the local market return is less than anticipated.

An international bond portfolio's return, therefore, consists of three components. The first two components are the local market return and the currency return. The local market return is simpy the weighted-average return in all the countries denominated in the local currencies. The weight applied to each market is the initial market value of the portfolio's holding in that country divided by the total initial value of the composite portfolio. The currency component of return in a portfolio can be measured the same way. It is the weighted-average return on the different currencies.

The third component of return on the composite portfolio is the weighted average of the product of the currency and local market returns. This component of return represents the foreign exchange return on the profits/loss made in the local markets. For instance, if the local market return in Japan were 13.79 percent and the currency return were 26.54 percent, the total return in the Japanese market would be greater than 40.33 percent. The actual portfolio return would be 43.99 percent. The extra 3.66 percent represents the currency gain on the 13.79 percent of local market return. In other words, the foreign exchange is not only relevant to the initial investment, but it is applied to the profit/loss in the local market also.

Once the three sources of return are identified, the total return on the composite fixed-income securities portfolio can be expressed as their sum. If the manager engages in hedging or currency swaps activities, the

TABLE 8–2
Sources of Return on Portfolio

	Market 1		Market N	Composite Portfolio	Benchmark
Total contribution	R(1)		R(N)	R(P) = ΣR(i)	r(P) = Σr(i)
External	r(1)	...	r(N)	r(P)	r(P)
Management	R(1) − r(1)		R(N) − r(N)	ΣR(i) − r(i)	0
Initial allocation					
Portfolio	a(1)	...	a(N)	100	
Benchmark	b(1)		b(N)		100
Sources of return in each country					
Total	R(1)		R(N)	R(P)	r(P)
Local market	RM(1)		RM(N)	ΣRM(i)	ΣrM(i)
Currency	RC(1)	...	RC(N)	ΣRC(i)	ΣrC(i)
Hedging	RH(1)		RH(N)	ΣRH(i)	0
Currency × Local	RM(1) × RC(1)		RM(N) × RC(N)	ΣRM(i) × RC(i)	ΣrM(i) × rC(i)
Components of local market return					
Total	R(1)	...	R(N)		
External	r(1)		r(N)		
Management					
Maturity	RD(1)		RD(N)		
Sector/quality	RS(1)	...	RS(N)		
Individual security	RI(1)		RI(N)		

Note:

R(i)	= Return on the portfolio in Country i.
r(i)	= Return on the benchmark in Country i.
R(P), r(P)	= Return on the composite portfolio and benchmark, respectively.
a(i)	= Initial allocation of portfolio in Country i.
b(i)	= Initial allocation of benchmark in Country i.
RM(C), rM(i)	= Local market return in Country i in the portfolio and the benchmark, respectively.
RC(i), rC(i)	= Currency return in Country i in the portfolio and the benchmark, respectively.
RH(i)	= Return from hedging activities in Country i.
RD(i), RS(i), RI(i)	= Maturity, sector/quality, and individual security selection return in Country i.

return from currency hedging can be treated as a fourth component. Finally, within each country, the total local market return can be divided into the external effect and the various management contributions, just as the single-currency case.

The framework of an international bond performance analysis is summarized in Table 8–2. Under this framework, the fixed-income securities in the portfolio are divided into their respective countries. Within each country or market, the total portfolio's return is disaggregated into external effect and manager's contribution. Alternatively, the country's

TABLE 8–3
An Example of International Bond Performance Analysis, January–December 1986

(Returns Measured in U.S. Dollars)

	United States	Japan	Germany	Composite Portfolio	Benchmark
Total return	15.92%	43.99%	38.62%	26.51%	26.01%
External	15.27	43.64	38.72	26.01	26.01
Management	0.65	0.35	– 0.10	0.50	0.00
Initial allocation					
Portfolio	61.00	32.41	6.59	100	
Benchmark	61.03	32.46	6.51		100
Sources of return in each country					
Total	15.92	43.99	38.62	26.51	26.01
Local market	15.92	13.79	9.04	14.78	14.31
Currency	0.00	26.54	27.13	10.39	10.38
Hedging	0.00	0.00	0.00	0.00	0.00
Currency × Local	0.00	3.66	2.45	1.35	1.32
Components of local market return					
Total	15.92	43.99	38.62		
External	15.27	43.64	38.72		
Management	0.65	0.35	– 0.10		
Maturity	0.10	0.22	– 0.17		
Sector/quality	– 0.20	0.00	0.00		
Individual security	0.75	0.13	0.07		

return can be separated into the individual components: local market return, currency return, currency return on local market profits/loses, and hedging return.

The composite portfolio's total return can be evaluated directly from the returns in various local markets. Each component of return in the aggregate portfolio can also be computed as the weighted-average sum of the components in the local markets. After the total return and the sources of return on the composite portfolio are constructed, they can be compared against the international benchmark to identify the specific areas of strength or weakness of the manager.

In Table 8–3, a numerical example of an international bond portfolio performance measurement and attribution analysis is provided. The hypothetical portfolio in this example consists of fixed-income securities from three countries: the United States, Japan, and Germany. All returns are measured in U.S. dollars. For instance, the composite portfolio's total return is 26.51 percent—about 40 percent of which is accounted for by currency appreciation. Moreover, the marginal contributions from the United States, Japan, and Germany are 15.92 percent, 43.99 percent, and 38.62 percent, respectively. Within the composite portfolio, the manager allocates the investment in almost the same distribution as the international benchmark. The total local market return and the currency return on the composite portfolio, therefore, are very close to the international benchmark.

In this example, the manager is running an indexed portfolio within each country. The portfolio's returns in each individual market, therefore, are very close to the local indixes. For instance, the management contribution in the local markets for the United States, Japan, and Germany are only 0.65 percent, 0.35 percent, and − 0.10 percent, respectively. A further disaggregation of the manager's contribution is provided in the bottom of Table 8–3.

ENDNOTES

1. See Gifford Fong, Charles Pearson, and Oldrich Vasicek, "Bond Performance: Analyzing Sources of Return," *Journal of Portfolio Management*, Spring 1983, pp. 46–50.
2. An example of such a bogey would be the Salomon Brothers world bond index.

CHAPTER 9

METHODS TO ENHANCE PASSIVELY MANAGED GLOBAL BOND PORTFOLIOS*

Christopher N. Orndorff

This chapter is for those investors who may want something more than the return of the passive portfolio and want to achieve that result with the smallest possible increase in risk. In the following pages, we will discuss benchmark selection and the rationale for seeking to enhance portfolio return and will introduce some basic tools that a global bond investor may utilize to add value.

The most important action is to choose the correct benchmark for your circumstances. Your current benchmark may not fit your risk and return preferences. How do you choose the correct benchmark? This question is best answered if you consider the reasons for your investment in global bonds. Are you "testing the waters" with a small amount of funds for a limited time? Is your investment long term for diversification? Are you making an asset allocation decision based on seeking the highest return? Or is the global bond market just too big to pass up? Your answers to these questions, among others, will decide what type of a benchmark is appropriate.

---

*The author wishes to thank Victor Filatov, James Lorie, and Michael Rosenberg for their helpful comments and suggestions on earlier versions of this chapter.

The existing benchmark indices were developed by consultants, broker/dealers, or banks. Their index construction technique could be theoretically as simple as an EXTEL[1] tape dump that would include every bond outstanding or one carefully constructed to screen for liquidity. Liquidity is important because it is difficult to go to a risk-neutral position relative to the benchmark if you can't buy over 50 percent of the bonds in the index! Examine the reasons for the inclusion or exclusion of global bond markets. Countries may be included in the index only if the broker/dealer has a primary dealership there; they may be excluded because the consultant never had a previous client invest there. Be sure to ask questions before choosing an existing benchmark.

An existing benchmark may not meet your needs. The available indices may be too broad or not weighted to fit your risk/return profile. In these cases, investors may want to design a benchmark themselves. The investor may not have to look beyond the subindices that comprise the available master index. Some available market indices are comprised of a number of subindices. These subindices may be categorized by market, sector, maturity, liquidity, or credit quality. If this still is not satisfactory, then you will have to start from scratch. Designing your own benchmark is not an easy task. It takes not only an honest appraisal of your objectives, but also a sophisticated knowledge of the global bond markets. You may wish to receive some advice from a consultant or investment manager with knowledge of global markets.

WHY ENHANCE THE BENCHMARK PORTFOLIO?

The most obvious reason is to add value. However, a more subtle argument may be made. Portfolio managers, investment committees, pension plan sponsors, and other investors are becoming more hesitant, in nearly all asset classes, to pursue strategies that may underperform their benchmark. This view—that the risk of underperformance is worse than the benefit of potential return to be gained from active strategies—has fueled the growth of indexing, or passive management.

Perhaps, though, what those investors really want is a way to skew the distribution of returns more to their favor. Let's assume a common interest rate decision to extend duration carries a normally distributed return spectrum. Risk-averse investors will not accept this actuarially fair

FIGURE 9–1

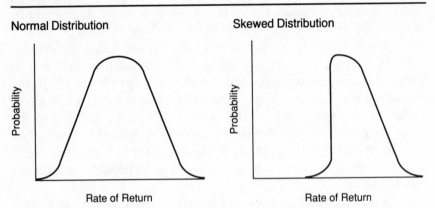

Normal Distribution

Skewed Distribution

gamble. They feel that the disutility experienced from the risk of loss is greater than the utility gained from the achievement of superior performance. This is a passive management client. Now let's assume there is a way to skew the return distribution so that the risk of underperformance is significantly diminished, while the potential for gain remains equally attractive. See Figure 9–1.

Would this be attractive to you? This is a simple example of what enhancement of passively managed global bond portfolios is all about.

MANAGING AGAINST A BENCHMARK

In our simple example, we presented an extreme case where the risk of underperformance was close to zero percent. In practice, these events do not occur frequently. When they do, it is referred to as *pure arbitrage* and not advertised. Pure arbitrage is like finding a $100 bill on the street; you pick it up, put it in your pocket, and keep going.

It is much more common to find a situation whereby the risk of underperformance is substantially reduced and positive gains may be achieved. The key to the successful management of these strategies is to quantify the risks and rewards involved and understand the dynamics of those variables as market events unfold. It is useful to know your break-even point(s) in the strategy and the maximum and minimum returns that can be achieved relative to the benchmark.

Six major decisions are made in the management of global bond portfolios. Enhancements can be achieved in each of these areas. The six decisions are currency, market, duration, yield curve, sector, and issue. We will explore each of these decisions in the following pages. Let's begin with the currency decision.

Currency Decision

Each benchmark will generally comprise a group of global bond markets with a corresponding basket of currencies, weighted in some defensible manner. Let's assume you are a U.S. dollar-based investor and your benchmark has the following market weights:

Country	Weight
Australia	10%
Canada	15
France	15
Japan	30
Germany	30

A decision to deviate from these weights, or to introduce a currency from a country not in the index, can be made to enhance the return. Of course, these decisions also introduce some risk. But this risk can be quantified.

Obviously, if you underweight a currency that depreciates and overweight a currency that appreciates, significant value can be added. The strategy could backfire, of course, and leave you to explain why you decided to pursue such a strategy. In fact, the currency decision can dominate all other sources of return. The results of one study noted that the currency component may represent up to 41 percent of the total return for a given global bond market.[2] That is why it is important to place some structure on the judgments you make with the currency decision. The investor may want to preestablish a maximum return differential below the benchmark that could be attributable to the currency decision. For example, the investor may choose to return the currency weights to a neutral position if the portfolio currency decision causes an underperformance relative to the benchmark of more than 0.5 percent, or 50 basis points.

What additional information do we need to quantify that risk? We need a correlation matrix with each currency in the index.[3] It would also be valuable to have some idea about the stability of those correlations over time. A stable correlation, or one that exhibits little change over time, can be used with greater confidence than one that changes materially. Stability is important to the investor who wants an accurate understanding of the true relationship between each currency in the benchmark.

Let's try a simple example. Assume that in the index above, you do not have a conviction for any currency except for the deutschemark (DEM) and the yen (JPY). You wish to overweight DEM to 35 percent and underweight JPY to 25 percent but remain neutral for other currencies. You have observed stable correlations between the DEM and JPY over time. What is your risk?

The difference between your potential portfolio return and the benchmark return is

$$AUD(W*aud - Waud) + CAD(W*cad - Wcad) + FFR(W*ffr - Wffr) + JPY(W*jpy - Wjpy) + DEM(W*dem - Wdem) \quad (1)$$

where

AUD = Return of the Australian dollar.
$W*aud$ = Adjusted weight of Australian dollar.
$Waud$ = Benchmark weight of Australian dollar.

Similar notation is used in the equation for each currency in the benchmark.

In this simple example, the above equation reduces to

$$JPY(W*jpy - Wjpy) + DEM(W*dem - Wdem) = Diff$$
So,   (2)
$$JPY(25\% - 30\%) \quad + DEM(35\% - 30\%) \quad = Diff$$

If the difference (Diff) is positive, you have made a wise choice in overweighting the DEM and underweighting the JPY. But what if the return to the DEM were 0.0 percent, and the return for the JPY were 6.0 percent, thereby achieving an underperformance of 6.0 percent (25 percent −30 percent) + 0.0 percent (35 percent −30 percent), or −0.30 percent? Would this be too large? Since our preestablished differential was −0.50 percent, we could comfortably proceed with our proposed change in weighting unless we expected the JPY return to exceed the DEM return by more than 10 percent, or 1,000 basis points.

Now consider the case of introducing a currency from a country not in the index. We need to perform the analysis previously described, and we also need to add to our correlation matrix the currency we wish to introduce. Keep in mind that the currency introduced will have a benchmark weight (W_{CUR}) of 0 percent. That makes this strategy especially risky and sensitive to return differentials in our algorithm.

Market Decision

The investor can deviate from the market weights by changing the fixed-income exposure and/or by changing the currency exposure. It is common to confuse the two decisions. The market decision may sometimes be a part of the currency decision. For instance, if the investor in our previous example decides to change the currency exposure by selling JPY bonds and buying DEM bonds, then he/she has also made a market decision. The investor feels that both the currency and the bond markets of DEM will outperform those of JPY. However, if the investor decides to change the currency exposure by currency hedging and does not buy or sell bonds, then it was only a currency decision, and our investor has remained market neutral. What if our investor sells JPY bonds but buys a bond from another market and hedges it into DEM? Our investor has made a combination of a market and a currency decision called a *cross-currency synthetic bond*. We will discuss such a strategy later in the chapter when we cover synthetic securities.

The tools that an investor utilizes in analyzing the risk involved in market decisions are similar to those used in the currency decision. For the investor in the previous example, Equation (1) may be used to estimate the risk of underperformance if bond market returns are substituted for currency returns. It is important to note that local bond returns are used, not returns imbedded with any currency component. The investor will also need a correlation matrix—and need to know something about its stability—to achieve a better grasp of the risks involved. Instead of currency movements, here the investor wants to understand the relationship of interest rate changes between each market.

Analogous to our currency example, the investor may choose to invest in a bond from a market not represented in the benchmark. This is risky, because the bond market exposure introduced will have a benchmark weight of 0 percent and will be sensitive to return differentials in our algorithm. We also need to add to our correlation matrix the bond market that we wish to introduce.

Duration Decision

Each market represented in the benchmark will have an average duration and convexity. A manager's deviation from those measures represents a decision to enhance the portfolio return. The investor should be careful not to directly compare duration and convexity measures for bonds denominated in separate currencies. Remember that durations represent price sensitivity to *domestic* yield fluctuations. This is discussed at greater length in the section on synthetic securities.

In addition to duration and convexity measures, the price volatility of a bond is also an important measure. (It is assumed that the reader has a working knowledge of these concepts.)[4] Managing the duration decision in non-U.S. markets is not substantially different than managing that decision in the U.S. market. In fact, it may be easier, since bonds with imbedded options are relatively scarce outside of the United States.

As with the currency decision, the investor may want to preestablish a maximum return differential below the benchmark that could be attributable to the duration decision. For example, the investor may choose to return the duration in each market to a neutral position if a duration decision causes as underperformance relative to the benchmark of more than 0.5 percent, or 50 basis points.

Assume our benchmark index for France has the following characteristics:

Yield   = 10.01 percent
Duration = 5.21   (Portfolio 1)
Convexity = 0.39

And we decide to extend to the following:

Yield   = 10.02 percent
Duration = 5.71   (Portfolio 2)
Convexity = 0.47

What does this do to our risk and return profile?

Parallel Yield Change	Annual Return		
	Base	Extended	Difference
+ 100 basis points	5.53%	5.05%	− 0.48%
+ 50 basis points	7.62	7.38	− 0.24
− 50 basis points	11.96	12.21	+ 0.25
− 100 basis points	14.20	14.72	+ 0.52

As you can see in Figure 9–2, the rewards may be significant for a modest increase in duration. Of course, a similar result could be achieved if interest rates increased and the investor had a modest decrease in duration. The potential risk of underperformance relative to the benchmark

FIGURE 9–2
Profit Analysis: Duration Decision

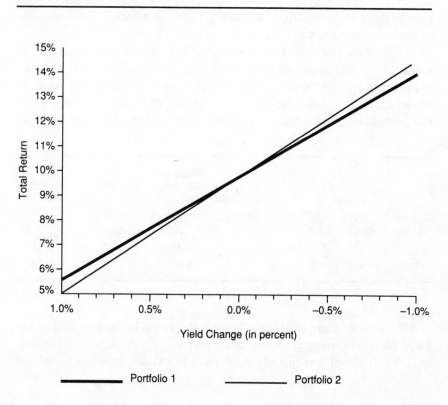

with duration changes may be great. However, from the preestablished maximum return differential of -0.50 percent, our investor would feel comfortable with the proposed increase in duration as long as he/she believed the probability of a 100-basis-point increase in interest rates was very low. Our investor was prudent to set a tolerance band for the duration range in each country.

Duration management also includes the composition of the cash flows comprising the summary portfolio duration statistic. What if the yield curve does not undergo a parallel shift? The construction of your portfolio could have a significant effect on the returns you achieve in such a scenario. This is best examined under another decision, the yield curve decision.

Yield Curve Decision

Another important method to enhance passively managed global bond portfolios is to take advantage of changing slopes and shapes of global yield curves. Just as there is nearly an infinite variety to the shapes of global yield curves, there is also a variety of techniques to take advantage of them. One of the most common ways is to construct a barbell portfolio.

A barbell portfolio concentrates cash flows on both ends of the yield curve. It is commonly utilized when the investor feels that the yield curve will become negatively sloped, or more negatively sloped. In the example below, the barbell maintains the duration-neutral position of the benchmark portfolio while adding yield and convexity.

	Weight	Yield to Maturity	Duration	Convexity
Canada 9.25% of 1–Mar–91	44.5%	10.47%	1.38	0.01
Canada 10.0% of 1–Jun–08	55.5	9.29	8.57	0.55
		9.82%	5.37	0.31
Benchmark—Canada		9.22%	5.37	0.18

Of course, there is risk involved. If the yields in the long end of the yield curve rise more than any other part of the curve, your trade will backfire. It is useful to quantify the amount that yields must go against you before this occurs. The following matrix reports estimates of the gain or loss in Canadian dollars versus the benchmark for each C$1,000,000 of barbell market value:[5]

		Pivotal Shift (in basis points)		
		− 25	0	+ 10
Parallel shift	+ 25	$10,166	$78	($3,847)
(in basis points)	0	10,478	0	(4,077)
	− 25	10,977	91	(4,143)

Note these results are based on a model that assumes instantaneous changes in the yield curve.

Sector Decision

A common method to enhance passively managed U.S. bond portfolios is through the sector decision. A U.S. investor can choose among agencies, mortgages, and corporates. Even within a sector like corporates, a U.S. investor has a myriad of choices: asset-backed corporates, telephones, finance companies, industrials, or utilities. The investor looking for the same variety and depth in non-U.S. markets will be disappointed.

The reason is that many foreign corporate issuers prefer to raise capital with equity, bank lines, or privately placed debt issues. For those issuers that choose to issue public debt, the ownership of that debt is often restricted.[6] A further obstacle placed in the way of global bond investors is the credit-monitoring process. Lack of accounting data and accounting standards significantly different than the U.S. market create a mine field that an investor must negotiate. Often this must be done alone, as most foreign issuers, except sovereign entities, carry no credit rating. Be sure to read the covenants for the bond, as they may materially differ from those found for U.S. corporations. To compound these problems, liquidity for these issues is spotty. And, withholding taxes are assessed and may not be reclaimable for corporate issues.

All of this news may sound discouraging, but there are ways to invest in this sector. One of the ways is through bulldog, samurai, or similar issues. A bulldog issue is a bond issued in the United Kingdom, denominated in pound sterling, by a non U.K. entity. A samurai bond is issued in Japan, denominated in yen, by a non-Japanese entity. These issues also have the advantage of being generally exempt from withholding taxes.

Another way to invest in this sector is through government-sponsored corporations. These may be corporations entirely owned by the government, such as banks and financial services companies, airlines, natural resource companies, or utilities. In some markets, these are referred to as crown corporations. While under government ownership, these corporations enjoy good liquidity (for the corporate market) and are generally regarded as safe investments by the market. However, the continuing global trend of deregulation and privitization implies that you should pay close attention to the words and actions of the government that has ownership in the corporation whose debt you purchased. If you are offered such an issue at an especially wide spread to government securities, be careful. Perhaps the government has made an indication that it intends to sell the corporation.

Agencies are not as problematic. They generally enjoy an explicit guarantee by the government and are much more liquid than any other class of nongovernment securities. They also usually carry the same withholding tax status as government obligations. Another type of agency securities is those issued by supranational agencies, such as the World Bank. Supranational agencies enjoy good liquidity and are denominated in a variety of currencies. Many are denominated in ECU[7].

The securitization of the mortgage market in non-U.S. countries is still in its infancy. While not currently useful to global investors, the mortgage sector may become an exciting addition to non-U.S. markets. It is certainly an important sector for investors seeking value in the U.S. bond market.[8]

The methods used to enhance portfolios with this sector are relatively simple: buy a sector when it is "cheap," and sell it when it is "rich." How does one recognize when a sector is cheap? A sector is cheap when it is trading at a yield spread relative to another sector than is greater than normal. For example, assume you observe that on-the-run, like-maturity government and agency bonds in Germany have the following relationship:

	Yield
Bundespost (postal service)	7.57%
Bundesrepublic (government)	7.35
Yield spread	0.22%

Let's assume that during the last five years, the highest spread observed was 25 basis points, the lowest spread observed was 5 basis points, and the spread has averaged 15 basis points. You could conclude that the Bundespost is cheap relative to a similar Bundesrepublic. You could conversely conclude that governments are rich relative to agencies, particularly Bundespost. As an investor, you are counting on the concept of reversion to the mean. That is, the yield spread will deviate around an average (mean) but will return to the average value eventually. It is important to note that just because one sector yields more than another does not imply that the sector is always cheap. If, in our example, the yield spread were eight basis points, then you could conclude that the Bundesrepublic was cheap relative to Bundespost.

Issue Decision

Another method to add value is through superior issue selection. This broad category includes synthetic securities as well as the traditional methods of issue selection. Some investors overlook this method, assuming global markets are always efficient and, therefore, no added value can be achieved by issue selection. Those investors will be surprised to learn that issue selection in any global bond market can achieve significant return enhancement. Perhaps global markets are not always so efficient?

More traditional methods of issue selection focus on a similar approach to choosing a cheap sector. In this approach, two securities within a sector are compared on a yield-spread basis to determine which issue is trading cheap. In the U.S. market, investors commonly use option-adjusted spreads to compare securities. As previously noted, most non-U.S. bonds rarely contain imbedded options. Therefore, yield-spread relationships are easier to calculate.

A refinement of the traditional method of intramarket issue selection for global bonds has been offered by the Bond Index Group of J. P. Morgan Securities, Inc.[9] They calculate a linear regression on a market cross-section of known cash flows and observable prices to estimate individual cash flow discount factors. The discount factors are modeled as nth degree polynomials. The estimates of discount factors are used to calculate theoretical prices.

$$MPj = \sum_{k = 1}^{K} Cjk\, Dk + \Delta j \qquad (3)$$

where

MPj = Gross market price.
Cjk = kth cash flow for bond j.
Dk = Average discount factor for all j corresponding to the kth cash flow.
Δj = Price difference or error term.
j = 1, 2, . . . J; J = Number of securities in the model.

This technique introduces price differences into the pricing equation. The price difference is obtained by subtracting the theoretical price estimated by the model from the actual market price. The differences occur because the model cannot explain all factors that influence the price. Some of those factors are permanent and due to coupon and liquidity effects; others are temporary. The model seeks to effectively measure the temporary component and use it to identify buying or selling opportunities. The model is not designed with high-frequency trading in mind but rather as a tool for investors to identify and add value beyond the index return.

A new method of using issue selection to enhance returns is to choose lendable securities. With the introduction of global securities lending, you may obtain securities-lending income by allowing your custodian to lend your bonds to interested parties. This aspect of issue selection has grown in importance with the introduction of government bond futures contracts in many markets. Borrowers of your securities use them to deliver against a short position in government bond futures. Of course, the advantage is additional income, but the disadvantage is the relative liquidity you have forgone. To sell the security you lent to the other party, you must give your custodian reasonable (the definition of which varies among custodians) notice that you wish to sell your bond(s).

CREATING SYNTHETIC SECURITIES

A *synthetic security* is a combination of two or more securities that, when combined, have characteristics similar to the instrument the combination is replicating. Why are synthetics important? Sometimes a synthetic security can be created at a price that is more favorable than that at which the actual security is trading in the market. Synthetics can be created in the derivative or cash security markets.

Let's begin by examining a cash strategy. Covered interest arbitrage is a transaction whereby the interest rate parity theorem is exploited so that the difference between the exchange agio and the interest agio is significantly non-zero. The interest rate parity theorem is represented by the expression

$$A \left[(F - S)/S \right] = (Rd - Rf)/(1 + Rf) \qquad (4)$$

where

F   = Forward exchange rate.
S   = Spot exchange rate.
A   = Factor to convert the absolute difference in the two exchange
      rates to an annualized value.
Rf = Foreign interest rate.
Rd = Domestic interest rate.

This is a simple cross-currency synthetic security. Note this strategy is riskless as long as the forward contract expires on the maturity date of the fixed-income security. The investor is purchasing an asset denominated in one currency and transforming that asset into one denominated in the currency of choice, or at least a currency where the exchange agio and the interest agio were not consistent.

A slightly different approach must be used for bonds with longer maturities. Fairly priced forward contracts rarely can be purchased or sold with an expiration date of greater than three years, so that limits the covered interest arbitrage market. However, the same concept is used to create a cross-currency synthetic bond. (Remember that a cross-currency synthetic bond is a unique combination of the currency decision and the market decision). One must be careful to evaluate the risk of such a strategy. Risk is present in the foreign exchange market because now the investor must choose to roll contracts. That is, the investor is not able to sell the currency forward to the maturity of the bond on purchase date, so he/she must choose a horizon that he/she is comfortable with and sell the currency forward to that date. When that contract expires, a new one must be put in place if the investor chooses to remain currency hedged. The risk occurs because the bond may have had a dramatic change in market value, so the amount of currency sold forward is too much (too little), leaving the investor overhedged (underhedged). Note this problem was alleviated in covered interest arbitrage because the expiration date and the maturity date coincided.

Another risk involves the bond itself. Remember that durations represent price sensitivity to *domestic* yield fluctuations. Therefore, the duration measure is not very useful across markets. All is not lost, however. The bond market research group at Salomon Brothers has suggested some tools that global bond investors may use to quantify the risk of such strategies.[10] One such tool is the use of local currency bond price volatilities instead of durations. This measure is virtually identical to the volatility of total returns on those assets. It provides an excellent measure of comparing risk for a cross-currency synthetic bond strategy. Another tool is the use of a regression beta on the duration proxy of the market you wish to replicate. The regression beta is not accurate for short time horizons, but over a longer period, it provides a reasonable assessment of risk. Combined with the intermarket correlation of yield changes, the investor now has the capability to create cross-currency synthetic bonds and reasonably assess the risk of the strategy. However, comparing risk across markets is the subject of continued research.

Derivative Securities

Derivative securities are probably the best way to create synthetics. Derivatives take two forms: exchange traded and nonexchange traded. Exchange traded derivatives include futures and options. Nonexchange-traded derivatives include swaps and over-the-counter options.

Futures contracts are traded on an exchange and available in many global bond markets. We will focus on deliverable contracts because they are the most common and the most flexible to use.

Deliverable contracts		
Government Bond Market	Exchange-Traded	Options on Futures
Canada	Montreal	No
France	Paris	Yes
Germany	London/Frankfurt	Yes
Japan	Tokyo	No
United Kingdom	London	Yes
United States	Chicago	Yes

Futures contracts can be used to hedge a portfolio of bonds, quickly change the duration of the portfolio, create leverage in the portfolio, or basis trade.

Hedging is accomplished by selling an appropriate number of futures contracts against a bond or a portfolio of bonds. Hedging a portfolio of bonds with futures can be accomplished with the following formula:[11]

$$(f \times C)/[1 + (r \times t)] \times (Pdur/Cdur) \qquad (5)$$

where

f   = Conversion factor for the bond.
C   = Price of the cheapest-to-deliver bond.
r   = Annualized financing rate from settlement to delivery.
t   = Term from settlement to delivery.
Pdur = Portfolio duration.
Cdur = Duration of the cheapest-to-deliver bond.

However, no hedge is perfect. In the market, yields on different bonds do not perfectly correlate. This may create a situation where the "hedge" suffers a loss or produces a gain. The risk that the futures contract does not perfectly track the bond, or portfolio of bonds, that the investor is attempting to hedge is called *basis risk*. Basis risk can be turned into opportunity, as some investors trade this relationship between the futures price and the bond price, adjusted for the conversion factor.

Futures are also used to quickly change the duration of the portfolio. The following formula is a basic calculation method to accomplish this result:

$$F = (PVBPt - PVBPc)/PVBPf \qquad (6)$$

where

F   = Number of futures contracts.
PVBPt = Price value of basis point of target duration generic security.
PVBPc = Price value of basis point of current portfolio.
PVBPf = Price value of basis point of futures contract.

By buying futures contracts, the investor will extend the duration of the portfolio. Conversely, selling futures contracts will decrease the duration of the portfolio.

Options on futures contracts are also traded on an exchange and are an excellent way to enhance return and skew the return distribution in your favor. (It is assumed that the reader has a knowledge of the basic gain/loss diagrams for puts and calls.)[12] Options may be used by themselves, combined with a cash market security, or combined with futures contracts to provide the desired risk and return distributions. A nearly infinite variety of option strategies exist, but, consistent with the scope of this chapter, we will focus on some basics.

Options can also be used to quickly change the duration of the portfolio. When dealing with options, the investor must be aware of the delta of the option. The *delta* is the rate of change of an option's price with respect to the price of the underlying asset. If we assume the number of options contracts multiplied by the delta of an option yields the futures-equivalent position of the option, then

$$0 = F/Delta \qquad (7)$$

where

0   = Number of options contracts.
F   = Number of futures contracts.
Delta = Delta of the option contract considered.

By buying calls or selling puts, the investor extends duration. By selling calls or buying puts, the investor reduces duration.

If the investor believes the markets will be upward trending, then the investor could play an option price spread. This may involve buying a call and selling a call with a higher strike price, both with the same expiration

FIGURE 9–3
Profit Analysis: Option Price Spread

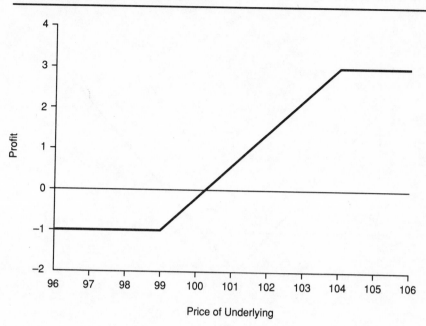

date. If our investor buys a June 98 call and sells a June 104 call, then the profile in Figure 9–3 is achieved.

Note the strategy generates limited downside risk and good upside potential. This strategy demonstrates the power of options.

Options can also be used to take advantage of changes in market volatility. If the investor feels volatility will increase, a common strategy is the *long straddle*. This strategy involves the purchase of one put and one call with the same expiration and the same strike price. Therefore, the payoff will be symmetric about the strike price. The profile in Figure 9–4 is achieved with such a strategy.

Of course, options have a cost, and that cost is depicted in the graph as the points below the 0 profit line.

It is important to note that the option strategies outlined above can be used with interest rate options and/or currency options. And, the variety of strategies available to the investor is so large that it would take another

FIGURE 9–4
Profit Analysis: Long Straddle

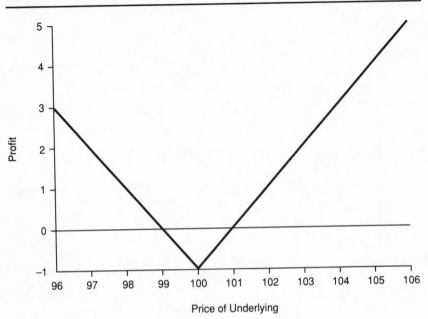

Price of Underlying

chapter (or another book) to discuss them all! The ability to implement option strategies in both the interest rate and currency markets
makes options a very important tool for investors seeking to enhance
return.

Options can also be traded on the over-the-counter market. These
contracts are generally between the investor and the broker/dealer and can
be customized to the investor's objectives. Many of the same strategies we
previously discussed are also possible with over-the-counter options.

Another nonexchange-traded derivative security is the swap. Swaps
can be on interest rates or currencies. A currency swap involves the
exchange of principal and fixed-rate interest payments in one currency for
principal and fixed-rate interest payments on an equivalent amount in
another currency. A currency swap is roughly equivalent to a series of forward contracts. The value of a swap can be determined from the term
structure of interest rates in each country and the spot exchange rate. Currency swaps may be used by the investor who wishes to create a cross-

currency synthetic security. A currency swap will eliminate the risk previously alluded to involving the "roll" of forward contracts in a cross-currency synthetic strategy.

Interest rate swaps generally involve the exchange of fixed-rate payments for variable-rate payments. Note that principal is normally not exchanged. The diagram in Figure 9–5 demonstrates the structure of an interest rate swap:

FIGURE 9–5
Interest Rate Swap Structure

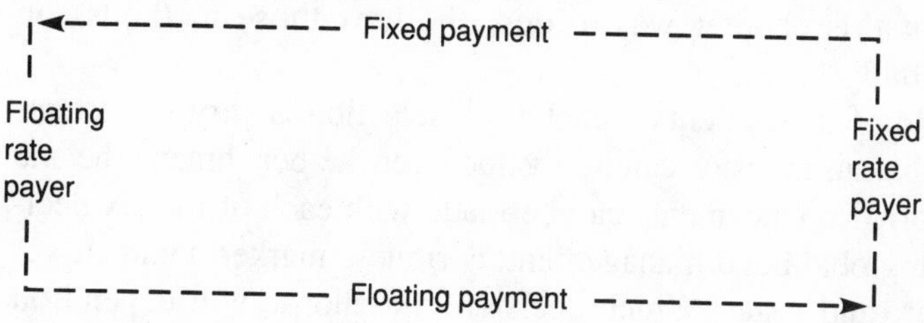

The fixed-rate payer is now effectively invested in a floating-rate asset, which was financed by the creation of a fixed-rate liability. The floating-rate payer now effectively has a fixed-rate investment. Interest rate swaps may be used by the investor who wishes to take a position on interest rate movements or to create a security that was not available in the marketplace.

When should an investor use synthetics? The investor should use a synthetic security when she can obtain a better return, or when it fits her risk profile. For example, in the interest rate swap above, the floating-rate payer may be able to create a higher-yielding fixed-rate asset than was available to the investor in the market. The investor using options may wish to change the portfolio risk profile and limit downside risk by purchasing a put option.

One last word about synthetic securities. It is critical to the success and profitability of the strategies that your global custodian accommodate the transactions necessary for the strategies. It is a sad fact that the capability of your global custodian may limit your effectiveness as a manager. Not all custodians are created equally or endowed with equally knowledgeable staff. With this in mind, be very selective about the global custodian that you hire. The same warning is applicable for your broker/ dealer. Many broker/dealers claim they are global, but only a select set truly are. Use an experienced broker/dealer, or you could create problems of disastrous proportions.

CONCLUSION

Throughout this chapter, basic methods of enhancement and ways to measure their risk were introduced. Many readers will note that these methods have been—and still are—in use in U.S. bond management. One purpose of this chapter was to describe how those methods can be applied globally.

In any field of investments, benchmark selection is very important. To the extent that an investor can add value over the benchmark, he/she will be better off. Enhancements can be made with each of the six decisions present in global bond management: currency, market, yield curve, duration, sector, and issue. Which decision you choose will depend on your insights and risk preferences.

Preestablished risk parameters may help you structure your decision making in a way that is consistent with your overall objectives for the portfolio. Probably the best way to obtain those parameters is to conduct some simulations on sample portfolios and observe the returns and the variability of those returns as the assets in the portfolio react to your simulated events.

Are enhancement strategies for you? Perhaps not all strategies may be consistent with your objectives for global bond investing. But the tools offered here can provide the investor with the means to win the loser's game.[13]

ENDNOTES

1. EXTEL Financial Ltd. is a London-based global data products company.
2. Cholerton, Pieraerts, and Solnick, "Why Invest in Foreign Currency Bonds?" *Journal of Portfolio Management*, Summer 1986, pp. 4–8.
3. The interested reader may find information on the construction of correlation matrices in *Quantitative Methods for Financial Analysts*, eds. Brown and Kritzman (Homewood, Ill.: Dow Jones-Irwin, 1987).

4. An excellent explanation of duration, convexity, and bond price volatility measures can be found in Kopprasch, *Understanding Duration and Volatility* (New York: Salomon Brothers, September 1985).

5. Matrix obtained from Bloomberg financial markets.

6. Nonresident investors are often prevented from participating in the original issue of the debt because of seasoning restrictions. Sometimes those restrictions are never lifted by the merchant banker.

7. European Currency Unit (ECU) is the official composite currency of the European Monetary System.

8. Interested readers will find a superb introduction to the U.S. mortgage market in Sullivan, Collins, and Smilow, "Mortgage Pass-Through Securities," in *Handbook of Fixed-Income Securities,* 2nd ed., Fabozzi and Pollack (Homewood, Ill.: Dow Jones-Irwin, 1987), pp. 382–403. A good introduction to the Canadian mortgage market is Boyle, "Valuing Canadian Mortgage-Backed Securities," *Financial Analysts Journal,* May/June 1989, pp. 55–60.

9. The model referred to can be found in Lobley, *J. P. Morgan Yield Curve Model* (New York: J. P. Morgan, September 15, 1989).

10. Gadkari, Spindel, and Thum, *Portfolio Optimization Relative to a Benchmark: Part I* (New York: Salomon Brothers, October 1988).

11. There are more-accurate techniques of hedging, but they are beyond the scope of this chapter.

12. The interested reader will find a good overview in *Options on Fixed-Income Securities* (New York: Morgan Stanley, October 1986).

13. Deference to Ellis, *Investment Policy: How to Win the Loser's Game* (Homewood, Ill.: Dow Jones-Irwin, 1985).

CHAPTER 10

DEFINITION AND CONTROL OF RISK MEASURES FOR ACTIVE PORTFOLIO BOND MANAGEMENT AND THE ROLE OF OPTIONS

Peter Vann

In this chapter, we discuss some of the risks in active portfolio management and a method to analyze option strategies used to enhance returns when forecasting market movements while controlling the risk of diminished returns if our market forecasts prove incorrect. Options have non-symmetric return characteristics and, thus, potentially provide useful tools for return enhancement and risk management. To illustrate the use of options, we consider the benchmark management approach where we aim to outperform a benchmark index. We have redefined the concept of risk for active benchmark management and present an analysis using the following risk measures:

Probability of underperformance of benchmark.

Market movement to outperform benchmark.

Maximum underperformance.

We consider portfolio returns from holding options to expiration to illustrate the use of the proposed risk measures. We believe an understanding of the basic risk measures we present should be obtained and then applied to the wide range of option strategies available; there is no free lunch, just the one that best suits the market forecast and risk/return requirements.

INTRODUCTION

To add value to a portfolio of securities, we normally forecast market movements and adjust our portfolio holdings to take advantage of our predictions. The discussion we present in this paper will analyze some simple methods to quantify the "risk" of a portfolio when we take active management decisions. We then focus on the use of options to adjust a portfolio's holdings to add value if our forecasts prove to be correct.

A number of instruments can be used to adjust a portfolio's holdings:

Physical securities.

Futures.

Options on the physical or futures.

Advanced techniques, such as dynamic asset and liability management (DALM) and construction of synthetic options using an optimal combination of options.

The use of physicals and futures to shift a portfolio's holdings has the advantage of capturing all of the upside, but we experience the full downside if our market views are incorrect. Options, by contrast, provide non-symmetric return payoffs and therefore can be used to enhance portfolio returns if we correctly predict market movements. Options can therefore be used to protect a portfolio from adverse market movements where adverse market movements for an actively managed portfolio can be attributed to our forecasts being incorrect.

To gain further insight into the use of options for return enhancement and risk management, we will:

Analyze the commonly used measures of risk.

Redefine risk.

Analyze various strategies when taking market views and discuss the return enhancement and control of the risk of poor returns.

We will provide a general discussion, which can be applied to any portfolio of securities, for example.

A diversified fund, domestic and/or international.

A specific asset class.

Part of an asset class, such as the currency component of an international fund.

Where quantitative data is required to help illustrate a discussion, examples will be provided in the fixed-interest (income) market.

RISK REVISITED

Common Measure of Risk

The most commonly used measure of risk of a financial security or portfolio of securities is the standard deviation of returns calculated using historical data over some time period; the returns may or may not be adjusted for the so-called risk-free rate determined by the rate of a short-term cash security. The standard deviation is a measure of the dispersion or spread of returns about the average return.

If the probability distribution of the calculated returns for a security display the characteristics of a normal distribution, then we can say that about two thirds of the time (0.6829, to be exact), the security's return was within 1 standard deviation of the mean return. Also, if the returns are normally distributed, then the mean and standard deviation are all that is required to uniquely describe the probability distribution of returns. Thus, for returns characterized by a normal distribution, the standard deviation provides one measure of the risk of not being close to the expected return, based on historical data.

If the calculated return does not have the characteristics of a normal distribution, then it is skewed to one side of the mean. For example, if we hold a bond and a put option on the bond, then from now to expiration we have a minimum return below which our returns will not fall. In this case, the standard deviation may not be as useful a measure of risk as can be seen from the following calculation.

We are holding a 10-year bond, and on January 1, 1989, we borrow money to purchase a put option on the bond with an expiration date of March 15, 1989. Based on historical yield movements, the expected return to March 15, 1989, is 2.57 percent, the minimum return is 0.13 percent, and the standard deviation of returns is 2.91 percent. The minimum return is only 0.84 of a standard deviation below the mean, and therefore the use of standard deviation as the sole measure to represent the dispersion of the returns about the mean does not represent the complete picture.

Redefining Risk

To assist in the discussion of risk, we will now consider the risk associated with the management of a portfolio of securities. Usually, various performance objectives and constraints are placed on the portfolio by the client. Consider the situation where the client has made the asset allocation decision and we, as the fund manager, have been delegated the responsibility of managing the fixed-interest component of the client's diversified portfolio. Let us also assume the client selects as a performance benchmark a published market index. We could propose that one measure of risk is not meeting the client's objectives for the fund. For example, if we chose to put all of the fund into cash, we are taking a major risk in that we may not produce a performance commensurate with that expected. Therefore, we are focusing our discussion on one of benchmark performance and the assessment of our portfolio's return versus the benchmark.

To outperform the benchmark index, we take a view on market movements and modify the portfolio holdings to gain from such movements. For example, if we are managing a fixed-interest portfolio and we expect interest rates to rise for bonds with term-to-maturities of longer than eight years, we could reduce our exposure to these long securities. Then, if the long rates do move in the expected manner, we could outperform the benchmark index. However, if our expectation is wrong and the long rates move down, then we will probably underperform the benchmark index.

If we are taking active views on market movements and modify the portfolio's holdings to take advantage of these views, then we are exposed to our views being incorrect. It would be desirable to be able to quantify the risk of the active bets we are taking. The main risk is that of underperforming the benchmark index when our views are incorrect. This measure of risk has direct relevance to the client's objectives for the fund if an appropriate benchmark is chosen such that the benchmark's performance will satisfy the client's objectives for the fund. We will assume the benchmark chosen is suitable, and we will use the probability of underperforming the benchmark as one measure of risk.

To illustrate the above comment on the choice of a suitable benchmark, consider a fund whose sole purpose is to fund future known liabilities. A benchmark portfolio could be chosen such that it will exactly match the liabilities of the fund (e.g., a fund of default-free zero-coupon bonds maturing on the dates of the liabilities). Such a benchmark represents a "neutral" position, which has no risk of not funding the liabilities. If liability coverage is an objective of the fund, then active management decisions are taken with the expectation of providing a return greater than that required to fund the liabilities. Such active management decisions should also consider the risk of not providing a return that will fund the liabilities.

As will be seen in the following sections, the probability of underperforming the benchmark, while an important measure of the risk of not meeting the client's objectives, should be considered in conjunction with other measures (such as the degree of underperformance and the market movement required for our option-adjusted portfolio to outperform the benchmark index). We will see that various trade-offs take place between these measures and that the trade-offs are necessary when planning strategies for using options to enhance returns and monitor the risk of underperformance. Note these risk measures are used at a micro level when considering buy and write strategies; we are applying a similar analysis at a macro level for the whole portfolio with the objective of controlling risk in active management.

The additional risk measures of probability of underperforming the benchmark index and the payoff and probability distribution diagrams can be used when the returns are not normally distributed, unlike the standard deviation, which is most useful with normally distributed returns.

ENHANCING RETURNS AND MANAGING RISK

We now consider active management about a simple benchmark of a 10-year bond. Payoff diagrams and return distributions are presented for actively managed portfolios, which will outperform the benchmark index if our market movement views are correct.

Enhancing Returns from the Simple Benchmark

As the benchmark index is a single 10-year bond, we will take that same bond in our portfolio and then include options to add value from correct predictions of market movements. An alternative method of adding value

TABLE 10-1
Active Option Strategies

View	Portfolio
Rates down	10-year bond, long call financed by borrowings
Rates steady	10-year bond, short call and put, invest option proceeds
Rates up	10-year bond, long put financed by borrowings

would be to buy or sell futures on 10-year bonds; however, we are exposed to both the upside if our active view is correct and the downside if our active view is incorrect.

The three views we will consider are interest movements up, down, and steady. In Table 10-1, we have described the portfolios we constructed to enhance returns if the views are correct. These portfolios are not unique; for example, we could just as easily have sold a put if we thought rates would decrease, thereby gaining the extra return from the option premium at all rates below the put's strike yield. However, this portfolio may be considered to have undesirable returns if our view was incorrect and rates rose.

The payoff diagrams and return distributions for the portfolios constructed for rates moving up, being steady, and moving down are shown in Figures 10-1A and B, 10-2A and B, and 10-3A and B, respectively. In each payoff and return distribution, the corresponding benchmark is also provided for comparison. In all instances, the options purchased are out of the money, with a strike yield 25 basis points from the current bond yield. As the options are all priced at their fair value and the implied volatility of the purchased options is the actual volatility, the expected returns for each of the portfolios is the expected return for the bond. This is shown in Table 10-2 together with the standard deviation of the return distributions.

Considerable differences exist between the standard deviations of the returns. This can be easily explained by analyzing the probability distribution of returns. Consider the portfolio of the bond and put; the return distribution is truncated by the put and shifted to the left (i.e., lower returns) by the loss of the cost of the put when the put expires out of the money. The net effect is to concentrate the distribution of returns closer to the mean return, thereby reducing the calculated standard deviation.

FIGURE 10–1A
Payoff Diagram—10-Year Bond and Put

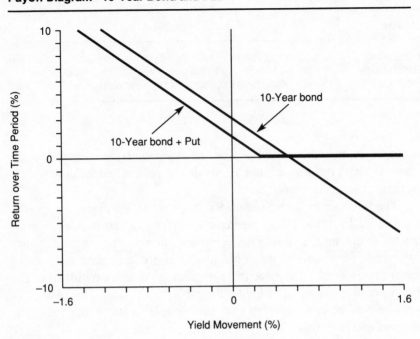

Yield Movement (%)

TABLE 10–2

Portfolio	Expected Average Return*	Expected Standard Deviation of Return
Benchmark portfolio	2.57	4.04
Portfolio for rates down	2.57	5.78
Portfolio for rates steady	2.57	4.38
Portfolio for rates up	2.57	2.91

*Note: Returns are not annualized.

However, the portfolio of long bond and call has the opposite charac-teristics; the extra return from the call with falling rates tends to spread the return distribution on the positive side, but the cost of the call tends to shift

FIGURE 10–1B
Probability Distribution of Returns—10-Year Bond and Put

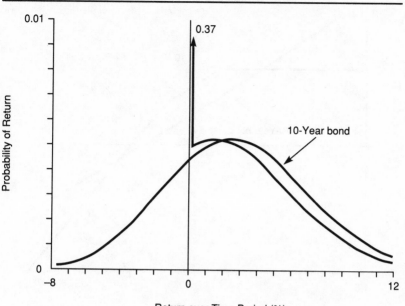

Return over Time Period (%)

the distribution to the other side—with the net result of the same average return and wider spread of returns.

Now, what is the impact if our view on market movements is incorrect? For the portfolios containing long options, we lose the cost of the option, and the impact of this can be quantified from the payoff diagrams. The portfolio with the put option underperforms the benchmark by about 1.0 percent, and the portfolio with the call option underperforms by 1.1 percent if our view is incorrect.

However, when we are short an option, as is the case for the portfolio that takes advantage of the yield being steady, the underperformance of the benchmark can be extensive if the market has large movements; but, as can be seen from the probability distribution (Figure 10-2B), the probability of these large movements is small. In this case, the probability of outperforming the benchmark is 50 percent, and we have a 50 percent probability of underperforming the benchmark. However, if our view is correct, we can outperform the benchmark index by 2.0 percent.

FIGURE 10–2A
Payoff Diagram—10-Year Bond and Put and Call

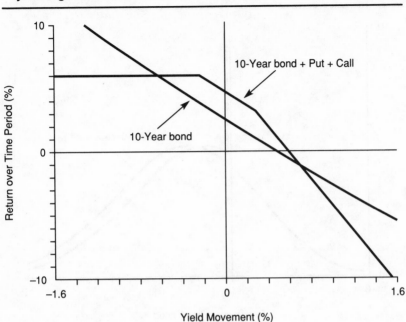

Yield Movement (%)

Managing Risk with the Simple Benchmark

In the last section, we saw that if our views are correct, we can easily obtain enhanced returns. But if our views are incorrect, what is the impact of our strategy? Are there other strategies that have a reduced risk of underperformance? We are primarily interested in the comparison of our portfolio's returns with those of the benchmark and the measures of the risk of underperformance. In the "Risk Revisited" section, we indicated that the appropriate measures may be the probability of underperforming the benchmark, the degree of underperformance, and the market movement required to outperform the benchmark index.

We now wish to further study the effect on these risk measures when using different options. Consider the case that rates will rise and a portfolio is constructed with a 10-year bond and a put option. In the previous section, we purchased an out-of-the-money put option with a strike yield

FIGURE 10–2B
Probability Distribution of Returns—10-Year Bond and Put and Call

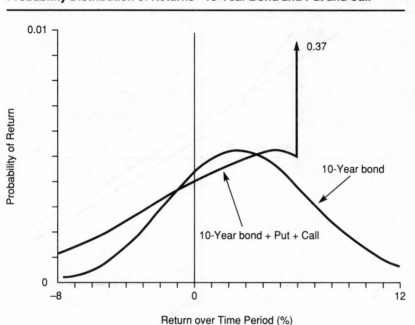

of 25 basis points more than the current market yield for the bond. We now also consider puts that are at the money and in the money by using strike yields at the current bond yield and 25 basis points less than the bond yield.

The payoffs for these three portfolios are shown in Figure 10–4. It is clearly seen that as the option used becomes more in the money, then the profit to be made if our view of rates rising is correct is greater—and our loss is greater if our view is incorrect. To help quantify this, we have calculated the probability of underperforming the benchmark index, the maximum underperformance, and the market movement required for the option strategy to outperform the benchmark; these amounts are provided in Table 10–3.

As can be seen from Table 10–3, there is a trade-off between the probability of loss (if the market moved randomly) and the yield movement required to outperform the benchmark with the loss that would be seen if the market moved against the strategy. The analysis of these

FIGURE 10–3A
Payoff Diagram—10-Year Bond and Call

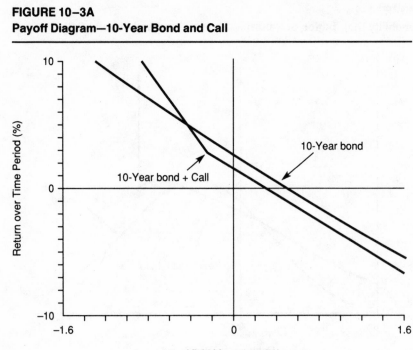

numbers can assist in choosing the appropriate option strategy to use that will match both our market movement view (both size of movement and confidence with our views) and the risk constraints imposed on the portfolio. A discussion of this trade-off is by itself a major topic, and we hope we have provided in this chapter a viewpoint from which to start.

TABLE 10–3
Risk Measures

Strike Yield Compared to Market	Maximum Loss If Underperform	Probability of Underperformance	Yield Movement to Overperform
+ 25 basis points	1.00%	0.71	+ 42 basis points
0	1.58	0.64	+ 29
− 25	2.36	0.59	+ 18

FIGURE 10–3B
Probability Distribution of Returns—10-Year Bond and Call

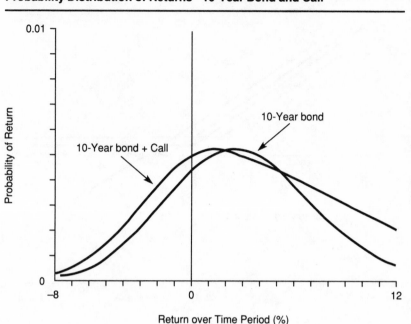

Return over Time Period (%)

SUMMARY AND CONCLUSIONS

We initially focused on the selection of risk measures for actively managed portfolios whose performance is compared to a benchmark. The concept of not meeting the performance objectives of a fund has been translated to the risk of underperforming the fund's benchmark under the assumption that the benchmark return will meet the portfolio's objectives.

Next, we used the nonsymmetric return characteristics of options as a tool to control the downside risk of active management decisions. We considered a simple fixed-interest portfolio's return compared to a simple benchmark of a 10-year bond.

If our market movement view is correct, then we can enhance returns. The degree of added return depends on the option strategy used (e.g., vary strike yield). The trade-off for the degree of enhanced return and probability of enhanced return is the magnitude of the loss if the view is incorrect. It is important to understand and quantify the trade-off to

FIGURE 10–4
Payoff Diagram—10-Year Bond and Various Puts

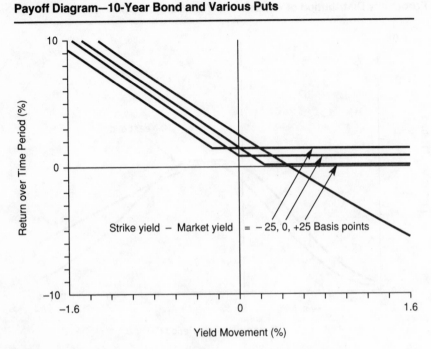

Yield Movement (%)

assist in deriving the desired strategy by considering not only the payoff but also the probability of underperforming the benchmark, the loss if we do underperform, and the minimum market movement required to outperform the benchmark. A thorough analysis of the trade-off should be performed in conjunction with the fund's constraints and the degree of confidence we place on our market views.

PART 3

OPTIMAL EQUITY PORTFOLIOS

CHAPTER 11

WORLD EQUITIES: THE PAST AND THE FUTURE

Roger G. Ibbotson
Laurence B. Siegel
Paul D. Kaplan

HISTORICAL PERSPECTIVE AND INSTITUTIONAL SETTING

The global character of the market for corporate equities is an age-old, not new, phenomenon. The principal stock exchanges of Europe antedate those of the United States. While several exchanges claim to be the oldest, the Paris Bourse has a record of price quotations going back to the 1600s and is the most venerable by that criterion.[1] The New York Stock Exchange, in contrast, dates back to 1792. Moreover, European investors—especially those on the Continent—have traditionally invested in each others' markets. Robeco, the publicly traded Netherlands-based international investment fund, is in its sixth decade, and private trusts have invested internationally for a longer period of time.

The current wave of equity globalization, then, really amounts to the integration of the noncontinental markets—the United States, Japan, and Britain, to name the largest—into an existing tradition of cross-border investing.[2] Changes in technology and other factors have, of course, changed and enriched the tradition. Yet, as Benjamin Friedman said, a time traveler from 1940 or even 1900 would be more at home in the financial markets of today than in practically any other part of modern society.[3]

173

This chapter will introduce the facts and current thinking about global equity investing and set the stage for detailed discussion of particular topics in the other chapters in this book. To that end, we present data on the market value (capitalization) and historical returns on the equity markets of the world. Our focus, however, is not limited to the past. We also raise some of the issues that we believe are important in making decisions about how to invest in the global equity markets of the future.

Characteristics of the National Markets

Most of the market value of securities trading takes place on organized exchanges. We can thus characterize the markets of the world, in a more or less satisfactory fashion, by looking at the attributes of the principal stock exchange of each country. Table 11–1 presents data for 32 countries. Note that while the large, developed countries account for the great majority of market capitalization and trading, stock market activity is found in almost every noncommunist country. There are additional, small markets not shown in Table 11–1.

The markets described in Table 11–1 are characterized not only by conventional measures (such as market capitalization, volume, and number of listings) but also by their trading institutions. These include the presence of continuous auctions, reliance on computer-directed trading, the role of specialists, the trading of futures and options, and the imposition of price limits and margin requirements. Cross-country differences in some of these institutions have been proposed as being influential in explaining price behavior.[4]

MARKET VALUES

The world equity market has grown phenomenally in the past generation, to a size approximating $6.5 trillion. In 1960, the U.S. stock market dominated the world, representing two thirds of world equity market value. In contrast, for several years in the late 1980s, the Japanese market was larger than that of the United States. European and other markets have also grown greatly in size and importance. Figure 11–1 shows the changing *relative* equity capitalizations in the United States and the major foreign markets from the end of 1985 (the first date for which we have reliable data) to the end of the first quarter of 1990.

The *absolute* sizes of the stock markets of the world as of the end of December 1985 and March 1990 are depicted in Figure 11–2. Perhaps the

FIGURE 11–1

Market Capitalizations of Stock Markets, December 1985–March 1990

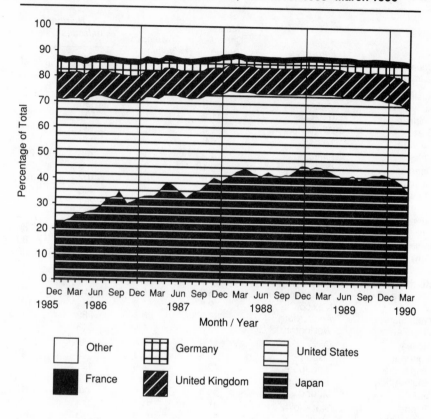

Month / Year

Legend:
- Other
- France
- Germany
- United Kingdom
- United States
- Japan

most notable fact shown in Figure 11–2 is the doubling of world equity market capitalization in just over four years. The chief source of this increase was capital appreciation, since new issues were not particularly strong over the period. In fact, the supply of U.S. equities actually shrank in several of the years as retirement of issues (by repurchase and various takeover mechanisms) exceeded new issuances.

As of early 1990, the United States and Japan are by far the largest markets, each with about $3 trillion in market capitalization.[5] The European market is also large, totaling nearly $2 trillion, but fragmented because of the large number of countries. Of the European countries, Great Britain has the lion's share of equity value, although the economies of Germany and France are larger as measured by GNP. The prominence of the British stock market is attributable to an ''equity culture,'' common

TABLE 11-1
Stock Markets of the World

Country	Largest Exchange	Market Capitali- zation ($ billion)	Trading Volume ($ billion)	Number of Issues Listed Domestic	Number of Issues Listed Total
Australia	Sydney	$ 137.4	$ 60.4	n/a	1,197
Austria	Vienna	7.5	1.9	96	138
Belgium	Brussels	41.3	11.7	191	331
Brazil	Rio de Janeiro	15.6	n/a	n/a	658
Canada	Toronto	76.8	n/a	1,628	1,695
Chile	Santiago	4.9	0.5	n/a	226
Denmark	Copenhagen	20.1	2.4	n/a	281
Finland	Helsinki	20.8	6.2	102	105
France	Paris	153.6	182.6	482	677
Germany	Frankfurt	190.0	283.3	281	522
Greece	Athens	1.2	n/a	n/a	114
Hong Kong	Hong Kong	54.0	47.8	273	288
India	New Delhi	8.4	0.1	n/a	2,180
Italy	Milan	161.7	56.6	n/a	286
Japan	Tokyo	2,724.2	2,028.6	1,533	1,621
Korea	Seoul	15.0	12.0	n/a	355
Malaysia	Kuala Lumpur	25.9	1.4	n/a	301
Mexico	Mexico City	2.3	1.6	n/a	191
Netherlands	Amsterdam	86.1	85.7	283	573
New Zealand	Wellington	13.5	1.4	318	416
Norway	Oslo	11.9	8.8	149	156
Portugal	Lisbon	0.8	n/a	n/a	40
Singapore	Singapore	42.7	4.9	127	321
South Africa	Johannesburg	89.4	6.3	n/a	n/a
Spain	Madrid	58.4	7.6	n/a	312
Sweden	Stockholm	48.9	21.3	164	171
Switzerland	Zurich	155.2	41.2	254	454
Taiwan	Taipei	18.6	23.0	n/a	145
Thailand	Bangkok	2.0	0.6	n/a	97
United Kingdom	London	674.1	386.5	1,911	2,577
United States	New York	2,216.0	1,873.0	2,174	2,244

Note: n/a = Not available. Market capitalizations as of 12/31/1987; trading volume and number of issues, 1987 data.

Source: The source of the trading institutions information is Richard Roll, "The International Crash of October 1987," *Financial Analysts Journal*, September–October 1988, pp. 19–35.

to the English-speaking countries and Japan, in which individuals and their agents (chiefly pension funds) have a capitalist bent and a correspondingly strong demand for corporate equities.

TABLE 11-1—*Concluded*

Country	Auction Mechanism	Official Specialists	Options/Futures Trading	Price Limits
Australia	Continuous	No	Yes	None
Austria	Single	Yes	No	5%
Belgium	Mixed	No	Few	10%
Brazil	—	—	—	—
Canada	Continuous	Yes	Yes	None
Chile	—	—	—	—
Denmark	Mixed	No	No	None
Finland	—	—	—	—
France	Mixed	Yes	Yes	4%
Germany	Continuous	Yes	Options	None
Greece	—	—	—	—
Hong Kong	Continuous	No	Futures	None
India	—	—	—	—
Italy	Mixed	No	No	10–20%
Japan	Continuous	Yes	No	10% down
Korea	—	—	—	—
Malaysia	Continuous	No	No	None
Mexico	Continuous	No	No	10%
Netherlands	Continuous	Yes	Options	Variable
New Zealand	Continuous	No	Futures	None
Norway	Single	No	No	None
Portugal	—	—	—	—
Singapore	Continuous	No	No	None
South Africa	Continuous	No	Options	None
Spain	Mixed	No	No	10%
Sweden	Mixed	No	Yes	None
Switzerland	Mixed	No	Yes	5%
Taiwan	—	—	—	—
Thailand	—	—	—	—
United Kingdom	Continuous	No	Yes	None
United States	Continuous	No	Yes	None

The size of the Japanese market is overstated because of cross-holdings (one company holding the stock of another). After correcting for cross-holdings, however, that market is still remarkably large relative to Japan's population and GNP. Likewise, the capitalization of Germany's stock market is mismeasured; it is understated because much

FIGURE 11.2
World Equity Market Capitalization, December 1985 and March 1990

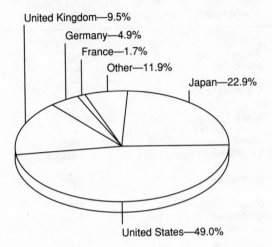

December 1985
(Total value $3.2 trillion)

United Kingdom—9.5%
Germany—4.9%
France—1.7%
Other—11.9%
Japan—22.9%
United States—49.0%

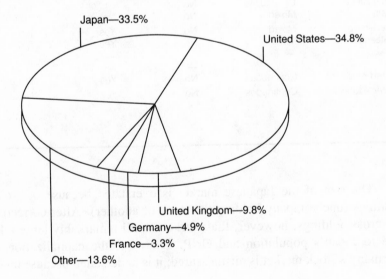

March 1990
(Total value $6.5 trillion)

Japan—33.5%
United States—34.8%
United Kingdom—9.8%
Germany—4.9%
France—3.3%
Other—13.6%

corporate equity is untraded and in private hands. Measurement problems like these make it difficult to compare the size of equity markets across countries.

Some of the most interesting and high-returning markets are the emerging markets, situated in countries attempting the transition from Third World to First World. Korea and Taiwan are the largest markets in the emerging group, each with a market capitalization a little smaller than that of Denmark. Special barriers exist, however, in some emerging markets; for example, it is difficult for non-Koreans to purchase Korean stocks. Investors often capture returns in emerging markets by holding shares of single-country mutual funds ("country funds") or of mutual funds that diversify across emerging markets.

Transnational Equity Benchmarks

To help understand the global equity market and to serve as a performance baseline or benchmark, world and multicountry indices have been constructed. Typically, these indices are weighted by market capitalization. Such a weighting scheme has two advantages: (1) the index is consistent with the assumptions of the capital asset pricing model and, consequently, a useful regressor in the context of that model and (2) it is macroconsistent, that is, every investor could hold the index.

However, alternatives to market-capitalization weights are attractive for a variety of reasons. Because investors are generally better informed about home-country opportunities than about those in foreign markets, it may be rational for investors to overweight their home country. Country-specific benchmarks using extra weight for the investor's home country may thus be useful.

Another issue is differing valuation among countries. The high P/E ratio of Japanese stocks is a case in point. Gross national product (GNP) or gross domestic product (GDP) weights, which consider the size of a country's whole economy to be the appropriate measure of its importance, overcome valuation differences and are gaining in popularity. A variation on this theme is to weight countries by their corporations' cash flows (or some other standardized earnings measure); this method assumes the size of the *corporate sector* of the economy is the relevant measure of a country's importance to investors.

TABLE 11-2
World Equities: Total Annual Returns in Local Currency, 1970-1989

Country	Geometric Mean	Arithmetic Mean	Standard Deviation
Australia	11.71%	15.01%	28.56%
Austria	10.43	13.23	29.34
Belgium	14.07	15.90	20.78
Canada	11.72	13.03	17.25
Denmark	16.87	21.84	38.31
France	14.20	21.79	44.15
Germany	8.77	11.57	25.82
Hong Kong	20.48	32.43	55.39
Italy	11.58	17.32	40.37
Japan	17.38	20.34	29.50
Mexico	41.31	62.48	94.20
Netherlands	12.71	15.06	23.80
Norway	14.89	23.30	51.96
Singapore	21.46	30.43	53.46
Spain	13.05	16.27	29.41
Sweden	17.04	19.85	26.41
Switzerland	5.32	7.65	22.70
United Kingdom	15.86	20.96	37.85
United States	10.69	12.00	16.75

HISTORICAL RETURNS

Long-Run Returns and Risk

Historical returns in the various stock markets range from spectacular to mediocre. Of the major countries shown in Table 11-2, Japan had the highest return in local currency terms, with a compound annual rate of 17.4 percent over the 1970-89 period.[6] The Swiss market fared the worst, with a compound annual return of 5.3 percent. The United States was below the middle of the pack. All returns are total returns (i.e., they assume the reinvestment of dividends) and are before transaction costs or taxes, including dividend taxes withheld at the source.

The standard deviation of annual returns, shown in Table 11-2, is a measure of the risk, or volatility, of a market. Mexican investors had the wildest ride, due chiefly to the stock market's boom-and-bust response to the almost continually crashing peso. Investors in Hong Kong, Norway,

TABLE 11-3
World Equities: Total Annual Returns in U.S. Dollars, 1970–1989

Country	Geometric Mean	Arithmetic Mean	Standard Deviation
Australia	9.78%	13.25%	28.24%
Austria	14.81	19.65	40.75
Belgium	16.00	18.28	24.96
Canada	11.29	12.62	17.39
Denmark	17.63	21.70	34.25
France	13.98	24.06	53.74
Germany	13.11	16.52	32.18
Hong Kong	18.94	30.93	55.44
Italy	7.71	14.98	47.41
Japan	22.86	27.32	36.55
Mexico	8.04	22.73	54.12
Netherlands	16.39	18.17	21.42
Norway	15.36	24.67	55.31
Singapore	24.45	32.92	53.73
Spain	10.56	15.56	37.19
Sweden	15.98	18.44	24.18
Switzerland	10.88	13.59	27.25
United Kingdom	13.58	18.67	35.47
United States	10.69	12.00	16.75

and Singapore also faced high levels of volatility but were rewarded with high returns. The U.S. and Canadian markets were the safest in local currency terms.

Translating returns to U.S. dollar terms, Japan was an even more dramatic winner, with a compound annual return of 22.9 percent. This reflects the appreciation of the yen against the dollar over the period, as well as the performance of the Japanese market. The worst performer over the 1970–89 period in U.S. dollar terms was Italy. Summary statistics of annual returns in U.S. dollars are shown in Table 11–3.

World Market Returns by Five-Year Periods

These compound annual returns do not reveal shorter-period trends, which are worth noting. Table 11–4 shows the compound annual return in U.S. dollars for each of 10 important countries' stock markets, where the

TABLE 11–4
Total Returns in Major Equity Markets over Five-Year Periods, 1970–1989

(Compound Annual Rates of Return in U.S. Dollars)

Country	1970–1974	1975–1979	1980–1984	1985–1989
Australia	− 7.31%	21.28%	3.99%	24.27%
Canada	4.41	18.02	7.01	16.35
France	− 0.59	22.35	− 13.91	61.19
Germany	4.91	15.87	1.37	32.82
Italy	− 9.37	− 1.28	6.58	41.16
Japan	15.78	18.78	17.07	41.49
Netherlands	− 0.25	24.25	12.89	31.16
Switzerland	3.80	22.66	− 3.67	23.25
United Kingdom	− 11.93	33.14	10.49	28.48
United States	− 3.42	13.30	14.66	19.64

1970–89 period is broken into four five-year periods.[7] In the first period, 1970 to 1974, the world equity markets stagnated and concluded with a bear market, different countries being impacted to different degrees. Great Britain had the worst crash in its history. Japan was the only really good performer.

In the second period, 1975 to 1979, all countries except Italy had good performance. Most of these positive returns are attributable to recovery from depressed stock price levels. Great Britain had a very strong recovery from its crash and was the big winner over this five-year period.

The third period, 1980 to 1984, had mixed results. Japan led with a return of 17.1 percent per year. The United States, which had been a laggard, came in second with a robust return of 14.7 percent per year. (Most of the U.S. return occurred in the dramatic upswing of mid-1982 to mid-1983.) The big loser was France, which experienced a devastating collapse in 1981 and 1982.

In the worldwide bull market starting in 1985, Japan led the way upward with an astonishing 41.5 percent per year return over 1985 to 1989. (France had a higher annual rate of return, 61.2 percent, and Italy was nearly as high at 41.2 percent, but much of these returns was a recovery from deeply depressed stock prices.) The returns of other countries

FIGURE 11-3

Growth of One Local Currency Unit Invested in Leading Stock Markets

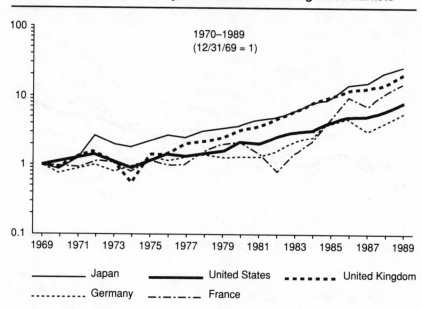

1970–1989
(12/31/69 = 1)

_____ Japan   _____ United States   ▪ ▪ ▪ ▪ ▪ ▪ ▪ United Kingdom

··········· Germany   _·_·_·_·_ France

were related to their performance in and after the price collapse of October 1987. The United States did not spring back quickly from the 1987 crash and was the second-lowest returning country over the period. (The lowest was Canada.) The European markets were all strong for the first time in the period studied.

Figure 11-3 illustrates the growth of one unit of money invested in the five leading equity markets at the end of 1969. Returns are in the local currency of the country indicated (i.e., in dollars, yen, francs, pounds sterling, or deutschemarks) and include reinvestment of dividends. As suggested by the summary statistics in Table 11-3, Japan was the big winner. Figure 11-4 presents the results for the same countries for the same period, but returns are translated to U.S. dollars.

Figures 11-5 and 11-6 show the historical risk/reward relationship for the various countries in local-currency and U.S. dollar terms, respectively. In general, the countries that were riskier to invest in had higher returns. However, the relation is loose: there is substantial dispersion of returns for countries with similar risk.

FIGURE 11–4
Growth of One U.S. Dollar Invested in Leading Stock Markets

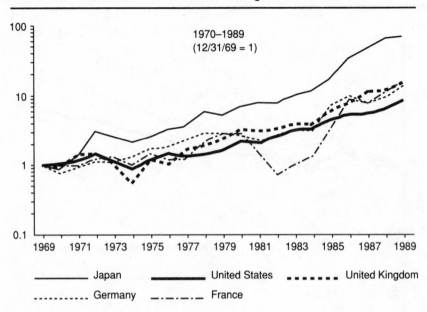

| | Japan | | United States | | United Kingdom |
| | Germany | | France | | |

Correlations of Returns

Table 11–5 shows the correlation coefficients of annual returns in 10 lead-ing equity markets from 1970 to 1989, where the returns are in local cur-rency. None of the correlations of the United States with another country is above 0.79, and the lowest is 0.38. Correlations of country pairs range from 0.08 (Britain and Italy) to 0.87 (Germany and Switzerland). Table 11–6 states the correlations of the U.S. dollar-translated annual returns of the same markets, again over the 1970–89 period. We discuss the expected future correlations of the countries later.

THE FUTURE OF WORLD EQUITY INVESTING

The Meaning of "Country" to the Investor

An old popular saying is that there is no stock market, just a market of stocks. Although this saying appears trivial or even wrong, it points out the confusion that many people experience when discussing causality.

FIGURE 11–5
Stock Market Performance, 1970–1989

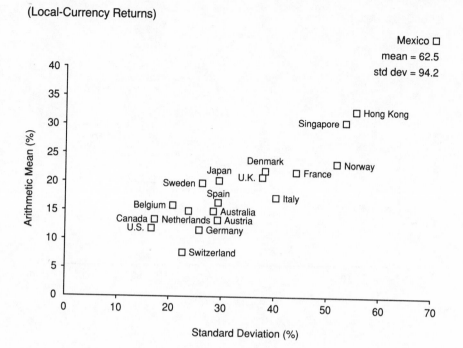

(Local-Currency Returns)

The stock market is sometimes said to cause a particular stock to rise or fall. It is equally valid to say that the movements of individual stocks are tallied up and the result is called the movement of the market.[8]

This kind of caution about causality is appropriate when discussing the world: it is reasonable to assert that there are no country markets, just a world market of stocks. One can cut up world equities any way one pleases: line of business, country, size, and so forth. Stocks have traditionally been classified by country for two reasons. First, investors, like most people, have great regard for nationality and nationhood. Second, in the past, the country in which a firm was domiciled was the single most powerful explanatory factor for that firm's return.[9]

If countries in the future have relatively open borders (with respect to people, goods, and capital), the sovereignty of a country is chiefly a mechanism for controlling the money supply. Under such conditions, *bonds* should be evaluated with respect to their country of issue, because

FIGURE 11–6
Stock Market Performance, 1970–1989

(U.S. Dollar Returns)

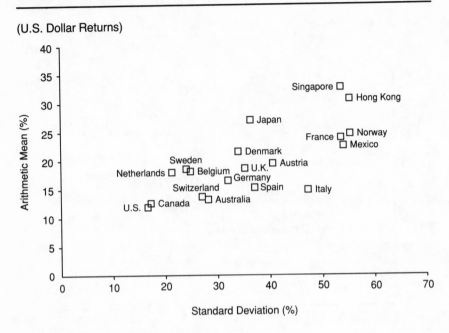

TABLE 11–5
Correlations of Total Annual Returns in Local Currency, 1970–1989

	1	2	3	4	5	6	7	8	9	10
1. Australia	1.00									
2. Canada	.73	1.00								
3. France	.75	.46	1.00							
4. Germany	.52	.26	.60	1.00						
5. Italy	.59	.36	.68	.44	1.00					
6. Japan	.28	.36	.37	.27	.20	1.00				
7. Netherlands	.73	.54	.56	.72	.39	.37	1.00			
8. Switzerland	.67	.57	.64	.87	.45	.40	.81	1.00		
9. United Kingdom	.51	.34	.29	.44	.08	.20	.68	.65	1.00	
10. United States	.66	.64	.45	.55	.46	.38	.76	.79	.64	1.00

they pay off in that country's currency (money). However, *equities* are claims to the assets of the firm, after satisfying bondholders and other creditors; they are claims to real economic assets—"stuff." In this frame-

TABLE 11–6
Correlations of Total Annual Returns in U.S. Dollars,
1970–1989

	1	2	3	4	5	6	7	8	9	10
1. Australia	1.00									
2. Canada	.69	1.00								
3. France	.56	.34	1.00							
4. Germany	.22	.10	.72	1.00						
5. Italy	.52	.28	.84	.60	1.00					
6. Japan	.39	.30	.46	.28	.43	1.00				
7. Netherlands	.61	.50	.76	.77	.62	.41	1.00			
8. Switzerland	.39	.31	.77	.91	.62	.43	.84	1.00		
9. United Kingdom	.56	.36	.37	.35	.26	.25	.62	.56	1.00	
10. United States	.54	.63	.38	.40	.41	.33	.76	.50	.60	1.00

work, a stock is currency independent and should be evaluated independently of its country of domicile.[10]

What, then, does the concept of "country" mean to the investor of the future?

- *Currency*. Firms in a country share the currency in which they earn their principal revenues and pay their principal expenses.[11]
- *Taxes*. Firms in a country are subject to similar tax rates and rules.
- *Central bank*. Firms in a country face similar inflation rates and credit conditions.
- *A set of laws*. Firms in a country have similar legal constraints on their behavior. These include regulation, antitrust, banking laws, and import/export restrictions. Laws applying to the investor are also common to the investors in a country.
- *A set of institutions and a culture*. As noted, the traditions associated with nationality affect the ways business is transacted and investment opportunities are evaluated.

It is also helpful to think about what a country is not:

- *A country is not a line of business*. Most large industrial countries are pretty much in the same line of business. The United States, Japan, Germany, United Kingdom, and even relatively small countries like Sweden all have major automobile and computer manufacturing companies. Likewise, all of them have highly developed service industries.

This does not mean a single country is sufficiently diversified to proxy a world portfolio. Countries may be diversified across industries but not within them. If one wants to place a bet on the automobile industry, it is inappropriate to invest only in Volvo. This company contains a great deal of unsystematic risk caused by the threat of competition from automobile companies outside Sweden. A properly diversified automobile company portfolio is a *world* portfolio of companies in that line of business.

- *A country is not a fortress (usually).* Barriers to investment are typically not insurmountable. They are just another cost, like labor costs and taxes. The cost of investing in a country with substantial barriers to investment must be weighed against the expected benefit from investing there.

Economic Issues in Global Equity Investing

Opportunities—Return and Diversification
Holding a world equity portfolio makes sense only under one of two conditions: (1) higher returns per unit risk are available internationally or (2) the world portfolio is more diversified than the domestic (say, U.S.) portfolio. If both conditions apply, so much the better.

In an equilibrium with prices set in a single world market, the first condition cannot hold. Investors would set prices such that the expected return on every stock and portfolio is proportionate to its systematic risk.[12] We call such a condition an *integrated world market*. It is, consequently, important to find out whether an integrated world market exists or can reasonably be expected to exist in the future.

The second issue, whether gains from diversification are available in world markets, is best addressed by looking at the conditions that cause countries to differ from each other. Even in an integrated world market, correlations of returns on stocks in different countries could be low if the countries focus on different lines of business. Anecdotal examples of such specialization abound. Switzerland is the world's banker, Japan its automobile manufacturer, and so forth. But, as noted earlier, the developed countries are probably less specialized than they are often believed to be: investors hear and remember the unusual, not the prosaic, features of each national economy.

Return—Is the World Market Integrated? In the absence of barriers—intentional or incidental—that cause markets to be segregated, it is reasonable to expect integrated markets. The expected return per unit risk in California is not likely to differ from that in Iowa, because stocks of companies from both states are compared, analyzed, and priced on the floor of the New York Stock Exchange and elsewhere around the United States. This proposition holds even though California and Iowa resemble each other very little. Expected returns on the stocks in the two states are linked by an institution, namely, the presence of a *single market* for these stocks. It may be safely presumed that the United States is internally an integrated market.

Between countries, barriers of all kinds have been erected, not necessarily with the intent of segregating stock markets, but typically with that result. Other barriers have simply arisen. Both kinds of barriers impose a substantial cost on the would-be global investor. Barriers of the first kind include trade restrictions, tariffs and taxes, capital controls, and outright prohibition of foreign investment. These barriers have formed a central part of the historical context of international investing.

The future of these barriers, however, is dim. Despite the misguided efforts of some governments to prop up these institutions, they are rapidly crumbling. In a world where the press of a key on a computer can send a billion dollars from Singapore to Riyadh via Los Angeles and London, intentional barriers to integrated markets make less and less sense. While the barriers are not yet gone, and some segregation of markets can be expected to be caused by them in the future, the movement is toward integration.

A body of literature on equity market segmentation supports this general view. When the 1960s and 70s (and, to some degree, the 1980s) are studied, the evidence for segregation or segmentation is strong.[13]

The crash of 1987 represented an about-face in market behavior. For the first time, all of the world's equity markets moved in the same direction at the same time; the only cross-country difference was magnitude.[14] The events of October 1987 are a powerful piece of evidence for the increasing integration of the world equity market.

Barriers that arise through cultural processes are less easily torn down. An example is the difference between countries in the way that investors perceive value. Investors in the United States are primarily long-run, total-return investors, with some consideration given to minimizing taxes.[15] In contrast, a substantial volume of Japanese investment is driven by the need to hold shares of suppliers, customers, and affiliated companies so that business relationships are enhanced.

Differences in the ways that investors perceive value produce arbitrage opportunities. Exploitation of these opportunities by global investors will cause the opportunities to shrink, and the barriers to decay, over time.

Can Gains from International Diversification Be Expected? As of this writing, the Berlin Wall has been torn down, and the economic unification of 11 or 12 European states is planned for a date less than three years away. The prospects for an integrated world market never looked brighter. In the previous section, we indicated that an integrated market, while reducing the costs of investing internationally, would also reduce the incentive to capture arbitrage profits from market segmentation. Yet a boom in international investing is occurring right now. The new breed of global investors must not be motivated by profits from arbitrage across barriers, but by *diversification*.

The prima facie evidence of a potential gain from diversification is the correlation structure of the assets into which one might diversify. Historically, as we saw in Tables 11–5 and 11–6, correlations of equity returns in different countries were sufficiently low to provide very large diversification gains. But the future, not the past, correlation matrix is the relevant information for making investment decisions now, and historical correlations are not necessarily the best forecasts of the future.

A helpful way of thinking about relating the past to the future is Bayesian forecasting. Our belief about the future (or prior belief, in Bayesian terms) is that correlations between countries' equity returns will be high for the reasons discussed above—integration of markets and the similarity of business mixes across countries. Observed correlations are quite low.[16] The best forecast of future correlations is that they will be higher than in the past. How much higher is a matter of judgment and depends on many factors.

Although correlations will be higher (and gains from diversification less) in the future than they were in the past, this does not weaken the argument for global diversification. All opportunities to diversify should be exploited, up to the point where the cost of diversification exceeds its benefit. With falling information and transaction costs across national borders, it seems very likely that the model equity portfolio of the future will be global. Specifically, rational investors will hold variants of a global portfolio. Variations come from differences in investors' risk tolerance, differences in taxes, and other clientele effects.

Currency Risk: To Hedge or Not to Hedge?

Hedging currency risk is an important topic in international equity management, due to the floating exchange rate environment that has prevailed for nearly two decades. There are at least four general approaches to hedging equities:

- Don't hedge.
- Hedge currency exposure as completely as possible.
- Hedge partially.
- Purchase currency insurance.

We will review each option critically.

Don't Hedge.   The case for not hedging is based on the proposition, noted earlier, that equities are claims to real economic goods ("stuff"). If this proposition is accepted, money is a *veil* that has no relevance; the real value of a stock is currency independent.[17] Hedging only costs money and does nothing.

We know this is not literally true. Returns on hedged portfolios differ from returns on unhedged portfolios, and the former were less risky over the period for which we have accurate data. It is not at all clear, however, that the past benefits of hedging are repeatable. There are not enough years of data to determine empirically whether hedging is a good idea.

Hedge as Fully as Possible.   The case for hedging rests on the idea that currency fluctuations are a risk that has no payoff. As with any other unsystematic or uncompensated risk, the investor should be willing to pay a price to get the risk to go away. The investor only wishes to make sure that the cost of the hedge does not exceed the expected benefit.[18]

Investors might cluster into clienteles based on differing expectations of the benefits of hedging and differing costs of hedging. One clientele might find hedging worthwhile, and the other not.

The case for hedging is often supported by the contention that holding foreign currency cannot consistently have a payoff. For each party holding a foreign currency (say, a U.S. investor holding yen), there is a counterparty (a Japanese investor holding dollars). Both cannot have a positive payoff! Some researchers interpret this to mean holding foreign currency is a zero-sum game—that is, both parties cannot have a positive *expected* payoff. But Jeremy Siegel showed that this is not true.[19] The expected payoff summing across the party and counterparty is positive. Thus, it may be desirable to have some currency exposure.

Hedge Partially. A position intermediate between not hedging and fully hedging is to hedge partially, that is, to protect a fraction of one's foreign portfolio from exposure to currency movements and leave the rest exposed. Fischer Black's chapter on universal hedging in this book presents a rigorous model in which all investors hedge partially in equilibrium.[20] Suppose British investors find a high correlation between the returns on Japanese stocks that they hold and the yen/pound exchange rate. Up to some point, they would be willing to pay Japanese investors a risk premium (by hedging against changes in the value of the yen) for bearing the currency risk. Also, there is some risk that Japanese investors would accept (by hedging against changes in the value of the pound) in exchange for receiving this risk premium. Investors in both countries would hedge until an equilibrium risk premium is established.

Black's model has two interesting features. First, the fraction of every investor's foreign portfolio that is hedged is the same, regardless of the country the investor lives in and the goods that he consumes. Second, this "universal hedging" constant is determined by a simple formula.

Use Currency Insurance. Currency insurance is a dynamic trading strategy that attempts to take advantage of currency movements in one's favor but avoid adverse movements. It is implemented in much the same way as portfolio insurance—by trading in futures or forward markets so as to replicate holding a long-term put option on the currency in question. David DeRosa's chapter in this book describes currency hedging in detail.

Currency insurance is relatively neutral with respect to holding an opinion on whether to hedge. (On average over time, the portfolio is partially hedged, so it is not completely neutral.) Currency insurance offers the best of both worlds—the hedged and the unhedged—but at a price. The price is the cost of the (synthesized) put. The investor must exercise judgment as to whether this price is worth paying.

Summary. All four of these approaches to hedging are used—there is a clientele for each of them. Since most behavior is purposeful, we would have to have a very strong theoretical or empirical basis for saying that any of these approaches are irrational. We have no such evidence. By identifying and characterizing the clienteles for different hedging strategies, we begin to shed light on the puzzle of foreign currency hedging.

Advice to the Investor

To conclude this overview of the future of world equities, we provide some specific advice. First, investors should regard global equities as their opportunity set and regard a global portfolio as their base case. In the distant past, barriers to global investing may have made a purely domestic portfolio desirable. The rules of the game have changed, and a global portfolio is, more and more, not just an option but a necessity.

The investor should be concerned with costs as well as with opportunities. Despite the globalization of the equity market, transaction and information costs differ among securities, countries, and industries. Paying high costs, especially repeatable costs (such as taxes), has a notable impact on the realized return to the investor. The investor should be on the lookout for ways to reduce any costs with which he or she is faced.

The selection of a global portfolio is often portrayed as an asset allocation, or top-down, problem. This approach is generally appropriate. In allocating assets globally, stocks are usually categorized by country (that is, the country in which the company is resident). This conforms to most of the mainstream thinking about global investing, but other ways of sorting stocks should not be ignored. Stocks can be categorized for asset allocation purposes along any dimension deemed relevant. These include line of business, place of doing business (for multinational companies), and firm size.

Because the choices and consequences relating to currency hedging are so complicated, it is more difficult to give advice on that topic. We anticipate that hedged, unhedged, partially hedged, and currency-insured portfolios will all have a place in the international investment world of the future.

ENDNOTES

1. The longest stock price history also belongs to France. Over-the-counter quotes for a French company, the water mill at Bazacle, are recorded sporadically from the 1100s and more or less continuously from the 1400s.

2. The current wave may be said to have started with John Templeton's pioneering efforts in the 1960s. It flourished in the 1980s (especially in the second half of the decade) but, in our view, has not yet fully come of age; we anticipate greater globalization.

3. Benjamin M. Friedman, "Postwar Changes in the American Financial Markets," in *The American Economy in Transition*, ed. Martin Feldstein (Chicago: University of Chicago Press, 1980).

4. Richard Roll, in "The International Crash of October 1987," *Financial Analysts Journal*, September–October 1988, found that when the beta of a country's stock market on the world market is *not* considered, trading institutions help explain the differential returns of countries in the crash. When beta is considered, the effect of trading institutions on return becomes statistically insignificant. The authors thank Professor Roll for permitting us to reprint some of his summary information on trading institutions, found in Table 3 of his article, in Table 11–1 here.

5. The data in Figure 11–2 indicate market capitalizations of about $2 trillion for both the United States and Japan. The indices used to compile this figure have limited breadth, and the comprehensive market capitalizations of the countries' equity markets are each closer to $3 trillion, as noted.

6. The smaller markets of Hong Kong, Mexico, and Singapore had higher returns. It should be noted that the 1970–89 period excludes the large decline in Japanese stock prices that occurred in early 1990.

7. Five-year increments are used to divide the study period for the convenience of having subperiods of equal length and to avoid imparting a subjective bias to the analysis. These increments do not correspond particularly well with economic events. The period studied more naturally divides into four major subperiods as follows:
   - 1970–1972, the final phase of the great postwar expansion.
   - 1973 to mid-1982, a period of worldwide stagnation and unprecedented inflation—"stagflation."
   - Mid-1982 to mid-1987, a powerful expansion.
   - Mid-1987 to the present, a period initiated by the global stock market crash but now difficult to characterize.

   The period of stagflation, lasting nearly a decade, can be further divided:
   - 1973–1974, a sharp contraction.
   - 1975–1978 or 1975–1980, a recovery.
   - 1979 or 1981 to mid-1982, another sharp contraction.

8. This assertion does not deny the importance of a stock's beta on the market as a means of *explaining* the return on the stock. It merely indicates that the beta is not necessarily the *cause* of the return.

9. See Bertrand Jacquillat and Bruno Solnik, "Multinationals Are Poor Tools for Diversification," *Journal of Portfolio Management*, Winter 1978. Note

that their study period, 1966 to 1974, is one in which barriers to international investing were generally high, and exchange rates were largely fixed.

10. Of course, there are many counterarguments. National barriers may not continue to crumble as they have started to do recently. National traditions may be more powerful in affecting ways of thinking about business and investing than we acknowledge here.

11. This assertion does not hold for multinational companies.

12. Systematic risk cannot be eliminated by holding a world portfolio.

13. See, for example, Donald R. Lessard, "World, National, and Industry Factors in Equity Returns," *Journal of Finance*, May 1974; Donald R. Lessard, "World, Country, and Industry Relationships in Equity Returns: Implications for Risk Reduction through International Diversification," *Financial Analysts Journal*, January/February 1976; and Bruno Solnik and A. de Freitas, "International Factors of Stock Price Behavior," in *Recent Developments in International Banking and Finance* vol. 2, eds. Sarkis J. Khoury and Alo Ghosh (Lexington, Mass.: Lexington Books, 1987).

14. As noted earlier, Richard Roll in "International Crash of October 1987" finds that the beta of a country on the world portfolio, measured *before* the crash, was the best predictor of the country's return in the crash.

15. The daily volume of transactions and the short-term volatility of the U.S. market make this assertion less than self-evident, but we believe *most* of the capitalization of the U.S. market is committed for the long term.

16. "Influential points"—data points having a large effect on the measure of correlation—may cause the forecast of future correlation to be over- or understated. For example, most of the correlation of Australian and British equities is attributable to their comovement in the crash/recovery cycle of 1974 and 75. If one removes those two years from the 1970–89 study period, the correlation of this country paid in local currency falls from 0.51 to 0.22.

   The question thus arises as to which correlation is a better forecast. The lower correlation appears to be a better forecast of the correlation over most periods; but in periods when there is a large market move (as there was in 1974 and 75), the higher correlation is the better forecast. Australian and British returns were similar in the crash of October 1987.

17. If, in the equity context, money is purely a veil, let's remove the veil. A Japanese investor buys a stock so he can purchase goods (say, rice) in the future. An American investor buys the same stock to get different goods (say, corn) in the future. The stock has, at every point in time, a rice price and a corn price. Changes in the corn price of rice (the real exchange rate) will cause these investors to experience different real returns on the same stock. This risk—the risk of change in the *real* exchange rate—is the only exchange risk that an investor in our money-free world would wish to hedge. This observa-

tion suggests that the effects of *any* hedging strategy on equity returns need to be evaluated in real terms.

18. This argument is directly applicable to hedging bonds but only applicable to equities by inference, as noted earlier.

19. See Jeremy J. Siegel, "Risk, Interest Rates, and the Forward Exchange," *Quarterly Journal of Economics*, May 1972. Siegel showed that risk premiums (summed across the parties) must exist because, in the absence of perfect foresight, the expected changes in currency values between two countries cannot add up to zero across the two countries. This fact has become known as Siegel's paradox.

20. As Black points out, his model assumes all changes in exchange rates are due to changes in the real exchange rate. Changes in the real exchange rate are the only exchange rate changes that equity investors should care to hedge against (see footnote 17). Historically, we have found that real exchange rates and nominal exchange rates have not always moved in the same direction in both the short run and the long run.

This suggests hedges on equity portfolios should be constructed from futures or options on index-linked bonds (bonds with payoffs tied to an inflation index). Index-linked bonds are required to construct a real exchange rate hedge.

CHAPTER 12

GLOBAL PASSIVE MANAGEMENT*

Brian R. Bruce
Heydon D. Traub
Larry L. Martin

This chapter discusses passive management. First, we will define passive management and discuss what makes it different from other forms of management. Second, we will analyze how passive strategies perform compared to active strategies. Third, we will explore different passive approaches, highlighting the most commonly used strategy: market-capitalization weighting.

PASSIVE MANAGEMENT

What is passive management? How does it differ from active or quantitative management? Investment management styles can be defined in terms of risk and judgment. Figure 12–1 shows the taxonomy of investment management styles and asset classes. It shows how you increase your judgment and risk by moving from strictly passive products (no judgment and low risk, as defined by variation from the accepted asset class benchmark) to active products (significant judgments and higher risk due to potentially large variation from the benchmark). The asset classes are the horizontal component. Bruce points out that nontraditional asset classes

* The authors would like to thank Jerry Pogue, Rob Arnott, and Kelly Morgan for their helpful comments.

FIGURE 12–1
Investment Management

Portfolio Level	Equity				Asset Allocation Portfolio Restructuring				
						Fixed			
	U.S. Large Cap	U.S. Small Cap	Venture Cap	International	U.S	International	Cash	Real Estate	Monetary Metals
Passive level	S&P 500	Russell 2000		EAFE	Shearson-Lehman	Goldman	T bills	Frank Russell	Gold
Enhanced passive level	Enhanced S&P 500				Enhanced Shearson		Enhanced Cash		
Quantitative level	Tilts	Tilts		Country Allocator	Dedicated/Immunized sector allocators				
Active	Income	Growth		Growth	Duration		Yield curve		

Note: Table entries are widely followed indices or examples of a style that exemplifies the category.

(real estate, venture capital) can fit in this framework along with the more traditional equities and fixed income.[1]

Active management relies on human judgment to determine portfolio holdings on an ongoing basis. Active funds take two forms: (1) "traditional" management, which relies on a manager's ability to look at the relevant information and judge a stock's value, or (2) quantitative management, which relies on human judgment to build a model and then apply this model in an objective manner. These funds may also make country and currency bets based on macroeconomic data. Other types of funds that are becoming popular include country allocation funds and active/passive funds. Country funds involve holding the security selection within a country passive and making an active country bet based on a quantitative model and/or a manager's judgment.

Passive funds use little judgment. Traditionally, the funds under management use capitalization to weight both countries and stocks. This minimizes turnover costs and the related drag on returns. Recently, in response to concerns regarding the huge capitalization of Japan relative to the rest of the world, funds have sprung up that weight the countries based on the gross national/domestic product or other somewhat arbitrary means to reduce the Japanese exposure.

Today, over 30 percent of the domestic equity assets of the 200 largest U.S. pension funds are indexed. InterSec estimates that 15 percent of the international funds are indexed. Currently, there are three major indices: Salomon-Frank Russell PMI index (SR–PMI), the Morgan Stanley Capital International Europe Asia Far East index (MSCI), and the Financial Times Europe-Pacific Basin index (FT–A). All three use market-capitalization weighting. They differ in the number of securities included and the number of countries covered. Figure 12–2 shows a comparison of the three.

REASONS FOR PASSIVE MANAGEMENT

Why invest in global passive funds? There are four primary reasons:

1. Diversification.
2. Cost.
3. Fees.
4. Performance.

FIGURE 12–2
International Indices

	MSCI	*FT–A*	*SR–PMI*
Countries	18	20	20
Securities	1,023	1,690	724
Market value	$3,500 billion	$4,400 billion	$2,600 billion
Other	Longest performance record	Broadest	Large capitalization; most liquid
Correlations with MSCI	1.00	.99	.99
Annualized returns 1987–89	20.9%	21.5%	20.5%

Source: State Street Bank and Trust Company.

Diversification

The first justification for global indexing is diversification. Since international equities have a low correlation with the S&P 500, they help lower the risk for a given level of return (or, conversely, they help raise the return for a given level of risk). Figure 12–3 shows the efficient frontier of the S&P 500 versus EAFE over the period 1979 to 1989. This clearly shows that due to the low correlations between markets, a mixture of domestic and international securities outperforms a 100 percent domestic portfolio.

Cost

Passive management is a less expensive way to operate in the investment business. Passive management is very system intensive. Browne states,

> Once systems are in place there is no need to hire large numbers of highly compensated investment analysts to seek out new ideas. This is quite the opposite of what is required in active management. Since active managers are marketing their services on a basis of adding more alpha than their competitors, it is essential for active managers to attract and retain highly compensated personnel who can convince the marketplace of their superiority. Passive management firms need not be managed on this "star" system, nor is there generally a need for as many professionals per unit of assets man-

FIGURE 12–3
Efficient Frontier S&P 500 with EAFE, 1979–1989

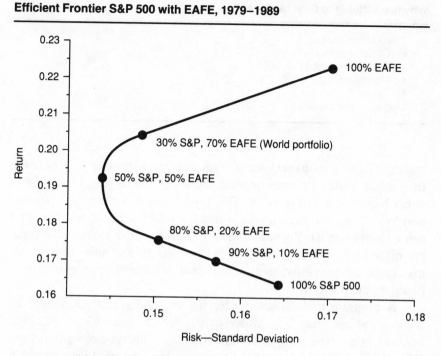

Source: State Street Bank and Trust Company.

aged. While the construction of complex systems can pose a formidable "barrier to entry," once the systems are in place great economies can be passed on to the client in the form of lower fees.[2]

Systems and personnel costs are fixed costs, which are lower with passive management. In addition to lower costs, passive managers are more likely to retain assets because they almost always meet their objectives. This allows passive managers to operate with lower fees.

One variable cost is also lower: transaction costs. As Traub points out, transaction costs can be broken down into four types: commissions, bid-offer spreads, market impact, and taxes (see Figure 12–4).

Transaction Cost 1

Commissions are a major reason why passive strategies are less costly to implement than active strategies. This stems from the use of program

FIGURE 12–4
Why Is It Difficult to Beat the Index?

---

1. Transaction costs.
   - Commissions.
   - Bid-offer spreads.
   - Market impact.
   - Taxes.
2. Management fees.

---

trading. Active managers trade with the block desk at a brokerage firm. Most trades are done because the active manager has a reason to either buy or sell that security. This type of trade is called an *information trade* (i.e., the person who is making it has some information that causes him to do it). Because of this information, the broker must price his offer or guarantee to reflect the possibility that this information may cause adverse movement of the security before he can purchase or liquidate the position.

A program trade is simply buying or selling a large number of securities at one time. It is utilized by passive managers who need either liquidity or a rebalancing of current holdings. This type of trade is considered informationless, since the person making the trade has no hidden information about the securities in which he wishes to transact. This difference can have a significant effect on the price of commission bids from brokers.

State Street Bank estimates that international program desks average 25 basis points for agency program bids versus 50 basis points for international block desks trading the same securities.

Transaction Cost 2

The next transaction cost is taxes. In the United States, there are no exchange taxes except minimal SEC fees on the sell side. Overseas, taxes are as high as 1 percent for both buys and sells. For example, Sweden has the highest tax structure of the EAFE markets. This is a major reason why global active managers trail their benchmarks by more than domestic managers do. Active strategies have a higher turnover than do passive strategies. If you have to pay up to 100 basis points to the local exchange every time you wish to trade, high turnover can significantly impact returns.

Transaction Cost 3

Bid-offer spreads also contribute to the cost of transacting. Spreads can be very high, especially in some small capitalization issues. In the United States, over 4 percent of all companies in the second- and third-thousand-largest names have bid-ask spreads larger than 4 percent. These spreads typically represent the largest part of the transaction cost, yet managers often overlook them when moving from one security to another because they cannot easily be measured. As with other costs, they are typically higher overseas. Based on data compiled at State Street Bank's asset management group, the weighted-average bid/ask is estimated to be at least 1.2 percent, which translates to a cost of 60 basis points each way. Realistically, we would expect an active manager to face higher bid/ask spreads since many active managers equally weight the holdings in their portfolios. This means a larger proportion of their dollars traded will involve smaller-capitalization stocks (as compared to an index fund), which have above average bid/ask spreads.

Transaction Cost 4

The last component of transaction cost is market impact. This is the most difficult part to measure, so we will not add it to the following transaction cost calculation. However, based on our experience managing both passive and active portfolios, market impact exists, and it is typically greater for active portfolios. The latter is true because active managers often take large positions relative to the size (capitalization) of a company. Since capitalization correlates highly with trading volume, we should expect smaller positions offered at a given price for small-cap stocks. This means the offer price is more likely to be ''impacted'' up for a small stock if a manager tries to accumulate a sizable position in a short amount of time. Also, we would expect that most active managers would not be willing to wait very long for fear that other investors will discover the ''bullish'' information (which has led them to want the stock) before they have bought all the desired shares.

Fees

Management fees also make it more difficult to beat the index. According to a recent SEI survey, international active fees average 68 basis points versus approximately 25 basis points for an EAFE index fund. SEI also

FIGURE 12–5
Annual Cost Comparison: Indexing versus Active Management

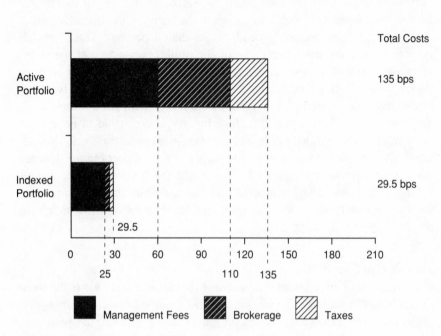

Source: State Street Bank and Trust Company.

found that the average domestic active fee was 58 basis points. Compare this to an average fee of 5 basis points for an S&P 500 index fund. Management fees alone constitute a drag in performance of over 40 basis points.

Total Cost for an International Trade

How this translates into total cost can be seen in Figure 12–5. The first cost is management fees. We conservatively estimate an active management fee of 60 basis points. Next, we figure the brokerage commission at 50 percent turnover and estimate a 50-basis-point (each way) commission. This equals a total cost of 50 basis points.

Finally, we estimate the weighted-average tax to trade (Australia, Germany, Hong Kong, Italy, Japan, Singapore, Sweden, Switzerland,

FIGURE 12–6
EAFE Performance versus Active Management

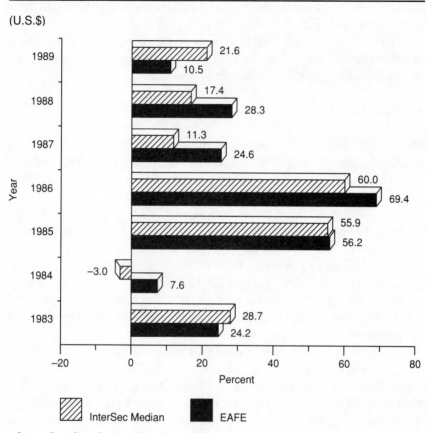

Source: State Street Bank and Trust Company.

and the United Kingdom tax trades) to be 25 basis points. Ignoring contributions and withdrawals, and assuming 50 percent turnover each way for an active manager, this causes a drag of 25 basis points for an active portfolio.

The total for the active portfolio is 135 basis points. This total ignores the important (but harder to quantify) market impact.

In analyzing costs for an EAFE index portfolio, we first look at turnover. The average percent change in the composition of the EAFE index is about 3 percent. This translates to turnover for an index fund of 6 percent. At a cost of 50 basis points for commssion and 25 basis points for taxes, the total cost is 4.5 basis points. Add on the management fee of 25 basis points for a total of 29.5.

Even assuming no market impact costs, an active portfolio must select stocks that outperform by 1.05 percent just to match a passive portfolio's returns. This is a large hurdle to overcome.

Performance

Perhaps the most convincing argument in favor of index funds is their results. Unlike the active investment manager, an index fund seeks to achieve returns identical to a specific benchmark. It achieves this objective by holding a basket of securities designed to track the index.

Looking at the most recent data from 1980 through 1989, the two most well-known global indices (the S&P 500 and EAFE) have easily beaten the median manager performance. Figures 12–6 and 12–7 show that the EAFE index has beaten the InterSec median manager by 196 basis points per year. In addition, from 1983 to 1987, the EAFE index was in the top 1 percent of the InterSec rankings of all investment managers. Figure 12–8 shows that the S&P 500 has beaten the SEI median manager by an average of 139 basis points per year.

A final advantage of index funds is the flexibility the strategy provides to add excess returns. The most straightforward method to add return is through securities lending. In Japan, lending fees in certain situations could add 250 to 300 basis points to a stock's return, according to State Street Bank's securities lending department (although we would expect this number to fall as more players enter this lucrative market). Lending in other countries is still in its infancy, but there is certainly significant opportunity to add value with little risk. Although active portfolios could lend securities, doing so adds a layer of complexity and potential problems that indexers do not face. Lending might impede the active manager's ability to transact on short notice because of delays in getting the stock back. On the other hand, a passive investor rarely needs to sell a stock, and, even if he does, he should have little urgency to transact because it is not an information-based trade. Other possibilities to add value to an index include futures arbitrage, options/warrant arbitrage, and index tilts, such as eliminating the most unattractive stocks from an indexed portfolio.

FIGURE 12-7
EAFE Index Performance versus InterSec Median

Year	EAFE	InterSec Median	Difference
1980	23.50%	28.80%	-5.30%
1981	-1.60	-1.90	0.30
1982	-1.20	3.90	-5.10
1983	24.20	28.70	-4.50
1984	7.60	-2.90	10.50
1985	56.20	55.90	0.30
1986	69.40	60.00	9.40
1987	24.60	11.30	13.30
1988	28.30	16.40	11.90
1989	10.50	21.60	-11.10
Average	24.1%	22.2%	1.9%

Source: State Street Bank and Trust Company.

FIGURE 12-8
S&P 500 Index Performance versus SEI Median

Year	S&P 500	SEI Median	Difference
1980	32.57%	30.60%	1.97%
1981	-5.34	-2.20	-3.14
1982	21.08	22.40	-1.32
1983	22.39	19.60	2.79
1984	6.11	1.50	4.61
1985	31.73	30.00	1.73
1986	18.55	16.70	1.85
1987	5.23	4.00	1.23
1988	16.83	16.80	0.03
1989	31.52	27.30	4.22
Average	18.1%	16.7%	1.4%

Source: State Street Bank and Trust Company.

PASSIVE STRATEGIES

The most popular passive strategy employed today is capitalization weighting. Is this the best method? Most research says yes, because it is the easiest and most cost-effective way. It is reasonable to own the capitalization percentage of each company. A benefit is that as a company's market value (and, therefore, its target weight) increases, the weight in the portfolio automatically matches it. Contrary to what some believe, a properly balanced passive portfolio does not need to buy more of a company when it goes up in value. This limits the turnover primarily to situations involving corporate actions (takeovers, bankruptcies, etc.) and dividend reinvestment.

Should you consider another method? GDP weighting is considered by many to have merit; however, this method typically has a 13 percent turnover. A third method is equal weighting. This method is usually dismissed due to the high transaction costs incurred when rebalancing. What follows is a fresh look at the subject to determine if it has any merit in the global context.

When investing in foreign markets, the purposes are to get exposure to assets less correlated with our stock market and to invest in the companies that produce some of the goods we consume. If a major goal is smaller correlation, why do so many people put most of their international eggs in one basket: Japan? Because Japan has the lowest statistical correlation. This may be due to the time frame involved. Most global data goes back only 20 to 30 years. During that period, Japan has moved up steadily, while the United States has moved up and down significantly. Ignoring the time frame and thinking about the intercorrelation between economies, perhaps an equal-weighted scheme should be considered.

Traditionally in the United States, the argument against an equal-weighted index fund has been its unnecessarily high turnover. Consider, however, this recent (February 1989 *U.S. Newsletter*) analysis from BARRA:

Rebalance Period	Excess Return	Annual Turnover
Monthly	2.8%	53.0%
Quarterly	2.4	24.3
Semiannually	2.4	12.0
Annually	2.4	5.7

BARRA's conclusion was that "Our initial examination showed that the equal-weighted S&P 500 outperformed the cap-weighted index by 2.8 percent per year over the past nine years." Turnover, when the equal-weighted rebalancing is held to annually, is down in the range for most capitalization-weighted funds.

What would happen if you looked at international country selection the same way? We analyzed the Morgan Stanley Capital International (MSCI) data from 1981 through 1988 using the simulation model provided by G. A. Pogue & Associates of Greenwich, Connecticut. The Pogue model allows the simulation of portfolios by building baskets of individual securities and making monthly rebalancings, taking into account taxes and transaction costs. It also recalculates the MSCI returns from the raw data. All of our analysis was with local-return portfolios, as we did not want any currency component to alter the analysis. For the period studied (constrained only by the unavailability of more data), the returns were virtually identical: 19.15 percent for equal weighting versus 19.38 percent for capitalization weighting. (Equal weighting means equal weighting the countries on an annual basis but capitalization weighting the securities within the countries and rebalancing the countries each month.)

Year	Equal Weighting	Capitalization Weighting
1981	9.27%	7.87%
1982	4.03	5.92
1983	39.87	28.65
1984	9.67	18.42
1985	40.82	25.36
1986	30.35	40.24
1987	−13.52	−3.41
1988	32.73	31.99
Average	19.15	19.38

Based on this information, several strategies appear to be worth investigation, although it will be tough to find any strategy that beats capitalization weighting.

CONCLUSION

A strong argument can be made for the use of passive funds in any investment strategy due to their lower costs compared to other styles of management. Passive funds should be considered the core portfolio for any global equity portfolio. Dean LeBaron, Andrew Rudd, Rex Sinquefield, Gary Bergstrom, Bob Aliber, and Hans Erickson will now look at other methods used to manage global equity portfolios.

ENDNOTES

1. Brian Bruce, "Tactical Asset Allocation: Trends and Prospects," *Investment Management Review*, September/October 1988, pp. 41-51.
2. Remi Browne, "The Theoretical Basis for Indexing," forthcoming article in *Investing Magazine*.
3. Heydon Traub, "The Outlook for International Passive Management," *Investment Management Review*, July/August 1988, pp. 62-67.

CHAPTER 13

APPLIED PORTFOLIO OPTIMIZATION

Hans L. Erickson

SECTION 1: INTRODUCTION

Portfolio optimization is a mathematical approach for constructing equity portfolios. This approach requires several inputs and a compute to determine the optimal portfolio based on the inputs. The inputs include a universe of possible stocks, the maximum weighting in any one stock, the benchmark portfolio, and a risk model. The risk model is the most important input, and it attempts to predict the comovements of stock prices. The optimization allows one to construct a portfolio that minimizes the statistical difference between the portfolio and the index. The portfolio optimization process is often considered a "black box," which blindly produces portfolios without regard to earnings reports, balance sheet information, new product development, and macroeconomic factors.

The most well-known application of portfolio optimization is indexing. Given an equity index (such as the Standard & Poors 500 or the NIKKEI 225), the goal is to find a small basket (in terms of number of stocks) that tracks the broader index. In the case of the NIKKEI 225 or the S&P 500, the presence of a futures contract makes indexing powerful. If a portfolio can be expected to behave very similarly to the index, then it can easily be hedged with futures. The use of optimization has been extended to cross-border indices, such as Morgan Stanley Capital International's Europe, Australia, and the Far East Index (EAFE). For non-U.S. portfolios, EAFE is often the standard by which portfolio managers are judged. The "risk" in managing such a portfolio is underperforming EAFE. As such, many managers want to use optimatization for portfolios that are very similar to EAFE.

The central theme of this chapter is that optimization should not be considered a black box, which limits human judgment by mechanically producing index baskets. Rather, it provides a fund manager with the capability to explore alternatives by providing analytical machinery for quickly constructing portfolios that meet client specifications. Judgment is enhanced because the optimization can create several portfolios for different scenarios and help isolate the effect of investment policy.

This chapter will focus on how the use of optimization allows a fund manager to combine the baisc indexing problem with investment policy concerns. Some typical investment policy statements and concerns to be addressed are:

"The optimal portfolio should have a P/E of 10.0 or less."

"The turnover in this rebalancing must be limited to 20 percent per year."

"A portfolio with fewer names is preferred." (For illustration purposes, assume the index has 200 names.)

"Europe is a good place to invest, but our accounting department is not large enough to implement procedures for every country."

"EAFE is the known benchmark for non-U.S. portfolios, but it is weighted too heavily in Japan."

Section 2 will describe the portfolio optimization process in general terms. Section 3 will then present examples of investment policy trade-offs. The case studies in Section 3 are done with Worldtrack, the global portfolio optimization system.

SECTION 2: THE OPTIMIZATION PROCESS

Overview

Portfolio optimization is a methodology for weighting a portfolio. As such, it could be compared to the more simplistic equal- or capital-weighting algorithms. However, there are two major differences. The most noticeable difference is that the algorithm (method) of determining

FIGURE 13–1
The Portfolio Optimization Process

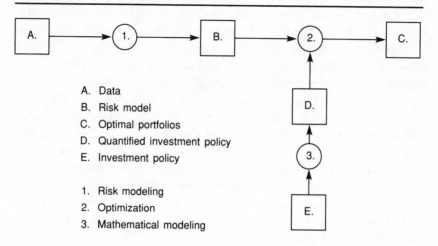

A. Data
B. Risk model
C. Optimal portfolios
D. Quantified investment policy
E. Investment policy

1. Risk modeling
2. Optimization
3. Mathematical modeling

the weights is mathematically more sophisticated in the case of portfolio optimization. The less obvious feature of portfolio optimization is that it increases flexibility in portfolio construction and enhances investor expertise.

A portfolio optimization system can be viewed as three processes. The first stage analyzes all current information and forms a risk model, which determines the statistical difference between the portfolio and the benchmark. The second stage incorporates the investment policy. Mathematical modeling techniques allow investment policy to be quantified. Finally, the optimization algorithm takes the risk model and quantified investor inputs and creates an optimal portfolio. These three processes are shown schematically in Figure 13–1. Section 3 will focus on specific instances of how investment policy enters the optimization process.

Risk Models

A *risk model* is a statistical model that attempts to predict the difference in performance between a portfolio and a benchmark. Of particular interest to risk modelers is the covariance of stock prices, rather than the simple return. The covariance of stock returns allows one to predict the difference between portfolio performance and benchmark performance. Suppose a risk model predicts 100 basis points of standard deviation between a portfolio designed to match EAFE and the actual EAFE index. The model does not attempt to predict whether the EAFE index will return 20 percent or whether EAFE will return − 20 percent. The only prediction is that the performance of the portfolio will closely mirror that of EAFE. Risk models apply to *any portfolio* in that the predicted difference can be calculated.

Three general classes of risk models have developed over the years. The traditional capital asset pricing model (CAPM) states that a stock's return is proportional to the return on the market. This implies a relationship for how two stocks will move relative to each other. If two stocks both increase 1.1 percent for a 1 percent increase in the market, then the two stocks are correlated. If one stock moves with the market and another stock moves against the market, the stocks are negatively correlated. The model has the advantage of being easy to understand, but it lacks enough detail to accurately predict returns.

The multifactor regression model attempted to correct the simplicity of the CAPM. In this model, the stock's return was correlated not just to the market but to several factors, such as price/book ratio, debt/equity ratio, or price/earnings ratio. While the multifactor model explained more of the returns, it was subject to overfitting. In particular, the specification of the factors was arbitrary, and the only use of statistics was in quantifying the relationships between the factors and returns.

The arbitrage pricing theory factor analysis model uses historical returns to determine the factors. In factor analysis, the factors are determined after examining historical returns. In this way, the sophisticated statistical theory is used to determine what factors are driving stock prices. Since the important factors are determined only from historical returns, the data used in the risk model is very accurate; returns are generated from prices, which are hard economic information. The difficulty is in naming the factors.

Investment Policy

Portfolio optimization can incorporate many investment policy objectives. As such, it should not be thought of as a black box but rather as a methodology to customize portfolios. Below are several investment policy decisions, which can be incorporated into the optimization process.

Selection of a Universe of Securities

The most basic investment policy is some statement as to which securities can potentially be part of the portfolio. This policy can be very relaxed, such as "all liquid stocks in the Financial Times Europe Index." It could also be very specific, such as a list of 50 stocks that an investor believes will perform well.

Selection of a Target

A second basic investment policy determines an appropriate benchmark. For single-country portfolios, this index is often a generally accepted one, such as the Standard & Poors 500 (United States) or TOPIX (Japan). For multicountry portfolios, various capitalization-weighted indices exist, but some investors prefer to create benchmarks that are not as heavily weighted in the developed markets. In all cases, the benchmark is the result of investment policy.

Upper/Lower Bounds

For each stock, the minimum and maximum holding is determined by investment policy. These bounds may be set by liquidity and transaction cost or by statutes govering the investment manager.

Portfolio Characteristics

The basic characteristics of the portfolio (such as its alpha or P/E) can be specified. There are two basic types of portfolio characteristics. *Fundamental* characteristics include debt/equity ratio, price/book ratio, and price/earnings ratio. *Statistical* characteristics include portfolio beta, alpha, or sensitivity to a specified factor in a multifactor model.

Top-Down Allocations

Investment policy can determine top-down allocations. For example, in a multicountry portfolio, the amount in each country can be explicitly stated. In a single-country portfolio, the percent in each industry can be explicitly stated.

Number of Stocks/Countries

The number of stocks in the final portfolio is also determined via investment policy. The motivation here is to limit accounting requirements and transaction costs. For multicountry portfolios, investment policy may dictate limits on the number of countries included in the portfolio.

Transaction Cost Assumptions
The transaction costs can be incorporated into the optimization. Stocks already in the portfolio may become relatively more attractive because holding them would require no transactions.

Turnover Considerations
Turnover is generally considered unfavorable. However, it is equally unfavorable to hold a portfolio that does not match primary client objectives, such as tracking an index or having low P/E. Only investment policy can determine the appropriate trade-off between meeting the objective and the turnover.

Optimal Portfolios

The quantified investment policy objectives, together with the risk model, make up the mathematical formulation of the problem. The role of optimization is to construct a portfolio that best meets the objectives. The central role of the optimization is to eliminate statistical differences between the portfolios and the target. Recall that the risk model predicts the statistical difference between a portfolio and the benchmark. The optimal portfolio will be the portfolio that meets all of the investor-specified characteristics and (based on these considerations) is the best match of the benchmark.

The mechanics of optimization are a quadratic programming algorithm. The algorithm focuses on *portfolio* characteristics, not individual stocks. Thus, if two index portfolios both have a tracking error of 100 basis points, the optimization algorithm would be indifferent between them. As a simple example, two companies in the same industry (e.g., Ford and General Motors) may both provide the diversification in the auto industry.

SECTION 3: EXAMPLES OF TRADE-OFF

Case I: S&P 500

An optimized portfolio can be tilted toward a particular characteristic. In this first example, a basket to track the S&P 500 is designed to favor stocks with low P/E. To the extent that the optimization is efficient, the two objectives will compete. For any portfolio value of P/E, there is a minimum level of risk. To decrease the portfolio P/E, the portfolio would have to be slightly adjusted, and, because the previous portfolio minimized risk, the risk would necessarily increase because of the adjustment.

The objective of low P/E enters the objective function in the expected return. To the extent that low P/E is considered an effective measure of return, a stock's P/E number will get converted into expected return. In this way, the problem is the same as trading off risk for return on an efficient frontier. For any given weight, the optimization determines an efficient P/E–tracking error combination. However, only investment policy can determine which "optimal combination" should be chosen.

The following risk/return trade-off focuses on the price/earnings ratio as a measure of outperformance. Baskets of 100 stocks were constructed from all of the S&P 500 stocks that had positive P/E. (Most stocks passed this screen. The biggest problem is the case of a company with slightly negative earnings. Since earnings is the divisor, P/E becomes a very large negative number.) The baskets were tilted index baskets that minimized tracking error and maximized return. The return was maximized via low P/E. Table 13–1 details the results of several optimizations with a varied tilt weight.

The risk–P/E trade-off is quite obvious and points out that several different portfolios are available. For smaller values of P/E, the marginal risk is greater. This means obtaining a portfolio with lower P/E becomes increasingly expensive in terms of risk. For higher P/E, the marginal decrease in risk is quite small, suggesting that some P/E can be given up with little or no increase in risk. For lower P/E, the marginal increase in risk is quite large, suggesting that very little P/E can be given up without an increase in risk.

Case II: Germany

Germany has recently received attention as a market with substantial potential. As such, many investors may want to hold a basket of securities that tracks a general German index, such as the Financial Times Germany index. A random basket of securities may perform better or worse than the index, but the goal in this case is to experience the returns of Germany and eliminate the exposure-specific stocks. The one problem is that maintaining a tracking basket could imply significant turnover and, therefore, high transaction costs.

TABLE 13–1
Risk/Return for Different P/E Values

(Tracking Error Is Relative to S&P 500)

P/E Weight	Predicted Tracking Error (percent)	P/E
0.2	1.00%	14.39
0.4	1.00	14.06
0.6	1.01	13.48
0.8	1.02	13.06
1.0	1.03	12.79
1.5	1.08	12.15
2.0	1.14	11.60
3.0	1.22	11.03
4.0	1.31	10.51
5.0	1.39	10.20
6.0	1.47	9.87
7.0	1.53	9.70

The investment policy can enter the optimization process by first looking at two extreme cases and then considering the range of alternatives defined by these cases. If the only goal was to minimize turnover, then the current German portfolio would be preferred. On the other hand, if tracking a German index was important, then an optimized basket would be preferred, and the turnover would be calculated ex post but would not influence. Suppose this turnover is x percent. Then, for turnover values between 0 percent and x percent, there are additional combinations of turnover and tracking error that may be preferred. After using the optimization to create these combinations, investment policy must enter the process again to determine the final combination.

In this particular case, the current portfolio has predicted tracking error of 208 basis points. With a rebalancing, the predicted tracking error can be virtually eliminated (17 basis points). However, this leads to turnover of 22.5 percent. Portfolio optimization constrains turnover to several different levels and minimizes the tracking error within the constraint. These results are shown in Table 13–2. The final selection of a turnover–tracking error combination is a judgment, which is complemented by optimizing the portfolio on 12 different assumptions about turnover.

TABLE 13–2
Turnover versus Tracking of FT Germany

(Initial Basket for This Case Is an Arbitrary German Basket)

Turnover (Percent)	Predicted Tracking Error (Percent)
0.0%	2.08%
2.0	1.25
4.0	0.97
6.0	0.80
8.0	0.63
10.0	0.54
12.0	0.46
14.0	0.40
16.0	0.34
18.0	0.28
20.0	0.22
Unconstrained (22.5%)	0.17

Case III: Pacific-X-Japan

The Financial Times Pacific-X-Japan index includes Hong Kong, Singapore, Malaysia, Australia, and New Zealand. Australia makes up the majority of the index, and Japan has greater capitalization than the entire index. Nonetheless, many view these countries as a viable source of return. To participate in the rewards (and risks) of this exciting region, an investor might want a portfolio to track a benchmark, such as the Financial Times Pacific-X-Japan index. Clearly, it is not sensible to buy all of the stocks (approximately 210) in the index to achieve excellent tracking. The following analysis will show several alternatives.

The number of stocks in a portfolio is another parameter subject to investment policy. In particular, as the number of stocks used increases, the tracking error decreases. The reasons for this are obvious. Suppose a 50-stock basket is constructed with a tracking error of x percent. A 60-stock-maximum basket could not possibly have a tracking error of more than x percent. It is more likely that the extra range in available stocks will lead to decreased risk via greater diversification. For any number of stocks, the optimization determines the best basket. However, investment policy must determine the number of names and weight this goal against tracking error.

TABLE 13–3:
Number of Stocks versus Tracking

(Predicted Tracking Error Is Relative to Financial
Times Pacific-X-Japan Index)

Number of Stocks	Predicted Tracking Error (Percent)
20	3.97%
30	2.86
40	2.41
50	2.09
60	1.91
70	1.80
80	1.68

As a final caveat, one should note it is not possible to prove that for a given maximum number of stocks, the risk will be minimized. (Solving this problem involves finding a solution to a mixed integer and quadratic optimization problem, which is mathematically impossible.) Approximation methods exist and give excellent results as far as minimizing the expected tracking error. These baskets also have excellent actual tracking error.

Table 13–3 shows the results. The difference between 20 and 30 stocks is 100-plus basis points of tracking error. However, the difference between 70 and 80 stocks is 12 basis points. Thus, the improvement in tracking error from adding more stocks decreases.

Case IV: Europe 1992

With the likelihood of unified Europe in 1992, the recent unification of a divided Germany, and unrest in the Soviet Union, eyes have turned to Europe as a potentially attractive investment alternative. Despite the plans for a unified economic and monetary system, each stock market currently has its own idiosyncrasies. Therefore, an investor who wants to participate in the broader benefits and risks of Europe may want to consider a portfolio that closely tracks a European benchmark but does not require one to own stock in every European country.

TABLE 13–4
FT Europe Index

Country
United Kingdom
Ireland
Norway
Sweden
Finland
Denmark
Austria
Germany
Switzerland
Netherlands
Belgium
France
Spain
Italy

The following study examines the trade-off between the number of *countries* and risk defined as the tracking error between the basket and the benchmark. The benchmark used for broader European price movements is the Financial Times Europe index. Table 13–4 displays the index countries. The United Kingdom, Germany, and France are the more heavily weighted countries. The optimization can generate a portfolio for any number of countries. However, only investment policy can determine the combination of number of countries and tracking error.

The analysis will determine the best *n*-country basket for selected *n*. The study considered *n* from 3 to 14. In addition, the number of stocks was limited to 200. One might hypothesize that the biggest *n*-country basket would have the *n* largest capitalized countries in the index. Although this is not necessarily the case, it is a likely result. The summary results are shown in Table 13–5. Obviously, as fewer countries were used, the tracking error increased.

The countries with the highest capitalization turned out to provide the best tracking in each of the portfolios. We used the following elimination algorithm: starting with the complete FT Europe universe, we built an optimized basket of 200 stocks. Countries that had "insignificant" weight were eliminated until there were only three left. Table 13–6 details the search.

TABLE 13–5:
Number of Countries versus Tracking

(Tracking Error Is Relative to Financial Times Europe)

Number of Countries	Percent of FT Europe Index in Universe	Predicted Tracking Error (Percent)
14	100%	1.07%
8	87	1.39
6	82	1.78
5	77	1.92
4	70	2.00
3	64	2.14

Case V: EAFE and Japan

EAFE consists of over 1,000 securities and includes 18 countries in Europe, Australia, and the Far East (see Table 13–7). Successful tracking baskets have been built with 200 to 300 stocks. For these baskets, there is no a priori reason why the weight in each country should match that of the index. However, it is often the case that weights are very close. This means more than 60 percent of the portfolio is likely to be placed in Japan. This lack of country diversification is often an appropriate source of concern for fund managers.

A constraint generally leads to increased tracking error. Suppose one wanted to build an EAFE basket but limit the amount held in Japan to 25 percent (even though it was about 60 percent of EAFE when this example was run). Without the constraint, the optimized basket would be very likely to have 60 percent or more in Japan. The constraint would imply that about 35 percent of the best tracking portfolio would have to be reallocated. Since the portfolio with 60 percent in Japan minimized the tracking error, the new portfolio would necessarily have more tracking error. The extent to which the portfolio is constrained can be compared to the tracking error. In this particular example, the amount held in Japan could be varied from 0 percent, 10 percent, . . . 60 percent. As the amount in Japan increased to 60 percent, the tracking error would decrease.

The investor may prefer to have 25 percent in Japan with larger tracking error. The bet is that a portfolio with 25 percent in Japan will out-

TABLE 13–6
Summary of Search

Index	Weight	Number of Countries					
		14	8	6	5	4	3
Austria	0.38	—	—	—	—	—	—
Belgium	2.77	2.66	—	—	—	—	—
Denmark	1.07	—	—	—	—	—	
Finland	.29	—	—	—	—		
France	11.93	12.87	14.05	14.81	15.91	20.85	22.60
Germany	13.96	16.98	15.31	16.63	18.75	19.17	26.59
Ireland	0.51	—	—	—	—	—	—
Italy	6.81	7.87	8.56	8.87	9.49	—	—
Netherlands	5.16	6.05	7.41	7.82	10.36	13.20	—
Norway	0.70	0.41	—	—	—	—	—
Spain	11.00	3.47	3.90	—	—	—	—
Sweden	1.63	1.16	1.15	—	—	—	—
Switzerland	5.01	5.84	6.76	7.45	—	—	—
United Kingdom	38.71	42.65	43.02	45.00	45.08	46.80	50.80
Tracking Error (%)	—	1.07	1.09	1.78	1.92	2.00	2.14

perform EAFE, so the tracking error will be due to outperformance of the portfolio. The investment policy determines a combination weight in Japan versus tracking error.

What if the weight in Japan were constrained to something less than 60 percent? How would the projected tracking results be affected? Table 13–8 shows the results of building a 200-stock EAFE basket with Japan constrained to 0 percent, 10 percent, 20 percent, 30 percent, 40 percent, 50 percent, and 60 percent. As in cases I, II, and III, an efficient frontier depicts the trade-off between the two competing objectives. In this particular case, the objectives are limiting the portfolio weight in Japan and tracking error relative to EAFE.

SECTION 4: CONCLUSION

Each case shows that portfolio optimization is a means of enhancing investment policy. The U.S. manager who favors low P/E stocks can now see exactly how much this preference costs in terms of tracking error. More importantly, the portfolio selects the minimized tracking error for

TABLE 13–7
EAFE Countries

Country
Australia
Austria
Belgium
Denmark
Finland
France
Germany
Hong Kong
Italy
Japan
Netherlands
New Zealand
Norway
Singapore/Malaysia
Spain
Sweden
Switzerland
United Kingdom

the level of P/E. Rebalancing a Germany portfolio can be done in such a way that turnover is explicitly considered. The Tiger fund can be constructed in several different ways now that the trade-off between number of countries and risk is quantified. In the case of the Europe fund, the exact number of countries may not be known prior to examining the consequences. The role of the optimization in this case was to show the effect of including a specified number of countries in the portfolio. Finally, in the case of the EAFE fund, the general policy was that a generic EAFE portfolio would be tantamount to betting on Japan. Again, the role of optimization was to quantify that policy; the trade-off between the percent of funds in Japan and risk was made implicit.

As the investment process becomes increasingly complex, optimization methods have been able to keep pace. Optimized portfolios are not limited to passive managers; rather, they are a form of active-structured portfolios. The action portion is the investment policy decision; the structured portion is the optimization algorithms that incorporate investment policy.

TABLE 13-8
Projected Tracking Error versus Weight in Japan

(Tracking Error Is Relative to EAFE)

Weight in Japan	Predicted Tracking Error (Percent)
0%	12.36%
10	9.00
20	6.15
30	3.95
40	2.49
50	1.49
60	0.82
Unconstrained	0.72

BIBLIOGRAPHY

Anita, M. "A Comparison of Risk-Modeling Approaches." *DAIS Investment Technology Conference.* LaQuinta, California: March 1990.

Blin, J., and S. Bender; "Portfolio Management with APT." *Advanced Portfolio Technologies Brochure.* New York: 1990.

Blin, J.; S. Bender; and H. Erickson. "A Unified Approach to Global Investing." *DAIS Investment Technology Conference.* LaQuinta, California: March 1990.

Blin, J., and G. M. Douglas. "Stock Returns versus Factors." *Investment Management Review,* November/December 1987, pp. 36–46.

Bradley, S. P.; A. C. Hax; and T. L. Magnanti. *Applied Mathematical Programming.* Reading, Mass.: Addison-Wesley Publishing, 1977.

Brown, S., and M. Kritzman. *Quantitative Methods for Financial Analysis.* Homewood, Ill.: Dow Jones-Irwin, 1990.

Cohen, J.; E. Zinbarg; and A. Zeikel. *Quantitative Methods for Financial Analysis.* Homewood, Ill.: Richard D. Irwin, 1990.

Douglas, G., and H. Erickson. "The Proper Calculation of Tracking Error." *Drexel Burnham Lambert, Global Analytics.* New York: September 1989.

Elton, E. J., and M. J. Gruber. *Modern Portfolio Theory.* New York: John Wiley & Sons, 1987.

Financial Times Limited, Goldman, Sachs and Co., and County NatWest/Wood Mackenzie. "The FT-Actuaries World Indices™." Copyright © 1987.

Rudd, A., and B. Rosenberg. "Realistic Portfolio Optimization." In *Portfolio Theory: 25 Years Later,* eds. E. J. Elton and M. J. Gruber. Amsterdam: North Holland, 1979.

"Tracking Indexes." *Global Finance,* March 1990, p. 40.

Traub, H. "The Outlook for International Passive Management." *Investment Management Review,* July/August 1988, pp. 62–67.

Von Hohenbalken, B. "A Finite Algorithm to Maximize Certain Pseudoconcave Functions on Polytopes." *Mathematical Programming* 9 (1975).

Worldtrack Users' Manual. New York: DAIS Group.

CHAPTER 14

THE RETURNS ON PERFORMANCE–BASED INTERNATIONAL EQUITY PORTFOLIOS*

Robert Z. Aliber

Two decisions are central in developing a diversified international portfolio of equities: (1) the choice of the weights for each country's equities in this portfolio and (2) whether the foreign exchange exposure associated with the ownership of foreign equities should be hedged. The choice of weights for the equities of individual firms once the weights for each country have been determined is less important, because the incremental returns from alternative weights for the equities of individual firms within a country are significantly smaller than the incremental returns from alternative weights for the equities of firms headquartered in different countries, as long as both portfolios are reasonably well diversified.

These two basic decisions—the choice of country weights and whether to hedge the foreign exchange exposure—have quite different impacts on the return and the risk of the diversified international portfolio of equities in the short run and in the long run. In the short run, the foreign exchange hedging decision is likely to have a major impact on the return on the portfolio, since the net cost of continually hedging the foreign exchange exposure is large; however, in the

---

*Ricardo Bekin provided immense help with the measurement of the returns on the several portfolios.

longer-run periods of more than three or four years, the cost of hedging the foreign exchange exposure is likely to be small.[1] The choice of country weights is likely to be more important in the long run, since in the short run the return on equities available in different countries will be dominated by changes in equity prices, which reflect a common world effect. In the longer run, however, country-specific factors are more important in the returns on the equities of firms headquartered in different countries; in the 1980s, equity prices in some industrial countries increased by a factor of five or six, or by two or three times the increase in equity prices in other countries.

A diversified international portfolio of equities can be developed on the model of the domestic index fund. The literal extension of this model from the national to the international would involve using the value of each national equity market as the basis of country weights. The index fund approach to the choice of country weights generally has as its counterpart the view that the foreign exchange exposure associated with the ownership of equities of firms headquartered in a foreign country should not be hedged on one of several rationale[2]; the international component of the equity portfolio is small relative to the total domestic portfolio, so changes in exchange rates have a modest impact on the U.S. dollar value of the foreign equities in the portfolio[3]; or that in the long run, changes in price of the U.S. dollar in terms of various foreign currencies are largely offsetting, with the increases in some years more or less matching the price decreases in other years.[4]

Economic intuition suggests that the returns from owning equities of firms headquartered in individual countries is likely to be related to the rates of economic growth of each of these countries. Thus, the returns from owning the equities of firms headquartered in the countries that achieve higher-than-average growth should be higher than the average return on equities for firms headquartered in every country.[5] Economic performance can be considered the input to the economic processes that lead to changes in equity prices.

The rationale for economic performance weights for a diversified international portfolio of equities is that the more rapid the rate of growth of national income within a country, the more rapid the increase in the profits of the firms headquartered within that country, and the higher the return on the equities of this set of firms. Moreover, the more rapid the rate of economic growth within a country, the more likely that the country's currency will appreciate. One rationale for the association between more rapid economic growth and currency appreciation is rapid productivity gains in tradable goods; a second is that the country's exports of securities will increase.[6]

The performance weights are based in part on the stylized facts about the Japanese economic developments in the 1970s and 80s. Rapid economic growth has been associated with a rapid growth of exports and with a surge in equity prices. The surge in exports facilitated the growth in national income by permitting increased imports, and some combination of the realized increase and the anticipated increase in national income and corporate profits induced investors to bid up prices of Japanese equities.

The probable efficient market rejoinder is that the prices of the shares of those firms headquartered in countries identified with superior economic performance already reflect the promise of superior performance. Otherwise, the return on the equities of rapid-growth firms would exceed the return on the equities of slower-growth firms after adjusting for risk. Hence, the return should not be higher—except for investors who own these equities when there was recognition of an improvement in economic performance.

This chapter asks whether developing the diversified international portfolio of equities using weights for national equities based on some measure of economic performance may provide a higher return than using market-value weights. This chapter reports an experiment on the return and the risk of various international equity portfolios constructed to reflect superior economic performance. The measures of economic performance include the rates of growth of national income, the rates of growth of exports, the rates of growth of exports of manufactured goods, and interest rates. Three different returns are developed for these different portfolios—the returns in the local currency, the returns in the U.S. dollars without hedging the foreign exchange exposure, and the returns in U.S. dollars with the foreign exchange exposure hedged.

The next section of the chapter discusses the foreign exchange exposure decision and its relation to the measure of economic performance. Then, the returns on the various portfolios are summarized. The relationship between the risk of these various portfolios is then discussed.

THE COST OF HEDGING THE FOREIGN
EXCHANGE EXPOSURE

The ownership of an equity of a firm headquartered in a foreign country is implicitly the ownership of a noninterest-bearing demand deposit denominated in the currency of this foreign country and the ownership of the equity. The investment alternatives to owning both the equity and the foreign currency demand deposit include owning the equity and shorting the demand deposit or owning only the demand deposit. (The investor might also own the demand deposit and short the foreign equity; as a practical matter, this combination seems inconsistent with the spirit of a diversified international portfolio of equities.) Consideration of these alternatives suggests that a relevant question is how much of the return on the foreign equity is attributable to ownership of the equity and how much to the ownership of the demand deposit denominated in this foreign currency.

The economics of the foreign exchange hedging decision centers on two questions—the first (and traditional) is whether there is a cost (which might be positive or negative) to hedging the foreign exchange exposure on a systematic basis in the long run. This translates into whether forward exchange rates are biased estimates of the spot exchange rates on the dates when the forward exchange contracts mature, for an extended series of forward exchange contracts. The second question is whether a systematic relationship exists between changes in the prices of equities of firms headquartered in a particular foreign country and changes in the price of the U.S. dollar in terms of the currency of this country.

The foreign exchange exposure implicit in the ownership of the equity of a firm headquartered in a foreign country can be hedged through a series of forward exchange contracts. When the investor buys the equity, at more or less the same time the investor sells in a forward exchange contract an amount of this foreign exchange that approximates the anticipated value of the foreign equity at the end of the investment period.[7] At the maturity of the forward exchange contract, the investors must deliver the foreign currency, and the investor would then receive domestic currency. In effect, the investor "uses" this domestic currency to buy the foreign currency, so there is "cash in" or "cash out" but only as forward exchange contracts are not effective predictors of spot exchange rates. As each forward contract matures, the investor repeats the process and again sells an amount of foreign currency that approximates the local-currency value of the foreign equity at the maturity of the investment period. The likelihood that the exchange rate in the forward contract would be identical with the spot exchange rate on the date when the forward contract matures is low. As a result, the hedging transaction incurs a loss if the value of the foreign currency in the spot exchange market is higher than the forward exchange rate; alternatively, the hedging transaction leads to a gain in the opposite case. Stating that there is no anticipated cost to a series of foreign exchange hedging transactions means the sum of the losses on one set of forward exchange contracts will approximate the sum of the gains on the other forward exchange contracts.[8]

A number of alternative or competing systematic relationships can be posited about the possible relationship between changes in equity prices and changes in foreign exchange values of national currencies, which vary with the scope or nature of economic shocks. An increase in the rate of economic growth within a country should be associated with an increase in the foreign exchange value of the country's currency and in the prices of equities of firms headquartered within a country; so, the change in the price of equities and the change in the foreign exchange value of the country's equities should be positively correlated. An increase in the inflation rate should be associated with an increase in the value of the country's equity prices and a decrease in the foreign exchange value of its currency; in this case, there is a negative correlation.

The second of these questions is relevant even if the answer to the first question is that there is no cost (positive or negative) to hedging the foreign exchange exposure in the long run. To the extent that changes in exchange rates are negatively correlated with changes in equity prices, the risk of holding foreign equities would be reduced, and without cost.

THE CONSTRUCTION OF A PERFORMANCE
PORTFOLIO

A large number of performance-based international equity portfolios can be constructed. The returns on these portfolios can be compared with the returns on the U.S. equity portfolio and with the returns on market-value-weighted portfolios.

The returns on the U.S. equity portfolio and those of 15 other countries were based on the stock price indexes reported in *International*

TABLE 14–1
Summary of Economic Performance Portfolio

1. Gross national product.
2. Rate of growth of GNP 1.
3. Rate of growth of GNP 2.
4. GNP adjusted by 2.
5. GNP adjusted by 3.
6. Market value adjusted by 2.
7. Market value adjusted by 3.
8. Exports.
9. Rate of growth of exports 1.
10. Rate of growth of exports 2.
11. Exports of manufactures.
12. Rate of growth of exports of manufactures 1.
13. Rate of growth of exports of manufactures 2.
14. Interest rates 1.
15. Interest rates 2.

Financial Statistics; this data source was used to measure the return in the form of price changes, and it ignores the return in the form of dividends and right issues. Monthly data were used for a 30-year period.[9] The exchange rates used to determine the total return to the U.S. investor also are obtained from *International Financial Statistics*; if the foreign exchange exposure is not hedged, then this component of the return is the return in the foreign currency adjusted for the difference between the spot exchange rate at the beginning of the month and the spot exchange rate at the beginning of the next month. If, instead, the foreign exchange exposure is hedged, the cost of hedging the exchange exposure is the difference between the forward exchange rate at the beginning of the month and the spot exchange rate at the beginning of the next month.

Returns on portfolios were calculated for six quinquinneal periods (1958–1962, 1963–1967, 1968–1972, 1973–1977, 1978–1982, 1983–1987) and for the inclusive 30-year period. The risk for each of these portfolios for the total period was also calculated.

The returns on the performance-based portfolios are compared with the returns on two benchmark portfolios: the U.S. equity portfolio and a portfolio based on the market values of national equities for these six periods and for the inclusive 30-year period. The performance portfolios are listed in Table 14–1.

Each country's weight in the GNP-weighted portfolio is proportional to its share of the GNP of this group of countries, based on the exchange rates prevailing at the end of each period. The rates of growth of GNP weights are constructed by initially assuming equal weights and then altering these weights by an amount reflecting the rate of change in the U.S. dollar GNP of each country. This technique is applied across time periods for each country: the weight is high or low versus other years for the same country (method 1) and across countries for each time period, which means the weight is high or low versus other countries for the same year (method 2).[10] The adjustment to value-weighted portfolios involves the same two approaches to the rate of growth of GNP. Several portfolios are constructed using exports of manufactures. The export growth rate weights are comparable to rates of growth of GNP. Two portfolios have weights based on interest rates.

The combination of 17 sets of portfolio weights—2 benchmark and 15 performance oriented—and three different types of returns—local currency, unhedged U.S. dollar, and hedged U.S. dollar—results in 51 portfolio returns for each five-year period. Some sets of weights are quite similar to other sets, and so the number of interesting cases is much smaller than the number of possible combinations.

THE LOCAL CURRENCY RETURNS ON
PERFORMANCE—BASED PORTFOLIOS

The return on the U.S. equity portfolio averages 7.3 percent for the 30-year period. The return on the market-value-weighted portfolio exceeds the return on the U.S. equity portfolio for five of the six five-year periods and by an annual average amount of 1.5 percent a year—which means the return on the non-U.S. equity portfolios may exceed the return on the U.S. equity portfolio by about 3 percent a year. The excess return on the GNP-weighted portfolio relative to the U.S. equity portfolio is 1.3 percent a year for the 30-year period, or 0.2 percent a year less than the market-value weights. Modifying the GNP weights to reflect the rate of growth of GNP increases the excess return slightly if method 2 is used—but there is a comparable increase in the excess return when this same type of adjustment is applied to market-value weights.

The return on the portfolio weighted by exports exceeds the return on the U.S. equity portfolio in four of the six five-year periods and by an annual average amount of 1.7 percent a year, or by 0.2 percent more than market-value weights. There is a modest improvement in the return if export weights are modified by the rate of growth of exports. There is a further modest increase in the excess return if portfolio weights are rates of growth of exports of manufactures.[11]

THE UNHEDGED U.S. DOLLAR RETURNS ON PERFORMANCE–BASED PORTFOLIOS

The return on the market-value-weighted portfolio exceeds the return on the U.S. equity portfolio during five of the six five-year periods and by 2.4 percent a year for the 30-year period. One inference—based on the comparison with the local currency returns on the same portfolios—is that as a group, foreign currencies appreciated by an average of 0.9 percent a year during the 30-year period; the return to the U.S. investor on the market value portfolio over the return on the U.S. equity portfolio included the 1.5 percent from the local currency return and 0.9 percent from the appreciation of the foreign currencies.

The excess of the return on the equally weighted portfolio over the return on the U.S. equity portfolio is about the same as the excess return with market-value weights. The use of GNP weights leads to an increase in the excess return comparable to that of market-value weights. Modifying the market-value weights and the GNP weights to reflect the rate of growth of GNP leads to an improvement in the excess return of 0.4 percent a year.

The use of exports as the basis for weights in the equity portfolio leads to an increase in the excess return over that on the U.S. equity portfolio by 3 percent a year for the 30-year period, or by 0.6 percent more than the market-value weights and the GNP weights. Modifying the export weights by the rates of growth of exports leads to an increase in the excess return of 0.5 percent a year, to an excess return of 3.5 percent a year.

If exports of manufactures are used as the weights, the excess return on the performance-based portfolio is 1 percent a year more than if exports are used as the basis of the weights. And, modifying the weights to reflect the rate of growth of exports of manufactures increases the return by an additional 0.4 percent a year if the second method of adjustment is used.

THE HEDGED U.S. DOLLAR RETURNS ON PERFORMANCE–BASED PORTFOLIOS

The return on the market-value-weighted portfolio exceeds the return on the U.S. equity portfolio for five of the six five-year periods and by an average of 1.2 percent a year, whereas the comparable difference is 1.5 percent a year in local currency returns and 2.4 percent a year on unhedged U.S. dollar returns.[12] The inference is that the cost of hedging the foreign exchange exposure averaged 1.2 percent a year, or 0.3 percent a year more than the average effective rate of appreciation of the various foreign currencies on a market-value-weighted basis. There is a modest increase in the return when the market-value weights are adjusted by the rate of growth of GNP.

The use of GNP weights and export weights also leads to higher returns than that on the U.S. equity portfolio, but by less than when the market-value weights are used. In contrast, the return on a portfolio based on exports of manufactures weights exceeds the return on the portfolio based on market-value weights by an average of 0.4 percent a year.

COMPARATIVE RETURNS ON PERFORMANCE PORTFOLIOS

The average annual returns of the major portfolio-weighting arrangements in terms of local currency, unhedged U.S. dollar, and hedged U.S. dollar are summarized in Table 14–2 for both the 30-year period and the 20-year period. The 20-year period also permits comparison of results of portfolios weighted by exports of manufactures.

For both periods, unhedged U.S. dollar returns exceed both local currency returns and hedged U.S. dollar returns. And, local currency returns generally are higher than hedged U.S. dollar returns.

The returns on portfolios based on market values are modestly higher than portfolios where each country has the same weight and portfolios

TABLE 14–2
Comparative Returns on Performance Portfolios

		Foreign Exchange	
	Local Currency Returns	Unhedged U.S. Dollar Returns	Hedged U.S. Dollar Returns
1958–1987			
Portfolio weights			
Market value	8.7	9.7	8.4
Equally weighted	8.7	9.6	7.5
1. Gross national product	8.5	9.5	8.1
8. Exports	8.9	10.3	8.1
11. Exports of manufactures	8.8	11.4	8.8
1968–1987			
Portfolio weights			
Market value	8.3	10.0	8.4
Equally weighted	9.3	10.9	8.6
1. Gross national product	8.4	9.9	8.3
8. Exports	8.8	11.0	8.9
11. Exports of manufactures	8.8	11.4	8.8

Note: The row numbers correspond with row numbers in Table 14–1.

based on GNP weights. The returns on portfolios based on export weights and export of manufactures weights for the 30-year period are higher than the returns based on market value, and even more strikingly for the 20-year period from 1968 to 1987.

THE RISK OF PERFORMANCE–BASED PORTFOLIOS

The risk of these portfolios as reflected in the standard deviations can be compared. An efficient portfolio has a higher average return and a lower standard deviation than other portfolios. In Table 14–3, the portfolio weights that lead to efficient portfolios are indicated by the asterisks for each of the six five-year periods and for the 30-year period.

TABLE 14–3
Efficient Portfolios

Portfolios	1958–1962	1963–1967	1968–1972	1973–1977	1978–1982	1983–1987	1958–1987
Local Currency Returns							
United States							
Market value		●				●	
Equally weighted	●	●			●	●	●
1. Gross national product		●			●	●	
8. Exports		●		●		●	
11. Exports of manufactures							
Unhedged U.S. Dollar Returns							
United States							
Market value		●				●	
Equally weighted	●	●		●	●	●	●
1. Gross national product		●		●	●	●	●
8. Exports				●		●	
11. Exports of manufactures							
Hedged U.S. Dollar Returns							
United States							
Market value		●				●	
Equally weighted	●	●		●	●	●	●
1. Gross national product		●			●	●	●
8. Exports				●	●		
11. Exports of manufactures							

Note: ● = Efficient portfolio.

The equally weighted portfolio is efficient for the 30-year period in terms of local currency returns. The market-value-weighted portfolio is efficient on an unhedged basis. The use of GNP weights also leads to an efficient portfolio. Both sets of portfolios are efficient when weights are modified to reflect the rate of growth of GNP.

The market-value-weighted portfolio is efficient on a hedged basis only when modified by the rate of growth of GNP. The GNP-weighted portfolio and the export-weighted portfolio are efficient in terms of unhedged U.S. dollar returns.

CONCLUSION

This chapter has examined whether diversified international portfolios based on performance weights lead to higher returns than those based on market-value weights. Fifteen different performance-weighted portfolios were constructed. Their returns were compared with the returns on a U.S. equity portfolio, with returns on equally weighted portfolios, and with the returns on a portfolio based on market-value weights for six five-year periods from 1958 through 1987, and for the 30-year period. The returns were calculated from changes in equity prices as reported in *International Financial Statistics*. Returns were presented in local currency, U.S. dollars on an unhedged basis, and U.S. dollars on a hedged basis.

The returns to the unhedged portfolios are significantly higher than the returns on the hedged portfolios; perhaps half of the excess of the return on the international portfolio over the return on the U.S. dollar portfolio reflects the appreciation of foreign currencies. And, the performance weights—both GNP weights and export weights, and especially exports of manufactures weights—dominate market-value weights by a significant amount. Equally weighted portfolios are as efficient as portfolios based on market value.

ENDNOTES

1. The cost of hedging the foreign exchange exposure is the return from not hedging this exposure. This cost is the difference between forward exchange rate and the spot exchange rate at the maturity of the forward exchange contract. If forward exchange rates on average are unbiased predictors of future

spot exchange rates, there is no cost of hedging. Similarly, if interest rate differentials more or less correspond with rate of change of the exchange rate, there is no cost of hedging. See Robert Z. Aliber, "The Debt Denomination Decision," in *Handbook of International Financial Management,* ed. Robert Z. Aliber (Homewood, Ill.: Dow Jones-Irwin, 1989).

2. This common world effect would be changes in world interest rates, and especially those induced by changes in interest rates on U.S. dollar securities.

3. For investors resident in smaller countries, the foreign component of the diversified portfolio of international equities might be 80 or 90 percent.

4. Stating that "changes in exchange rates" are more or less offsetting in the long run is not the same as stating that the forward exchange rate is an unbiased predictor of the future spot exchange rate. Nor is it the same as stating that the real exchange rate is constant in the long run.

5. This proposition might be viewed as the cousin of the proposition that the returns of portfolios of "growth stocks" exceed the returns on "nongrowth stocks." If so, then why investors own "nongrowth stocks" on a risk-adjusted basis is a puzzle.

6. For further discussion on the relation between the national rates of economic growth and changes in real exchange rates, see Robert Z. Aliber, *The Multinational Paradigm,* Chicago: University of Chicago Press, 1990.

7. The maturity of the forward contract is not especially significant, for these contracts can be rolled over as they mature. Transactions costs are trivially low.

8. The empirical data are mixed on whether forward exchange rates are biased predictors or forecasts of the spot exchange rates on the maturity of the forward contracts.

9. The return on the portfolio of international equities will primarily reflect the returns on the portfolios of equities of firms headquartered in one of the five major countries: the United States, Canada, Japan, Great Britain, and Germany. In 1970, these five countries accounted for 85 percent of the market value of the equities of all countries; in 1985, these five countries accounted for 90 percent of the combined market values. And the major reason for the increasing share of the market value of these five countries is the surge in the market value of Japanese equities in the 1980s.

10. The details of these adjustments are more complex. The idea is to overweight the higher-than-average performers and underweight the below-average performers. The constraint is that no country is ever eliminated from inclusion in the portfolio.

First, obtain in weights and basis for adjustment (one value per country per year). Then, compute mean and standard deviation of the adjustment basis across countries or across periods, depending on the method desired. Next, standardize the basis by subtracting the mean and dividing by the standard deviation. Then, pick an adjustment factor, which was the largest number such that the lowest adjusted weight is zero. (For example; if the lowest standardized basis is ~ 2.5, the adjustment factor is 40 percent, since 100 percent divided by 2.5 equals 40 percent.) Next, compute the adjusted weights using the following formula:

$$\text{Adjusted weight} = \text{Weight} * (1 + \text{standard basis} * \text{Factor})$$

(Continuing the above example, if Sweden in 1975 has a weight of 5 percent and a standardized basis of 1.2, its adjusted weight is 7.4 percent.) And, if necessary, for each year multiply the adjusted weights by a constant so they add up to 100 percent. The resulting rescaled adjusted weights are the ones used in forming the portfolios.

11. Data on exports of manufactures are available for only a 20-year period.
12. The one five-year period that is an exception is 1978 to 1982, when the U.S. dollar appreciated sharply.

CHAPTER 15

STOCK RETURN ANOMALIES IN NON-U.S. MARKETS

Gary L. Bergstrom
Ronald D. Frashure
John R. Chisholm

Compelling evidence now exists that a number of quantifiable stock selection methodologies have been able to "add value" in the U.S. equity market. Jacobs and Levy, for example, in an article published in the May–June 1988 *Financial Analysts Journal*[1], tested for the presence of extraordinary returns to 25 possible stock selection attributes or "anomalies" using advanced multivariate regression methodologies. Their study encompassed the 108-month time period from January 1978 through December 1986 for a universe of 1,500 large-capitalization U.S. stocks. They found that "tilting" an equity portfolio to take advantage of each of the following anomalies would have resulted in statistically significant incremental return over the time interval investigated:

Low price/earning ratios.

Small size.

Security analyst neglect.

Low price/sales ratio.

Trends in analysts' consensus earnings estimates.

Earnings "torpedo."

Risk-adjusted relative strength.

Residual or specific return reversal.

A number of other studies of the U.S. equity market have been done over a long period of time on these and many other stock selection anomalies. Among the more noteworthy and rigorous are the following efforts.

The incremental return benefits from low price/earnings ratios have been well documented since the mid-1960s by, for example, Miller and Widmann, McWilliams, Breen, and others.[2] Basu tested low P/E in a capital asset pricing model framework.[3] Practitioners such as Dreman and Hagin have provided further documentation of the performance advantages of a low-P/E approach.[4] More recently, Goodman and Peavy have shown that in the domestic equity market, low-P/E securities have provided positive excess return across all risk levels.[5]

The benefits of a low-P/E portfolio tilt have been so well documented that such a strategy has been incorporated into the approaches of a number of successful investment management firms operating in the U.S. equity market.

Rosenberg, Reid, and Lanstein also have researched price/book ratios (stated as book/price in their work for computational reasons) as a factor in an efficacious valuation framework for U.S. equities.[6] Their finding is that book/price strategy and a "specific return reversal" strategy, subject to careful tests, lead to the "inescapable conclusion" that prices on the NYSE are inefficient.

Security analyst neglect has been amply documented to add incremental return in U.S. equity selection. The above-average performance in domestic markets of stocks that are not widely followed by analysts and are generally ignored by financial institutions has been researched by Arbel and Strebel[7], Arbel[8], and Dowen and Bauman.[9] (Reference 9 also discusses the relationship among abnormal returns derived from analyst neglect, low P/E, and small capitalization.)

Price/sales ratios have been tested and found efficacious as a stock selection criterion in the U.S. stock market.[10]

In domestic markets, the efficacy of recent trends in consensus earnings forecasts as a highly consistent security timing indicator has been researched by several authors. For example, Kerrigan found, using the domestic I/B/E/S database of security analysts' forecasts, that there were strong month-to-month trends in consensus earnings forecasts.[11] Using this information, he was able to add additional value to a simple P/E valuation model. As the sample stocks were all large, widely followed companies, he concluded that the results of the study appeared to challenge the efficient-market hypothesis.

A similar line of enquiry was later followed by Arnott, who also used the domestic I/B/E/S database in his work.[12] A striking finding from his research is that while the U.S. equity market is relatively efficient in discounting the current earnings consensus, the startling fact is that it reflects essentially none of the information in recent shifts in consensus.

Arnott's work on the potential value added from exploiting shifts in the consensus of earnings estimates has been validated by Benesh and Peterson.[13] Also utilizing the domestic I/B/E/S database for their research, the authors found,

> An examination of analysts' revisions of their forecasts indicates that forecasts for the eventual top-performing firms become more optimistic as time passes, while forecasts for the worst-performing firms become more pessimistic as time passes. . . . This suggests that investors may improve their performance by immediately purchasing stocks that have experienced an upward revision in the consensus forecast and selling stocks for which the consensus forecast has been revised downward.

While the direction and magnitude of recent earnings-estimate changes can be a useful tool, there is significant evidence that historical or projected earnings growth alone is of little or no effectiveness in portfolio management. Little, for example, in one of the few published studies with a focus on foreign markets, found that the earnings trends of a large number of British companies were of no use in predicting their future course.[14] Similarly, Brealey examined the percentage changes in earnings of a large sample of American industrial companies between 1945 and 1964.[15] He too found that the directions of the earnings trends were not sustained but actually showed a slight tendency toward reversal.

Elton, Gruber, and Gutelkin authored a thorough study on projected earnings growth and stock returns using domestic I/B/E/S data.[16] They found no relationship between forecasted year-over-year earnings growth and subsequent returns. Zacks also reached this important conclusion in separate research.[17]

The earnings "torpedo" factor takes its name from a 1984 research report by Hagin,[18] who explained that "a *torpedo stock* is our term for a stock that you do not see coming until it plows a hole in your portfolio." Commenting on what causes a stock to become so risky, Hagin noted that stocks become torpedoes when very high earnings expectations give way to subsequent earnings disappointments. The higher the expectation for earnings growth, the deeper the disappointment if the expectation is not realized. Hagin's study showed that a portfolio of high-expectation stocks picked solely on the basis of forecasted strong year-ahead earnings gains is predestined to contain a significant number of torpedo stocks—the effects of which can damage the portfolio through their devastating performance.

When used with care, there is evidence that price momentum variables can improve results from valuation-centered strategies in the U.S. equity market. Bohan as well as Brush and Boles have found benefits from using relative strength as a selection factor for domestic stocks. In later work, Brush examined eight relative-strength models in the U.S. market and concluded that they are legitimate candidates for inclusion in multicomponent equity-ranking approaches.[19] He also observed that short-term models (such as those based on the last one-month's relative strength) show perverse performance over the next month—a conclusion consistent with the research on specific return reversal.

The concept of specific return reversal (as discussed by Rosenberg, Reid, and Lanstein in previously cited reference 6) is fairly simple. This strategy calculates the difference between the actual return for the previous month for a stock and an expected return based on common factors in the stock market in that month. This differential return is the "specific return" that is unique to the stock. The strategy expects the specific return to reverse in the subsequent month. It therefore favors stocks that experienced negative specific return in the prior month. To give an example of how this works, let us assume the case of an equity market that is up 4 percent in a given month. A particular stock in that market should have been up, say, 5 percent based on its industry, size, P/E, financial leverage, and other common fundamental factors. If the stock were, in fact, down 3 percent, part of the resulting negative specific return of 8 percent would be expected to be made up by higher performance in the following month.

The rationale for specific return reversal is also simple. Strong empirical evidence suggests that the stock market overreacts, as documented by such authors as DeBondt and Thaler (and numerous other students of experimental psychology, markets, and crowd behavior).[20] This overreaction tends to be followed by a period of excess returns as results regress to the mean.

Since international equity markets are generally even less efficiently priced than the U.S. stock market, exploiting such anomalies on a systematic basis in foreign investing should be even more rewarding.

METHODOLOGIES FOR TESTING STOCK SELECTION ANOMALIES

Whether one is seeking to isolate exploitable stock selection anomalies in the U.S. equity market or elsewhere, many potential problems with testing methodologies must be overcome to devise practically workable investment strategies that can add value. Key issues and problem areas include the following:

1. Database errors must be corrected. Even a very small number of pricing errors, such as those due to corporate actions, can dramatically affect summary results. A related problem is whether to systematically truncate extreme data values or outliers, which are often due to such errors.

2. Delayed database revisions may result in a research study assuming knowledge of certain information (such as earnings values) that would not actually be available to a stock selector until later in time.

3. Database revisions are only one source of "look-ahead" bias. Other examples frequently cited include the common problem of assuming knowledge of the past calendar year's earnings as of say January 31 of the subsequent year when some companies do not actually report earnings publicly until February or March.

4. Survivorship bias can arise in the sample universe to be tested for a number of reasons. It is particularly common when companies are selected retrospectively. This procedure often eliminates firms that have gone bankrupt or been merged out of existence, leading to substantial distortions in results. Therefore, it is essential that test samples be composed of a properly representative group of companies that were actually available for purchase at each point in time. Moreover, subsequent dropouts—whether due to mergers, restructuring, bankruptcy, or other developments—must be properly accounted for.

5. Industry and economic sector effects must be recognized. Obviously, these common factors influence stock returns significantly. Therefore, whenever possible, these effects should be accounted for explicitly in testing for stock selection anomalies. This is particularly important in testing for the statistical significance of results.

6. Multicollinearity of anomalies should be considered. Many anomalies are positively correlated with each other; many low-P/E ratio companies also have low price/sales ratios, for example. The statistical procedures employed should take this reality into account whenever possible.

7. Assumptions regarding the statistical characteristics of the phenomena being tested should not be made. Many anomalies have statistical distributions that are highly skewed or non-normal in nature. Special adjustments for infrequent trading are also important, especially for less-liquid stocks. It is important to recognize these characteristics and to employ the statistical methodologies most appropriate for the type of data being tested.

8. In-sample or out-of-sample testing procedures? With modern information-processing technologies, it is now easy to test one data sample repetitively until statistically "significant" stock anomalies appear. This far too commonly employed data-mining approach can lead to egregious problems. It is essential to have both a lengthy development or in-sample period for detecting anomalies and a significant out-of-sample or hold-out period with which to develop conviction that anomalies you have detected are not simply statistical artifacts that work only over one limited time interval.

9. Transactions costs to actually implement an investment strategy designed to capture anomalies must be carefully considered. The time-variant nature of such costs must also be explicitly recognized. Strategies that were uneconomic with the high-fixed-rate commissions and taxes existing in many world equity markets in the late 1970s may be quite attractive in the much-lower-transaction-cost environment possible in the 1990s.

10. In studies of equity-pricing anomalies in foreign equity markets, a number of issues arise that do not have to be addressed in U.S. research. Some of the major ones include the different tax structures across markets; the universe of stocks that foreign investors can actually purchase; the foreign exchange rates assumed, if necessary, for evaluation purposes; and, finally, timing issues. To cite one obvious example, when shorter-term anomalies using daily market data are being studied, it is critical that one be aware of each market's opening and closing times and the time differentials between all the global markets being analyzed.

ANOMALIES IN NON-U.S. EQUITY MARKETS

In general, there is much less careful, scientifically based empirical research on stock selection anomalies for equity markets outside the United States. At the same time, many knowledgeable capital market observers believe that most foreign equity markets are rather less efficient than the U.S. market. The opinion that there should be significant anomalies available to exploit is often advanced, based on one or more of the following observations:

1. Statistical databases on non-U.S. stocks are still typically inferior to those available in the United States on various counts. Accu-

FIGURE 15–1

The Low-P/E Effect in Four Major Markets, December 31, 1974–December 31, 1989

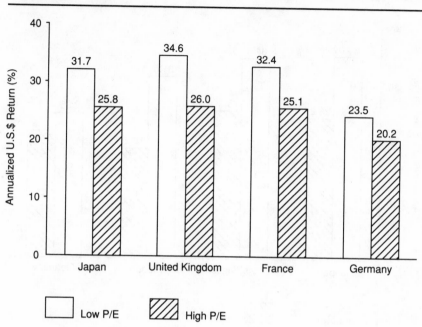

racy, timeliness, length and breadth of coverage, and cost are often cited as major problems with non-U.S. equity market databases.

2. Transaction costs in virtually all foreign equity markets have been significantly higher than in the United States. Recent substantial declines in these trading costs, however, may now make anomaly-capture strategies more attractive to investors.

3. The number of sophisticated academic researchers and investment practitioners who are rigorously testing for anomalies and then actually moving to exploit them is still far fewer abroad than in the United States.

SOME EMPIRICAL EVIDENCE

Figures 15–1, 15–2, and 15–3 present the results of some rudimentary tests over the 1974–89 period of three well-known and -documented U.S. stock return anomalies—low P/E, low P/B, and the small-stock

FIGURE 15–2
The Low-P/B Effect in Four Major Markets, December 31, 1974–December 31, 1989

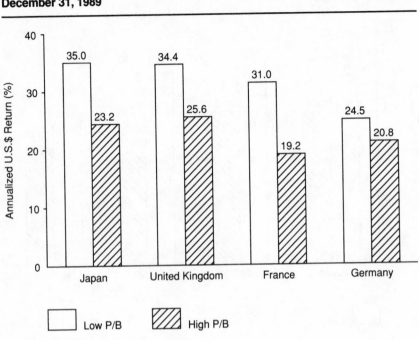

effect. Each was tested in four large foreign equity markets (Japan, the United Kingdom, France, and West Germany). Briefly, each test consists of contrasting the total annual returns in U.S. dollars of the two extreme quintiles in the database on each variable. In Figure 15–1, the lowest quintile P/E stocks in Japan (equally weighted) returned 31.7 percent per annum, for example, while the highest P/E quintile returned only 25.8 percent. New high- and low-quintile portfolios were constructed on January 1 of each year based on all individual stock data published in the end of December issue of the *Morgan Stanley Capital International Perspective Service*. Because these test portfolios were rebalanced only once a year, no transaction costs were deducted from these results. To the extent possible, however, we adhered to all the other testing caveats discussed previously.

Figures 15–4, 15–5, and 15–6 summarize the results of three similar tests for calendar year 1989 only. As is clear, not all of these anomalies worked in 1989. The small capitalization "tilt," for example, did not add

FIGURE 15–3
The Small-Stock Effect in Four Major Markets, December 31, 1974–December 31, 1989

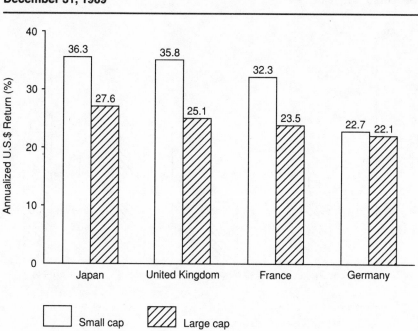

value in the U.K. market in 1989, but it rewarded investors handsomely in the other three markets.

During the 1974–89 time period, it appears that each of these three anomalies could have been advantageous to investors. While this evidence is intriguing and suggestive of opportunity, much additional work is necessary to take these anomalies out of the laboratory and actually implement them productively in large portfolios. This is but one of the reasons why, in our view, it will be a long time before many of these phenomena will cease to be beneficial.

ENDNOTES

1. Bruce J. Jacobs and Kenneth N. Levy, "Disentangling Equity Return Regularities: New Insights and Investment Opportunities," *Financial Analysts Journal*, May–June 1988, pp. 18–42.

FIGURE 15–4
The Low-P/E Effect in Four Major Markets, January 1, 1989–December 31, 1989

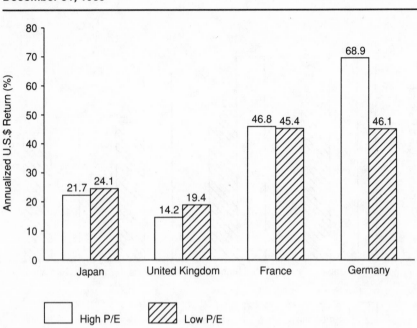

2. Paul F. Miller and Ernest R. Widmann, "Price Performance Bond Issue," *Commercial and Financial Chronicle*, September 29, 1966, pp. 26–28; James D. McWilliams, "Prices, Earnings, and P/E Ratios," *Financial Analysts Journal*, May–June 1966, pp. 137–42; and William Breen, "Low Price/Earnings Ratios and Industry Relatives," *Financial Analysts Journal*, July–August 1968, pp. 125–27.

3. Sanjoy Basu, "Investment Performance of Common Stocks in Relation to Their Price/Earnings Ratios: A Test of the Efficient Market Hypothesis," *Journal of Finance*, June 1977, pp. 663–82; and "The Relationship between Earnings' Yields, Market Value, and the Returns for NYSE Stocks: Further Evidence," *Journal of Financial Economics*, June 1983, pp. 129–56.

4. David Dreman, *The New Contrarian Investment Strategy* (New York: Random House, 1982); and Robert L. Hagin, "P/E and Size Effects," Kidder, Peabody & Co. research report, January 4, 1983.

5. David A. Goodman and John W. Peavy III, "The Risk-Universal Nature of the P/E Effect," *Journal of Portfolio Management*, Summer 1985, pp. 14–23.

FIGURE 15–5
The Low-P/B Effect in Four Major Markets, January 1, 1989–
December 31, 1989

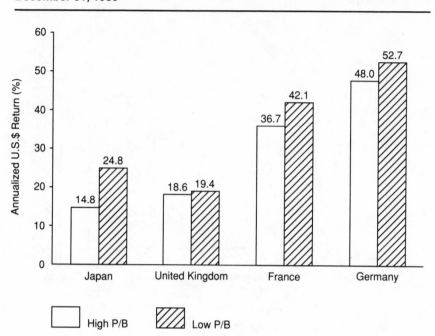

6. Barr Rosenberg, Kenneth Reid, and Ronald Lanstein, "Persuasive Evidence of Market Inefficiency," *Journal of Portfolio Management*, Spring 1985, pp. 9–16.
7. Avner Arbel and Paul Strebel, "Pay Attention to Neglected Firms!" *Journal of Portfolio Management*, Winter 1983, pp. 37–42.
8. Avner Arbel, "Generic Stocks: An Old Product in a New Package," *Journal of Portfolio Management*, Summer 1985, pp. 4–13.
9. Richard J. Dowen and W. Scott Bauman, "The Relative Importance of Size, P/E, and Neglect," *Journal of Portfolio Management*, Spring 1986, pp. 30–34.
10. A. J. Senchack, Jr., and John D. Martin, "The Relative Performance of the PSR and PER Investment Strategies," *Financial Analysts Journal*, March–April 1987, pp. 46–56.
11. Thomas J. Kerrigan, "When Forecasting Earnings, It Pays to Watch Forecasts," *Journal of Portfolio Management*, Summer 1984, pp. 19–25.
12. Robert D. Arnott, "The Use and Misuses of Consensus Earnings," *Journal of Portfolio Management*, Spring 1985, pp. 18–27.

FIGURE 15–6
The Small-Stock Effect in Four Major Markets, January 1, 1989–
December 31, 1989

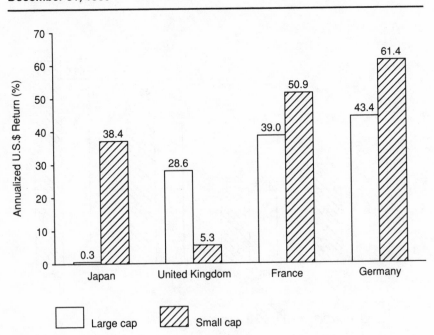

13. Gary A. Benesh and Pamela P. Peterson, "On the Relation between Earnings Changes, Analysts' Forecasts, and Stock Price Fluctuations," *Financial Analysts Journal*, November–December 1986, pp. 23–39.

14. I. M. D. Little, "Higgledy-Piggledy Growth," *Bulletin of the Oxford University Institute of Economics and Statistics*, November 1962.

15. Richard A. Brealey, *An Introduction to Risk and Return from Common Stocks* (Cambridge, Mass.: MIT Press, 1968).

16. Edwin J. Elton, Martin J. Gruber, and Mustafa Gutelkin, "Expectations and Share Prices," *Management Science*, September 1981, pp. 975–87.

17. Leonard Zacks, "EPS Forecasts—Accuracy Is Not Enough," *Financial Analysts Journal*, March–April 1979, pp. 53–55.

18. Robert L. Hagin, "The Subtle Risk of High Expected Growth—How to Avoid 'Torpedo Stocks,' " Kidder, Peabody & Co. research report, March 30, 1984.

19. James Bohan, "Relative Strength: Further Positive Evidence," *Journal of Portfolio Management*, Fall 1981, pp. 36–39; and John S. Brush and Keith E. Boles, "The Predictive Power in Relative Strength and CAPM," *Journal of Portfolio Management*, Summer 1983, pp. 20–23.

20. Werner F. M. DeBondt and Richard Thaler, "Does the Stock Market Overreact?" *Journal of Finance*, July 1985, pp. 793–805.

CHAPTER 16

THE GAINS FROM INTERNATIONAL SMALL-COMPANY DIVERSIFICATION

Rex A. Sinquefield

INTRODUCTION

This chapter examines the potential gains from diversifying internationally and, in particular, diversifying into small-company portfolios around the world. Historical data indicates that the tendency of small firms to outperform large firms, first reported by Rolf Banz for the United States, is a worldwide phenomenon occurring independently from place to place.[1] Our analysis indicates that a worldwide small-company strategy diversifies the "typical" domestic (U.S.) portfolio at least as well as large-company strategies, such as EAFE- or FT-A–based index funds. It further shows that most sponsors can invest about 30 percent of their total portfolio internationally without increasing portfolio risk. Total portfolio expected returns can increase over 2 percent per year.

Our perspective in this chapter is that of the U.S. sponsor who accepts currency risk. We do not examine the effects of currency hedging. Our underlying data consist of total quarterly returns for the period 1970 through 1987 for six major domestic and foreign asset classes: small-firm portfolios in the United States, Japan, and United Kingdom; EAFE; S&P 500; and U.S. intermediate fixed income.[2] For Japan and the United Kingdom, small companies can be loosely thought of as companies in the "smaller half" of the Tokyo and London stock exchanges, respectively. For the United States, *small* refers to the smallest fifth of companies on the NYSE. In recent years, it includes companies of equivalent size from the AMEX and OTC. The S&P 500 serves the large U.S. asset class. EAFE is the Morgan Stanley European, Australian, and Far East index. U.S. fixed income, USTR5, is a five-year U.S. Treasury note with an average maturity of four and a half years. For the most part, our data exclude the effects of trading costs and foreign withholding taxes. The data source section of the chapter describes all series.

Our analysis differs from nearly all other analyses in two respects. First, previous work often assumes the high ex post returns of foreign (non-U.S.) markets will continue, and these expectations become part of the case for international diversification. This assumption is hard to justify and introduces potential biases. We correct for these biases. Second, our work measures portfolio risk directly in terms of the magnitude and probability of loss, whereas other analyses rely exclusively on less-intuitive measures, such as standard deviation. We believe our approach is more useful for portfolio decision making.

In Section 1, we summarize historical returns for the various asset classes and then restate these returns to make them consistent with asset-pricing models and, therefore, more useful for evaluating international diversification. In Section 2, we conduct several simple experiments to show how the probability of loss falls as we shift a model portfolio from domestic assets to large- and/or small-company foreign portfolios. This allows us to estimate how portfolio returns can increase because of better diversification.

SECTION 1: HOW TO THINK INTERNATIONALLY ABOUT EXPECTED RETURNS

To measure the gains from diversification, we need to assign expected returns to each asset class. Historical data is key to this effort. We propose a simple model of expected returns that is consistent with previous studies of historical data and with existing financial theory.

For our purposes, assume there are only two risk classes of securities: small firms and large firms. The expected dollar return is the same for all small-firm portfolios regardless of the country of origin. Thus, in dollars the expected return on Japanese small firms equals the expected return on

TABLE 16–1
A Simple Model of Expected Returns

Asset	Expected Annual Return
Five-year U.S. Treasury	8.0%
+ Equity risk premium	4.5
= Large-company stocks (S&P 500)	12.5%
+ Small-company premium	4.5
= Small-company stocks	17.0%

International
Expected dollar return on large companies is the same country to country.

Expected small-company premium in dollars is the same country to country.

Therefore, expected dollar return on small companies is the same country to country.

U.K. small firms, which equals the expected return on U.S. small firms. Likewise, for large-firm groups, the expected dollar returns are the same across countries. Therefore, the difference in expected dollar returns between large and small firms—the expected small-company premium—is the same across countries.

The latter statement is consistent with the data for the last 18 years for the United States, Japan, and the United Kingdom. The average premium is about 4.5 percent. This is also about the average value for 1956 to 1987 for the United Kingdom and the United States, the only countries for which reliable data is available prior to 1970. According to our model and these historical results, the expected dollar return of small firms equals the expected return of large firms plus 4.5 percent per year. We assume the expected return of large firms equals the expected return on a riskless asset plus an equity risk premium. For the riskless asset, we use the five-year U.S. Treasury, whose expected return we assume to be 8 percent. We assume the risk premium equals 4.5 percent per year. Table 16–1 shows the entire model.

This model says that for any country, the expected dollar return on large-company stocks is 12.5 percent, and the expected dollar return on small-company stocks is 17 percent.

How should we estimate future risk levels? Research shows that estimates of risk from historical return series are far more reliable than the corresponding estimates of expected returns.[3] Thus, while we "impose" an expected return model, we can accept the historical return distributions as working estimates of future risk levels.

We apply this model to restate historical returns by forcing compound returns for each series to closely conform to our model but without changing any other statistical properties. We arbitrarily anchor all series to the S&P 500 (choosing any other series as the anchor would not change our results). We reduce the five-year Treasury series so that its quarterly compound return is 1 percent below the S&P 500 quarterly return. EAFE is adjusted so its quarterly compound return equals that of the S&P 500. Each of the small-company series are adjusted so each of their quarterly compound returns exceeds the S&P 500 (and EAFE) by 1 percent. These adjustments cause the annual compound returns to correspond to the 4.5 percent spreads given in our simple model. The actual procedure is to add or subtract a constant (different for each asset) from each quarterly return so that we obtain the desired quarterly (and annual) compound return.

Table 16-2 gives annual compound returns, quarterly compound returns, and quarterly standard deviations for the original series and the restated series.

SECTION 2: HOW MUCH SHOULD SPONSORS INVEST INTERNATIONALLY; AND HOW MUCH DOES IT PAY?

The ultimate test of diversification is how it changes an investor's prediversification portfolio. For the typical sponsor, this is an all-domestic portfolio, which we arbitrarily represent as a portfolio of 60 percent equity/40 percent fixed income, comprising 50 percent S&P 500, 10 percent U.S. small companies, and 40 percent five-year U.S. Treasuries. We designate this initial portfolio "USALL."

We observe the effects of diversification by comparing our USALL portfolio before and after the addition of international large or small firms. For international large firms, we use EAFE returns, and for small firms, we use a 50-50 combination of Japanese and U.K. small firms. Tables 16-3 and 16-4 give results for five strategies, designated S1 through S5 and E1 through E5. Both S1 and E1 correspond to USALL. Panel A of each table shows the portfolio allocations for the appropriate five

TABLE 16–2
Asset Returns, Original and Restated, 1970–1987

Asset	Annual Compound Return	Quarterly Compound Return	Quarterly Standard Deviation
S&P 500			
Original	10.3	2.5	9.3
Restated	10.3	2.5	9.3
Five-year Treasuries			
Original	9.4	2.3	3.8
Restated	6.1	1.5	3.8
D910			
Original	13.1	3.1	15.4
Restated	15.0	3.6	15.4
EAFE			
Original	15.9	3.8	9.7
Restated	10.4	2.5	9.7
Japan small ($)			
Original	28.8	6.5	12.5
Restated	14.9	3.5	12.5
U.K. small ($)			
Original	21.2	4.9	15.2
Restated	15.1	3.6	15.2

strategies. Each strategy increases exposure to international assets by 10 percent and decreases exposure to the S&P 500 and five-year U.S. Treasuries by 5 percent each. These weights are arbitrary.

Panel B gives the realized results for portfolio combinations in Panel A for the 1970–87 period. Table 16–3 shows that the frequency of losses diminishes as we add small firms. The distribution of quarterly returns gives the frequency of returns that fall within specified intervals. For example, S1, the all-domestic portfolio, has three quarterly returns in the range −20 percent to −10 percent, and 20 returns in-between −10 percent and 0 percent. Obviously, a loser in the (−20 percent, −10 percent) interval has more adverse wealth effects than a loser in the (−10 percent, 0) interval. We adjust for these differences and summarize the number of negatives in the column "Number of Equivalent Losers." Each return in the (−10 percent, 0) interval counts as one loss; each return in the (−20 percent, −10 percent) interval counts as 3.2 losses. This measure shows

TABLE 16–3

Diversifying a U.S. Portfolio (USALL) into International Small Companies (Japan Small/United Kingdom Small, 50/50)

(Underlying Data: Restated Quarterly Returns in Dollars, 1970–1987)

Panel A

	S&P 500	D9-10	5-Year Treasuries	International Small (Japan/United Kingdom, 50/50)
USALL S1	50%	10%	40%	0
S2	45	10	35	10
S3	40	10	30	20
S4	35	10	25	30
S5	30	10	20	40

Panel B

Distribution of Quarterly Returns

	Number of Equivalent Losers	=> <	−20 −10	−10 0	0 10	10 20	20 30	Compound Annual Return (%)
USALL S1	30		3	20	40	9	0	9.6%
S2	29		3	19	42	7	1	10.6
S3	27		4	14	45	8	1	11.4
S4	28		5	12	44	10	1	12.3
S5	30		5	14	41	11	1	13.1

Panel A shows the portfolio allocations for five strategies, S1 through S5. Each successive strategy increases exposure to the small-firm couplet (Japan/U.K., small, 50/50) by 10 percent and decreases exposure to the S&P 500 and five-year U.S. Treasuries by 5 percent each. These weights are arbitrary.

Panel B gives the realized results for the portfolio combinations in Panel A for the period from 1970 through 1987. The distribution of quarterly returns gives the frequency of quarterly returns that fall within the specified intervals. The column "Number of Equivalent Losers" summarizes the number of negative quarterly returns. Each return in the interval (−10 percent, 0) counts as one loss; each return in the (−20 percent, −10 percent) interval counts as 3.2 losses. In effect, this tells us how the magnitude and frequency of losses change as we add international small firms. By this measure, risk is less than S1 until we reach S5, where international small firms are 40 percent of the total portfolio.

that risk is below that of S1 for strategies S2 through S4. Beyond this, risk rises (S5 has as many equivalent losers as S1). If we assume a hypothetical investor will accept portfolio risk equal to that of S1—his starting position—then, based on Table 16–3, he would stop at S4 (or S5); that is,

TABLE 16–4

Diversifying a U.S. Portfolio (USALL) into International Large Companies (EAFE)

(Underlying Data: Restated Quarterly Returns in Dollars, 1970–1987)

Panel A

	S&P 500	D9-10	5-Year Treasuries	EAFE
USALL E1	50%	10%	40%	0
E2	45	10	35	10
E3	40	10	30	20
E4	35	10	25	30
E5	30	10	20	40

Panel B

Distribution of Quarterly Returns

	Number of =>	−20	−10	0	10	20	Compound Annual
	Equivalent Losers <	−10	0	10	20	30	Return (%)
USALL E1	30	3	20	40	9	0	9.6%
E2	30	3	21	39	9	0	9.9
E3	28	3	18	43	7	1	10.2
E4	28	4	15	44	8	1	10.4
E5	30	5	14	45	7	1	10.6

Panel A shows the portfolio allocations for five strategies, E1 through E5. Each successive strategy increases exposure to EAFE by 10 percent and decreases exposure to the S&P 500 and five-year U.S. Treasuries by 5 percent each. These weights are arbitrary.

Panel B gives the realized results for the portfolio combinations in Panel A for the period from 1970 through 1987. The distribution of quarterly returns gives the frequency of quarterly returns that fall within the specified intervals. The column "Number of Equivalent Losers" summarizes the number of negative quarterly returns. Each return in the interval (− 10 percent, 0) counts as one loss; each return in the (− 20 percent, − 10 percent) interval counts as 3.2 losses. In effect, this tells us how the magnitude and frequency of losses changes as we add international small firms. By this measure, risk is less than E1 until we reach E5, where international small firms are 40 percent of the total portfolio.

he would invest up to 30 percent or 40 percent of his portfolio in the international small couplet.

We repeat this experiment using international large firms (EAFE index total returns) in place of international small firms. With EAFE (Table 16–4), one could shift somewhere between 30 percent and 40 percent to large companies before matching the risk levels of E1.

The central message from our experiments is that either asset group—large foreign companies or small foreign companies, although the latter is limited to just two countries at this point—seems to provide U.S. domestic portfolios with a large fraction of the impressive diversification benefits of international investing. How much of each group to use depends on a sponsor's needs for performance versus liquidity. Large international firms provide liquidity; small international firms provide higher expected returns.

Diversification pays by allowing greater portfolio exposure to higher expected return assets without concomitant increases in risk. Our simple model of expected returns indicates that a shift from fixed income to large companies (in any country) increases expected returns 4.5 percent per year. A shift from any large companies or fixed income to small companies increases expected returns, respectively, 4.5 percent of 9 percent per year.

We can illustrate this with an example. Compare strategies S4 and E4—a shift of 30 percent of USALL (15 percent from the S&P 500 and 15 percent from fixed income) to, respectively, the small international couplet or EAFE. Each of these portfolios has less risk than USALL. The "Compound Annual Return" column in Panel B of Tables 16–3 and 16–4 shows how expected returns increase as international exposure increases.

The gains from any of these are impressive. For example, S4 returns 12.3 percent versus 9.1 percent of S1. In these particular examples, more than half the gain is due to shifts from fixed income to international equities. The portfolio equity/debt ratio shifts from 60/40 to 75/25 with no increase in risk.

SECTION 3: CONCLUSION

International diversification to large or small firms pays because international equities replace domestic fixed income as well as domestic equities. International small companies replace either group more effectively than international large companies because they are less correlated with either group than are international large companies. Furthermore, the ultimate gain relates not just to return differences between small and large companies internationally, but also to return differences between small international companies and all domestic asset classes, because each of the latter will be somewhat reduced as we add small international firms to our portfolio.

DATA SOURCES

S&P 500 Index (1926–1987)
Roger G. Ibbotson and Rex A. Sinquefield, *Stocks, Bonds, Bills, and Inflation: The Past and The Future* (Charlottesville, Va.: The Financial Analysts Research Foundation, 1982). Updates courtesy of *SBBI Yearbook* (Chicago: Ibbotson Associates, 1988).

Small-Company Stocks—Size Deciles 9 and 10 (1926–1987)
1926–1981: Smallest quintile NYSE (plus AMEX equivalent 1963–1981). Courtesy of Rolf Banz, Dimensional Asset Management Ltd.

1982–1987: Small-company portfolio returns net of all fees.

EAFE Index (1969–1987)
Europe, Australia, and Far East index courtesy of Morgan Stanley Capital International (includes gross dividends).

Japanese Small-Company Stocks (1970–1987)
1970–March 1986: Smaller-half, first section Tokyo Stock Exchange, courtesy of The Nomura Securities Investment Trust Management Company Ltd., Tokyo.

April 1986–1987: Japanese small-company portfolio returns net of all fees.

Japanese Large-Company Stocks (1970–1987)
1970–June 1986: Larger-half, first section Tokyo Stock Exchange, courtesy of The Nomura Securities Investment Trust Management Company Ltd., Tokyo.

July 1986–1987: Morgan Stanley Capital International index.

U.K. Small-Company Stocks (1956–1987)
1956–March 1986: Hoare Govett Smaller-Companies index, courtesy of London School of Business.

April 1986–1987: U.K. small-company portfolio net of all fees.

U.K. Large-Company Stocks—FT-A All Shares Index (1956–1987)
Financial Times All Shares index, courtesy of Rolf Banz, Dimensional Asset Management Ltd.

Intermediate-Term Government Bonds (1952–1987)
July 1952–December 1987: *Stocks, Bonds, Bills, and Inflation Yearbook* (Chicago: Ibbotson Associates, 1988).

ENDNOTES

1. R. Banz, ''The Relationship between Return and Market Value of Common Stocks,'' *Journal of Financial Economics* 9, 1981, pp. 3–18.
2. R. G. Ibbotson, and Rex A. Sinquefield, *Stocks, Bonds, Bills, and Inflation: Historical Returns (1926–1987)* (Homewood, Ill.: Dow Jones-Irwin, 1989); and The Research Foundation of the Institute of Chartered Financial Analysts, Charlottesville, Virginia. Updates courtesy of Ibbotson Associates, *SBBI Yearbook,* Chicago.
3. R. C. Merton, ''On Estimating the Expected Return on the Market,'' *Journal of Financial Economics* 8, 1980, pp. 323–61.

CHAPTER 17

INTERNATIONAL INVESTING: THE CASE FOR THE EMERGING MARKETS

Andrew Rudd

INTRODUCTION

Portfolio managers working for private wealthy individuals and institutional investors—such as pension funds, insurance companies, and mutual funds in the developed countries—control an enormous pool of assets. This pool is currently estimated to total approximately $7.5 trillion in assets at institutions in Europe, the United States, and Japan.[1] The size of the pool is anticipated to grow substantially so that by the end of the century, total institutional assets are anticipated to comfortably exceed $20 trillion.

The allocation of these assets to both asset categories and countries is the major strategic investment decision faced by portfolio managers. Typically, the decision is made sequentially. In broad terms, the hierarchy of subdecisions can be outlined as follows: First, an asset allocation problem is solved. The solution to this problem is a proportional allocation of the fund to the major asset categories. These asset categories will certainly cover cash and equivalents, bonds, and equities but may also include real estate, venture capital, precious metals, and oil and gas investments. The next step is to make a finer allocation within each asset category to either regions or individual country markets (or, in certain cases—such as low-capitalization stocks or mortgage-backed securities—to significant sectors within country markets). The final allocation decision is to actually select the individual assets from within each sector, country, or region.

Another sequence of decisions relating to the implementation of the portfolio may parallel the allocation problem. These decisions would consider the style of management, such as whether, for example, active or passive management would be employed or whether external specialist investment managers should be hired. Because the two decision sequences are related, a solution to one problem may impact the specification of the other problem. For example, regulatory issues or the lack of an identifiable specialist portfolio manager may prevent certain sectors or assets from being exploited; these would, therefore, be removed from the allocation decision.

Unfortunately, this asset allocation decision process may be suboptimal, since by its very structure the sequential nature of decision making may rule out an alternative at one level that should be considered at another later level.[2] In addition, some forms of management (such as tactical asset allocation and other dynamic strategies) may not conveniently fit into this structure at all.

A criticism more relevant to this chapter is that the sequential decision-making structure is innately conservative and potentially forces overdiversification on the fund. As a result, allocations to relatively risky assets or asset classes may be rejected on the basis of a limited set of opportunities at one level of the decision hierarchy—even though, when analyzed in the context of the aggregate fund, the correlation structure of some of these risky classes may lead to beneficial risk-reward trade-offs. It is likely that investment in the emerging markets is one of the victims of this conservative asset allocation framework.

For example, in the United States an allocation of 55 percent to equities, 35 percent to fixed income, and 10 percent to cash would be a reasonable allocation for a large corporate pension plan. The 55 percent commitment to equities may be split 65 percent to 35 percent in terms of domestic versus foreign exposure. If 0.5 percent of the total plan were allocated to emerging markets, then it seems unlikely that the overall risk of the plan would increase significantly, although the contribution to total returns may be meaningful. However, the 0.5 percent of the total plan translates into an almost 1 percent holding in the equity portfolio or almost 3 percent of the international portfolio. The managers of these subportfolios may be overwhelmed by the potential increase in risk arising from this size of commitment and be unwilling, as a result of their specialized perspective, to allocate as much to emerging markets.

A recent estimate suggests that approximately $8 billion may be invested in specialized funds concentrating in the emerging markets, which, when incremented by the amount of investment taking place outside of these funds, would lead to a total value of about $15 billion of nonresident assets in these markets.[3] This amounts to an allocation of only 0.2 percent of the overall $7.5 trillion institutional investment portfolio.

To justify an increased allocation, several related issues should be examined. These include the size of the markets and their relationship with the developed markets in the rest of the world. Are emerging markets a separate asset class? How similar are they to the developed markets of equities and bonds? This chapter concentrates on these statistical issues. In addition, there are, of course, many practical details relating to the restrictions on capital movements, taxation, and so on. These latter topics are not treated here since many excellent sources of this information are available.[4]

MARKET CAPITALIZATION

Relatively few studies have been made of global investment opportunities.[5] In general, these have been single projects to isolate the relative proportions of the different asset categories as of a particular time. For the purposes of the ongoing monitoring of the emerging markets, these studies are not particularly useful.

A more useful benchmark that has been updated annually is the multiple markets index (MMI) originally developed at First Chicago Investment Advisors and continued at Brinson Partners.[6] Their aim was to develop a measure of the investable capital markets, consisting of "primary wealth-generating assets where sufficient markets have developed and legal hurdles do not prohibit meaningful investment by tax-exempt investors."[7]

Table 17–1 shows the size of the investable capital market as represented by the MMI as of the end of 1989. As can be seen, the equity proportion comprises 42.8 percent of the total, or $10.1 trillion. The non-U.S. equity component is based on the Morgan Stanley Capital International (MSCI) universe.

The developed global equity markets are usually represented by the Financial Times-Actuaries (FT-A) world index or the Morgan Stanley Capital International world index. The universes underlying these indices

TABLE 17–1
The Investable Capital Markets

	(Percentage)
U.S. equity	13.7%
Non-U.S. equity	29.1
Dollar bonds	22.0
Nondollar bonds	21.6
Real estate	6.9
Cash equivalents	6.6
Venture capital	0.1
Total: $23.7 trillion	
As of December 31, 1989 (preliminary)	

Source: Brinson Partners.

comprise in excess of 2,000 large companies domiciled in some 20 or so major markets around the world. The market value of the 2,393 companies included in the Financial Times-Actuaries world index as of the end of December 1989 was $7.6 trillion.

One of the difficulties in determining the value of any particular market is deciding exactly what constitutes "the market." As we shall see, this definitional problem will be servere when we consider the emerging markets. However, the problem is still evident in the developed markets. For example, Table 17–2 shows the size of the Japanese equity market as of the end of February 1990. The values recorded by MSCI and FT-A are given, together with the information available on BARRA's Japanese database of listed equities. The values differ dramatically, and even the larger figure fails to capture the true size of the entire Japanese market since it omits at least the Japanese OTC companies. Nevertheless, it is almost twice the estimate provided by the narrower definition used by MSCI.

The aim of the two major indices is to capture a significant proportion of each country's market. From the definition of the indices, somewhat confirmed by the data in Table 17–2, it would appear that they capture some 70 percent of the total market in each country. Applying this ratio uniformly would indicate that the size of the investable equity markets as represented by the MMI should be closer to $14.4 trillion.

Let us now turn to the emerging markets. The first definitional ambiguity concerns exactly what an emerging market is. There is no generally

TABLE 17–2
The Japanese Equity Market, February 28, 1990

	MSCI	FT–A	BARRA
Number of assets	265	455	1,980
Value	$2.0 trillion	$2.67 trillion	$3.8 trillion

Source: BARRA.

accepted definition. However, the traditional list of markets is usually accepted to be those compiled by the International Finance Corporation (IFC) and belonging to the IFC composite index.[8] Table 17–3 shows the list of markets broken down into four groupings: Latin America, East Asia, South Asia, and Europe/Mideast/Africa.

TABLE 17–3
Emerging Stock Markets

Latin America
  Argentina
  Brazil
  Chile
  Colombia
  Mexico
  Venezuela
East Asia
  Korea
  Philippines
  Taiwan
South Asia
  India
  Malaysia
  Pakistan
  Thailand
Europe/Mideast/Africa
  Greece
  Jordan
  Nigeria
  Portugal
  Turkey
  Zimbabwe

Source: IFC.

TABLE 17–4
Potential Emerging Markets

Latin America/Caribbean
  Costa Rica
  Jamaica
  Peru
  Trinidad and Tobago
  Uruguay

East Asia
  People's Republic of China
  Vietnam

South Asia
  Bangladesh
  Indonesia
  Papua New Guinea
  Sri Lanka

Europe/Mideast/Africa

Bahrain	Ivory Coast	Morocco
Cyprus	Kenya	Tunisia
Egypt	Kuwait	United Arab Emirates
Hungary	Malta	Yugoslavia

This listing of emerging markets is by no means complete or unambiguous. For example, it is interesting to note that two of the IFC markets, Mexico and Malaysia, are included in the accepted global indices for the developed markets. Table 17–4 shows additional countries that have stock markets and could legitimately be classed within the emerging market category. Indeed, assets in many of these markets are now held within available country funds or comprise part of certain institutional portfolios.

A potentially more rewarding definition of an emerging market—at least for investment rather than developmental economics purposes—may be one essentially outside of those covered by the accepted global indices and on which reliable data can be located and updated reasonably accurately and frequently. For this reason, the IFC compilation carries considerable weight since they maintain a database of the larger assets within these countries, usually listed on the principal exchanges.[9] Table 17–5 shows the total market size and number of listed companies within the countries covered by the IFC.

It is immediately apparent that the larger of these markets are in East Asia—Taiwan and Korea being the two most prominent. Currently, direct

TABLE 17–5
Emerging Stock Markets, December 1989

Market	Capitalization (U.S.$ billion)	Number of Listed Companies
Latin America		
Argentina	$ 4.2	178
Brazil*	44.4	592
Chile	9.6	213
Colombia	1.1	82
Mexico	22.6	203
Venezuela	1.2	60
Subtotal	83.1	1,328
East Asia		
Korea	140.9	626
Philippines	12.0	144
Taiwan, China	237.0	181
Subtotal	389.9	951
South Asia		
India†	27.3	6,000
Malaysia	39.8	251
Pakistan	2.5	440
Thailand	25.6	175
Subtotal	95.2	6,866
Europe/Mideast/Africa		
Greece	6.4	119
Jordan	2.2	106
Nigeria	1.0	111
Portugal	10.6	182
Turkey	6.8	50
Zimbabwe	1.1	54
Subtotal	28.1	622
World	$ 596.3	9,767

* Sao Paulo.
† Bombay only.

Source: IFC.

foreign investment in these two markets is difficult and usually only available through country funds. For example, four country funds are readily available in Taiwan. Two (the Formosa fund and Taipei fund) are listed in London, while the other two (the Taiwan fund and the R.O.C. Taiwan fund) are listed on the New York Stock Exchange. The total market capitalization of these funds as of the end of 1989 was about $1.1 billion. In several of the other markets, most notably India and Brazil, either investment is possible only through country funds or access is severely restricted.

The largest market in terms of assets is the Indian market. Approximately 6,000 companies are listed on the Bombay Stock Exchange.[10] However, traditionally only about 400 or so are accepted as potential investment opportunities for institutional investors.

The total number of companies listed among the emerging markets is almost 10,000; however, when one accepts the reduction in size of the Indian market, a better estimate may be of the order of 7,000 companies.[11]

The total value of the emerging market universe is approximately $600 billion, a little less that 10 percent of the developed market capitalization as represented by the accepted global indices. Over 60 percent of the world emerging market capitalization is accounted for by the East Asian markets, principally Korea and Taiwan.

COVARIANCE STRUCTURE OF THE EMERGING MARKETS

The principal determinants of the value of adding a new asset class within an existing portfolio are (1) the covariance structure between the new asset class and the existing asset classes and (2) the covariance structure within the new class. In short, how distinct is the new class relative to the other classes, and how homogeneous is it? In general, a new asset class that is quite unlike the existing investment opportunities while being heterogeneous is potentially most valuable. Our concerns here are the characteristics of the emerging equity markets as a new asset class and the comparison of the characteristics with those of the developed equity markets.

When dealing with international investment, treatment of the currency gives rise to some major conceptual and analytical issues. This is certainly the case with regard to the developed markets; in the emerging markets, this becomes more acute, particularly when currencies are traded at different rates for different purposes and are far from freely convertible.

Fortunately, it is possible to separate the currency decision from the local-market investment decisions.[12] By separating the currency component, one can isolate difficulties that are specifically related to the foreign exchange market from those relating to within-market asset selection. For our purposes here, it also enables us to make a more measured comparison between the developed markets and the emerging markets. Our approach, therefore, is to look initially at the covariance structure of the emerging markets in local currency terms and, separately, the characteristics of the currencies.

Table 17–6 shows the correlations between the emerging markets in local currency terms with, on the diagonal, annualized standard deviations of the returns. This data is generated from the indices constructed by the IFC.

The results are startling. First, examine the annual standard deviations. In some countries, particularly Turkey and Argentina, the risk is enormous. Other countries, notably Pakistan and Colombia, show much less risk. Indeed, these latter two markets show risk levels equal to or below those of the developed markets (see Table 17–8). Presumably, much of this apparent lack of variability is the result of the trading practices in these local markets, particularly the lack of continuous trading.

The correlation structure shows some large negative values (for example, -0.46 between Korea and Pakistan, and -0.57 between Zimbabwe and Venezuela). These large negative correlations would suggest that extremely low-risk portfolios could be constructed by mixing these country markets into an aggregate portfolio. In many of these cases, there is no strong economic reason why these large negative correlations should exist. Indeed, likely many of these results are the outcome of applying straightforward statistical methodology on data series that are noisy. Presumably, if more sophisticated methodology is applied to estimate the correlation structure between these markets, many of the large negative correlations would become more reasonable.[13]

The same situation probably occurs for some of the positive correlations. However, it is notable that within the Latin American markets, Brazil, Chile, and Mexico do appear quite highly related, while Colombia, Venezuela, and Argentina appear to have quite different characteristics.

Table 17–7 provides some information on the remaining component of emerging market investment, namely, the impact of the currency decision. Again, the off-diagonal elements show the correlations between the various currency returns, while the diagonal elements represent the annualized standard deviation of currency returns from a U.S. perspective.

TABLE 17-6
Correlation of Emerging Market Returns

	ARG	BRA	CHI	COL	GRE	IND	JOR	KOR	MAL	MEX	NIG	PAK	PHI	POR	TAI	THA	TUR	VEN	ZIM
ARG	264.45	-0.21	-0.02	-0.07	0.16	0.23	-0.09	-0.13	0.15	0.27	-0.05	0.13	-0.11	-0.04	-0.01	0.08	-0.05	0.06	-0.31
BRA		112.18	0.58	0.00	0.20	0.03	0.26	-0.16	0.51	0.33	0.54	-0.04	0.04	0.20	0.31	0.27	0.54	-0.06	-0.12
CHI			75.09	0.46	0.26	-0.27	0.62	-0.22	0.58	0.49	0.25	0.21	0.05	0.05	-0.03	0.14	0.26	-0.22	0.77
COL				19.35	0.38	-0.30	0.15	-0.01	-0.12	-0.03	0.04	0.21	-0.09	0.24	0.30	0.00	0.14	0.14	0.36
GRE					69.70	-0.23	0.45	-0.25	0.04	0.42	0.68	0.07	-0.07	0.03	0.38	0.51	0.22	0.22	-0.26
IND						32.34	-0.19	0.31	0.24	0.27	0.09	0.43	-0.21	-0.24	-0.27	-0.11	0.50	0.24	-0.40
JOR							37.04	-0.08	0.00	-0.01	0.54	-0.46	0.11	-0.33	-0.02	0.13	0.48	-0.16	0.47
KOR								76.29	0.07	0.49	0.24	0.50	-0.21	0.05	0.02	-0.15	0.55	0.33	-0.26
MAL									28.28	0.47	0.11	0.21	0.18	0.17	0.20	0.19	0.21	-0.24	-0.31
MEX										80.80	0.24	0.22	-0.27	0.28	0.41	0.49	0.14	0.07	-0.42
NIG											43.32	-0.08	-0.34	-0.37	0.03	0.39	0.86	0.35	-0.40
PAK												9.77	-0.50	0.10	0.13	0.10	0.20	0.11	-0.34
PHI													28.53	0.22	-0.18	-0.22	-0.42	-0.25	0.20
POR														82.21	0.49	0.17	-0.13	0.21	-0.03
TAI															65.70	0.47	0.12	-0.32	-0.26
THA																65.26	0.14	0.10	-0.23
TUR																	309.61	0.09	0.03
VEN																		37.45	-0.57
ZIM																			26.42

Note: Diagonal elements represent annualized standard deviation of returns.

Source: BARRA, March 1990.

TABLE 17–7
Correlation of Emerging Market Currency Returns

	ARG	BRA	CHI	COL	GRE	IND	JOR	KOR	MAL	MEX	NIG	PAK	PHI	POR	TAI	THA	TUR	VEN	ZIM
ARG	61.84																		
BRA	-0.10	33.66																	
CHI	0.41	0.09	7.79																
COL	-0.40	0.04	-0.18	4.24															
GRE	-0.07	-0.18	-0.30	0.33	10.92														
IND	0.07	-0.15	-0.22	0.18	0.62	4.05													
JOR	-0.02	0.05	-0.17	-0.09	-0.07	0.31	11.32												
KOR	0.20	0.36	0.02	0.02	0.12	-0.03	-0.06	3.30											
MAL	-0.37	0.07	-0.08	0.24	0.65	0.33	-0.01	-0.03	3.27										
MEX	-0.08	-0.17	0.09	-0.07	-0.28	-0.30	-0.14	-0.04	-0.29	20.40									
NIG	-0.19	0.11	-0.34	0.03	0.28	-0.01	0.18	-0.09	0.12	0.00	17.51								
PAK	0.26	-0.28	-0.35	-0.15	0.48	0.56	0.33	0.06	-0.01	-0.21	0.34	3.74							
PHI	0.39	0.01	0.35	-0.21	-0.25	-0.14	0.12	0.06	-0.18	0.16	-0.12	0.08	2.71						
POR	0.00	-0.22	-0.27	0.20	0.96	0.61	-0.12	0.09	0.63	-0.27	0.21	0.51	-0.21	11.44					
TAI	-0.16	0.32	0.05	0.04	-0.02	-0.09	0.12	0.28	-0.06	-0.16	-0.43	0.20	-0.02		4.20				
THA	0.28	-0.14	-0.22	0.01	0.76	0.41	-0.12	0.25	0.38	-0.22	0.24	0.60	0.04	0.85	-0.04	2.30			
TUR	-0.30	-0.38	-0.18	0.16	0.31	0.18	-0.20	-0.47	0.45	-0.15	-0.03	-0.11	-0.47	0.37	0.11	0.09	6.46		
VEN	-0.07	0.14	-0.17	-0.09	0.33	0.49	0.07	0.14	0.39	-0.68	-0.04	0.26	-0.21	0.39	0.31	0.31	0.24	17.22	
ZIM	-0.19	0.12	-0.33	0.44	0.82	0.46	-0.06	0.27	0.53	-0.14	0.15	0.24	-0.33	0.73	0.02	0.55	0.10	0.18	6.06

Note: Diagonal elements represent annualized standard deviation of returns.

Source: BARRA, March 1990.

The risk of the various currencies can be quite substantial, notably for Argentina and Brazil. Other countries show remarkably low volatility, arising mostly as a result of pegging (or partial pegging) relative to the U.S. dollar. We again notice what appear to be anomalous results with regard to the correlation matrix. (Why should Greece and India have very high positive correlations on their exchange rates?) We also observe some substantial negative correlations.

The overriding impression is of a quite disparate group of relationships with heterogeneous risk levels. How similar are these markets and currencies to the developed markets and currencies? To answer this question, a similar analysis was performed on the MSCI indexes.

Tables 17–8 and 17–9 show similar parameters for the MSCI countries and their respective currencies. Again, the equity market returns are in local currency terms and are computed similarly to the methods employed for the emerging markets.

The correlations between the MSCI indices show much less dispersion than the correlations for the emerging market indices. For example, there are few negative correlations, with the smallest being − 0.20. Similar qualitative results seem to apply to the currency structure (Table 17–9) relative to the emerging market currencies.

Another intriguing question is the relationship between the emerging markets and the developed world. To get a better understanding of how these markets were related to the developed world, the correlations between the IFC emerging market return indices and the Financial Times-Actuaries world index were computed. The two sets of indices were based in U.S. dollars. Table 17–10 shows these correlations. In general, these correlations are all quite low, and some are reasonably negative. Intriguingly, there appears to be no regional similarity between these markets. This is similar to what is observed with the individual country correlations earlier. Notice the positive correlations between Korea and the Philippines and the negative one for Taiwan.

Table 17–11 presents similar results but, in contrast to the previous table, lists the correlations between the developed country markets (as represented by the respective country MSCI index) and the IFC index of all the emerging markets, again measured in U.S. dollars. Hence, it shows the potential diversification for investors in the different developed markets when investing in an emerging markets "index fund" of all 19 markets.

TABLE 17–8
Correlation of MSCI Market Returns

	AUS	AUT	BEL	CAN	DEN	FIN	FRA	GER	HKG	ITA	JPN	NET	NOR	NZE	SAG	SIN	SPA	SWE	SWI	UKI	USA
AUS	24.77																				
AUT	0.26	31.11																			
BEL	0.40	0.07	22.16																		
CAN	0.60	0.13	0.51	16.48																	
DEN	0.18	-0.09	0.19	0.21	18.75																
FIN	0.36	0.15	-0.02	-0.02	0.22	16.62															
FRA	0.35	0.28	0.66	0.54	0.25	0.00	24.68														
GER	0.43	0.45	0.58	0.37	0.18	-0.02	0.65	24.78													
HKG	0.59	0.31	0.41	0.49	0.07	0.16	0.35	0.32	30.82												
ITA	0.30	0.23	0.51	0.33	0.20	0.08	0.55	0.48	0.13	24.95											
JPN	0.23	-0.21	0.48	0.34	0.23	0.02	0.44	0.25	0.20	0.40	19.18										
NET	0.56	0.28	0.60	0.72	0.12	0.18	0.53	0.62	0.49	0.42	0.43	18.57									
NOR	0.53	0.36	0.52	0.53	0.12	0.41	0.34	0.51	0.48	0.22	0.26	0.68	27.22								
NZE	0.69	0.23	-0.12	0.22	-0.20	0.13	-0.22	-0.14	0.04	0.32	-0.02	0.23	0.23	29.11							
SAG	0.32	0.07	0.09	0.20	0.13	0.14	0.22	0.09	0.57	0.16	0.28	0.14	0.14	0.31	35.56						
SIN	0.56	0.07	0.45	0.49	0.15	0.39	0.25	0.24	0.30	0.40	0.30	0.50	0.60	0.57	0.31	29.16					
SPA	0.57	0.11	0.55	0.19	0.19	0.33	0.46	0.41	0.38	0.43	0.24	0.30	0.26	0.24	0.21	0.59	26.18				
SWE	0.57	0.24	0.53	0.49	-0.01	0.41	0.43	0.43	0.49	0.24	0.13	0.54	0.67	0.29	0.47	0.45	0.47	22.14			
SWI	0.50	0.40	0.59	0.62	0.30	0.01	0.77	0.45	0.49	0.24	0.18	0.57	0.77	0.24	0.18	0.34	0.42	0.53	20.64		
UKI	0.55	0.18	0.57	0.70	0.11	0.10	0.57	0.45	0.57	0.39	0.35	0.60	0.24	0.35	0.07	0.63	0.34	0.54	0.59	20.85	
USA	0.45	0.12	0.61	0.77	0.23	-0.09	0.60	0.46	0.51	0.37	0.41	0.71	0.55	0.05	0.06	0.60	0.56	0.49	0.65	0.78	17.74

Note: Diagonal elements represent annualized standard deviation of returns.

Source: BARRA, March 1990.

TABLE 17–9
Correlation of MSCI Currency Returns

	AUS	AUT	BEL	CAN	DEN	FIN	FRA	GER	HKG	ITA	JPN	NET	NOR	NZE	SAG	SIN	SPA	SWE	SWI	UKI
AUS	12.58	0.07	0.09	0.26	0.07	0.15	0.08	0.04	0.03	0.00	0.07	0.06	0.17	0.45	0.28	0.09	0.11	0.13	-0.02	0.22
AUT		13.03	0.97	0.03	0.99	0.92	0.98	1.00	0.15	0.80	0.81	0.99	0.90	0.23	0.15	0.57	0.93	0.96	0.95	0.77
BEL			12.77	0.07	0.97	0.90	0.96	0.97	0.15	0.81	0.77	0.98	0.90	0.28	0.15	0.56	0.90	0.95	0.92	0.75
CAN				3.97	0.05	0.06	0.00	0.02	0.06	0.06	0.03	0.05	0.10	0.32	0.06	0.03	0.12	0.08	0.00	0.17
DEN					12.59	0.92	0.98	0.99	0.14	0.81	0.79	0.98	0.91	0.24	0.13	0.59	0.91	0.97	0.94	0.80
FIN						10.48	0.92	0.91	0.11	0.76	0.79	0.90	0.94	0.34	0.20	0.63	0.88	0.95	0.86	0.85
FRA							12.21	0.98	0.13	0.78	0.80	0.97	0.91	0.25	0.16	0.60	0.92	0.96	0.94	0.79
GER								13.09	0.16	0.80	0.80	0.99	0.90	0.20	0.12	0.57	0.93	0.96	0.95	0.76
HKG									0.84	0.18	0.06	0.19	0.06	-0.08	-0.08	0.34	0.11	0.07	0.18	0.02
ITA										19.50	0.61	0.81	0.80	0.18	0.13	0.43	0.76	0.77	0.74	0.56
JPN											13.64	0.79	0.74	0.25	0.07	0.52	0.78	0.84	0.83	0.68
NET												13.13	0.89	0.22	0.12	0.56	0.91	0.95	0.94	0.74
NOR													10.84	0.34	0.25	0.60	0.88	0.93	0.84	0.81
NZE														15.47	0.26	0.10	0.25	0.30	0.20	0.37
SAG															36.24	0.02	0.22	0.14	0.09	0.17
SIN																4.66	0.53	0.60	0.58	0.57
SPA																	11.92	0.92	0.88	0.80
SWE																		9.17	0.93	0.86
SWI																			14.17	0.76
UKI																				13.75

Note: Diagonal elements represent annualized standard deviation of returns.

Source: BARRA, March 1990.

TABLE 17–10
Correlation between IFC Emerging Markets Total Return Indices and the FT-A World Index

(US$)

	Correlation
Latin America	
Argentina	− 0.31
Brazil	0.06
Chile	− 0.23
Colombia	− 0.07
Mexico	0.02
· Venezuela	0.09
Europe/Mideast/Africa	
Greece	0.07
Jordan	0.28
Portugal	0.32
Turkey	− 0.11
Nigeria	− 0.32
Zimbabwe	0.21
East Asia	
Korea	0.28
Philippines	0.33
Taiwan	− 0.32
South Asia	
India	− 0.08
Malaysia	0.37
Pakistan	− 0.02
Thailand	0.19

The pattern of correlations is much as one would expect from the results to date. The emerging markets as a group are, in general, correlated lowly with each of the developed markets. The highest correlations are with Sweden, Norway, Japan, the Netherlands, and Belgium. But even these correlations are not exceptional relative to the correlations among the developed markets.

More interesting are the correlations between the emerging markets and the developed bond markets. Table 17–12 shows the correlations with the Salomon Brothers world government bond indices. They are all very negative, suggesting that the emerging markets substantially hedge the movements in each of the local bond markets. A similar result holds for

TABLE 17–11
**Correlation between IFC Emerging Markets Index and
the Morgan Stanley Capital International Country
Indices**

(U.S.$)

Country	Correlation
Australia	−0.11
Austria	0.20
Belgium	0.20
Canada	−0.30
Denmark	−0.16
France	0.09
Germany	0.13
Hong Kong	0.00
Italy	−0.09
Japan	0.21
Netherlands	0.20
Norway	0.26
Singapore	0.13
Spain	0.02
Sweden	0.35
Switzerland	0.04
United Kingdom	0.07
United States	0.10

gold and silver; the correlations, again in U.S. dollars, are -0.49 and -0.42, respectively. The correlation with platinum is low, at 0.17, but not as low as with the other two precious metals.

WITHIN–MARKET AND ACROSS–MARKET ANALYSES

Another set of important issues relates to the structure of the individual markets in terms of their heterogeneity. In particular, the potential diversification value of a particular market depends on how related the price movements of stocks are within the given economy. If the stocks show considerable commonality, then the market factor is likely to be very prominent and the nondiversifiable proportion of risk is likely to be large.

TABLE 17–12
Correlation between IFC Emerging Markets Index and
the Salomon Brothers World Government Bond Index

(U.S.$) Country	Correlation
Australia	−0.33
Germany	−0.38
Japan	−0.36
Netherlands	−0.40
Switzerland	−0.54
United Kingdom	−0.19
United States	−0.18

For example, in the United States approximately 30 percent of a typical stock's return variance will be systematic and nondiversifiable.

Very little econometric work has been done in this area, so the results must be viewed as tentative.[14] Nevertheless, Table 17–13 shows the average R-square for each of the 19 emerging markets relative to an equal-weighted index. A high R-square indicates the market factor is important in explaining the returns of individual stocks, while a low R-square suggests the market is quite heterogeneous and has comparatively little influence in explaining individual asset return. As a comparison, the average R-square for the United States on a comparable basis would be about 0.31.

Interestingly, in most countries the market is very influential. Over half the countries achieve an R-square of 30 percent or greater, and in only two (Jordan and Pakistan) is the R-square less than 20 percent. These results suggest that risk prediction and modern analytical methods are as applicable in these markets as in the developed markets.

From the earlier analyses, it appears that many of the markets are quite highly correlated at the country level. Does this fact have any influence on the relationship between the individual stocks across countries? In other words, will the country factors continue to be prominent in a multicurrency framework? And, how important are the industry groups in explaining the return variance?

To test this hypothesis, we examined the four major emerging markets in the Far East (Korea, Taiwan, Thailand, and Malaysia), where we believe the data is scrutinized carefully and of high quality. In the test, we

TABLE 17–13
Average R-Square Relative to Equal-Weighted Country Index

Country	R-Square
Argentina	0.44
Brazil	0.41
Chile	0.33
Colombia	0.22
Greece	0.24
India	0.28
Jordan	0.16
Korea	0.33
Malaysia	0.35
Mexico	0.34
Nigeria	0.23
Pakistan	0.12
Philippines	0.28
Portugal	0.38
Taiwan	0.47
Thailand	0.32
Turkey	0.47
Venezuela	0.26
Zimbabwe	0.21

used the IFC economic sector assignments, which allocate companies entirely to one of nine sectors.

We observed an average adjusted R-square of 0.45 for the country factors alone, which improved to 0.47 for the country and sector model. These are high R-squares and give some confidence to the notion that these markets can be modeled as the developed markets. However, research in this area is in its infancy, and definitive results will have to wait on more detailed experiments.

MANAGEMENT STYLE IN THE EMERGING MARKETS

Currently, foreign investment in the emerging markets has been undertaken by active managers, working on either a regional basis or an individual country basis. In almost every case, the preferred approach has been to invest actively.

The obvious rationale for active management rests on the observation that these markets are informationally inefficient. Hence, with superior knowledge or research, it should not be difficult to beat the indices of the individual markets. Since the number of portfolios investing in these markets is relatively small, it appears still to be an open question as to exactly how informationally inefficient these markets are and, vice versa, whether foreign portfolio managers, even acting with the advice of local partners, can outperform local benchmarks.

An alternative approach that has not gained much favor to date is of passive investing in these markets.[15] Initially, the lack of informational efficiency is an apparent disadvantage that could not be overcome by the other advantages of passive investment. In particular, many of these markets are high-transaction-cost markets, where commissions, taxes, and other impediments can often be quite substantial. In these cases, the lower turnover of passive investing would appear to be an advantage.

In addition, passive investing would appear to not only pick the losers but also share in the winners. Only if insiders and superior research can continually outperform the index—or, in other words, cause a wealth transfer from the underperforming assets and investors holding them to the remaining assets—would passive investment fail. It may well be the case that for many investors domiciled in foreign countries, the hiring of an active manager who does exercise sufficient skill to outperform the indices would be hard to monitor and control. From this point of view, the averaging process implicit in passive investment may be beneficial because it occurs at lower risk than active management.

As indicated above, however, the actual benefit of passive versus active benefit, or vice versa, is an empirical matter. To the extent that individual stock selection is so beneficial, then it should be obvious in reported performance figures.

SUMMARY

Some of the least-explored areas by institutional investors around the world are the emerging stock markets. Although individual investors have been able to invest in these markets through closed-ended country funds and open-ended mutual funds or unit trusts, institutional investors have not invested much time or money in these markets. Indeed, current estimates are that less than one quarter of 1 percent of institutional funds are invested in the emerging markets.

These markets are admittedly small by global standards. Although there are a large number of assets, the total value is of the order of 10 percent of the developed markets. Moreover, the cost of exploiting these assets is bound to be large, in terms of both high transactions costs and high search and management fees.

Nevertheless, the emerging markets do appear to display characteristics quite unlike those of the developed markets. In general, the diversification opportunities afforded by the emerging markets appear large. The application of simple statistical methodologies—which are, unfortunately, prone to noise in the data—show substantial numbers of small positive and negative correlations, implying substantial diversification opportunities. Mitigating these diversification opportunities is the inherent risk of these markets. In general, they are several times riskier than the developed markets, even allowing for currency returns, which are often pegged relative to the dollar.

Although the empirical analyses of these markets are extremely limited, the market factor appears to be equally or more prominent as in the developed markets. Moreover, industry membership has similar value for risk prediction as observed elsewhere. In short, empirical research to date, together with market sentiment, indicates that these markets have significant appeal to institutional investors.

ENDNOTES

1. "Foreign Portfolio Investment in Emerging Equity Markets," Study Group Series No. 5 (Helsinki: World Institute for Development Economics Research of the United Nations University, March 1989).
2. Aspects of this problem are covered in Andrew Rudd, "Investment Techniques for the Future," presentation to the National Association of Pension Funds, 1987 Investment Conference, Eastbourne, United Kingdom, February 6, 1987.
3. See "Foreign Portfolio Investment in Emerging Equity Markets."
4. See particularly, *Emerging Stock Markets Factbook, 1990* (Washington, D.C.: International Finance Corporation, April 1990).
5. One particularly relevant source is R. Ibbotson and L. Siegel, "The World Market Wealth Portfolio," *Journal of Portfolio Management,* Winter 1983, pp. 5–17.

6. The rationale for the index is described in G. Brinson, J. Diermeier, and G. Schlarbaum, "A Composite Portfolio Benchmark for Pension Plans," *Financial Analysts Journal*, March/April 1986, pp. 15–24.

7. Ibid., p. 17.

8. The index is supported by the Capital Markets Department of the International Financial Corporation, 1818 H Street, N.W., Washington, D.C. 20433.

9. To make matters more confusing, many emerging markets have important exchanges in several cities that list companies other than those listed on what is usually regarded as the principal exchange. This applies to Brazil, India, and Portugal, among other countries.

10. In addition, there are around another 5,000 companies listed on the Calcutta, Delhi, and Madras exchanges.

11. The emerging markets in countries shown in Table 17–4 may have in total approximately 2,000 companies listed on their exchanges.

12. See R. Grinold, A. Rudd, and D. Stefek, "Global Factors: Fact or Fiction?" *Journal of Portfolio Management*, Fall 1989, pp. 79–88, for a further description of separating the two components.

13. Ibid.

14. One useful reference is Vihang Errunza and Prasad Padmanabhan, "Further Evidence on Benefits of Portfolio Investments in Emerging Markets," *Financial Analysts Journal*, July/August 1988, pp. 76–78.

15. Index funds, attracting primarily individual investors, are available for the Pacific Rim markets.

CHAPTER 18

THE UNIVERSAL VALUATION MODEL: A BLUEPRINT FOR GLOBAL INVESTMENT STRATEGY

Dean LeBaron
Lawrence S. Speidell

As we accelerate toward the 21st century, the investor's paradox is that his world is both growing and shrinking. The twin forces of capital and technology are reshaping traditional investment thinking. At last capitalism seems to have hit full stride as socialist and communist regimes have stumbled in the economic race. This has unleashed equity bull markets in emerging countries around the globe, and it has spawned exciting new equity markets in emerging countries hoping to become the ''next'' Japan, the ''next'' Korea, or the ''next'' Taiwan. The result has been a tremendous increase in the size of the investor's world of capital and capital flows. Meanwhile, the progress of technology has speeded communication, shrunk distances, and leapt country boundaries, making possible simultaneous news delivery and investment transactions anywhere around the world. In the future, it will not make any difference where you are or where you trade. With a telephone line or line-of-sight to a satellite, you can link to any global market. At Batterymarch, our trading computer runs 22.5 hours a day and has even been linked for trading from a mountain top in Switzerland.

The Investors Map of the World (Figure 18–1) shows a geography far different than the world atlas. Many countries loom larger than the area of

FIGURE 18–1 1988 Market Capitalization, Developed and Emerging Markets

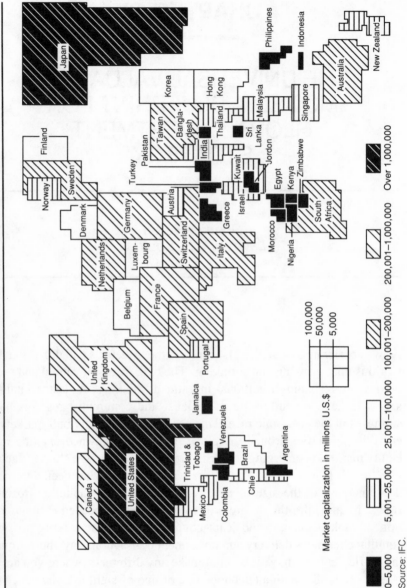

Source: IFC.

their land mass, with Japan now the largest of all. Meanwhile, small countries like Luxembourg and Taiwan have taken on significant stature in the investor's world due to the success of their financial markets. Today this map omits the communist world, but soon that may change given recent developments.

As the investor's world is being changed by capital and technology, investor's thinking is changing as well. Local techniques and styles are giving way to global analysis, and we are on the brink of a universal valuation model that will unify financial analysis and integrate capital flows around the world. This will draw on three distinct styles of investing presently practiced, and the ultimate model will be shaped by the forces of regulation, disclosure, and the world's view of the role of the corporation.

THE THREE STYLES OF INVESTING

The U.S. market has long been the leader in investment analysis and technology. Although this may change as the Japanese market surpasses ours in size, we have nonetheless set a pattern followed by the rest of the world.

The past 20 years have seen three specific periods during which the U.S. market has been dominated by one of the three major classes of investors: individuals, institutions, and corporations. Each period has had its own character and has set the stage for the regime to follow. The stages are summarized in Figure 18–2.

Phase I: Individual Investing

The first phase, from 1945 to 1965, saw markets dominated by individual investors. There were substantial pent-up savings and an inadequate supply of goods. Savings went into financial instruments, and individual investors dominated the character of equity markets. Good news and name recognition were highly prized; the pricing of securities was immaterial.

We witnessed a huge bull market (curiously, against the forecast of an inevitable postwar depression) characterized by brand loyalty, seeming disregard for financial ratios, and attraction to measures of forecast growth.

Valuation was less important than expectations. Not until the mid-1960s did *The Wall Street Journal* start publishing price/earnings ratios.

FIGURE 18–2
Stages of U.S. Equity Market

Phase I: 1945–1965
  Investor: Individual
  Valuation: Stock supply and demand
  Technology: Telephone
  Information source: Newspaper

Phase II: 1965–1985
  Investor: Institutional
  Valuation: Quantitative
  Technology: Mainframe computer
  Information source: Econometric database

Phase III: 1985–Present
  Investor: Corporate
  Valuation: Asset-based
  Technology: Data communications
  Information source: Real-time market feeds

On the same page, one could find valuations of 70 times earnings and 2 times earnings for companies growing at the same rate. Stock in America's premier companies was highly prized and in short supply. The market was based on loyalty to individual companies, much as in today's Japanese market.

The age of individual investing in the United States began with "Blue Chips" and ended with "GoGo Stocks"; since then, individuals have cut their holdings of common stocks in half. However, a new buyer emerged to set the tone of the U.S. market in the 1970s and early 80s.

Phase II: Institutional Investing

The institutional investor began with trust and mutual funds serving the individual, but institutional growth exploded due to massive funding of pension plans in the 1970s. Initially, institutions practiced the same style as individuals, leading to a speculative bubble in growth stocks in 1973. That, however, set the stage for the most dramatic influence on investing since Graham and Dodd's famous text, *Security Analysis*, in 1934: the computer. Initially with cumbersome mainframe computers, but then with handheld calculators and personal computers, institutions explored financial data to uncover pockets of undervaluation. The reach of databases into corners of the market provided a uniform yardstick for financial comparisons, which showed many areas of opportunity. The first number-crunching led to simple techniques: the small-stock effect, the low–price/earnings effect, and so on. These gave way to more complex calculations using developments by the academic community that were adopted on Wall Street in the form of dividend discount models, option pricing strategies, and the like.

One could, in effect, put the institutional investor on a silicon substrate and build that person into a computer. America's best institutional investors could operate tirelessly day after day for a very, very small price.

Markets became speculative in the sense that they were only price conscious; the names of companies became immaterial. After all, at some institutions all transactions are done by machine; and machines do not bother with names—they merely do the arithmetic.

As some of the earlier inefficiencies in pricing have been arbitraged away, institutions have begun chasing smaller and smaller profit opportunities with larger and larger volumes over shorter and shorter time periods. Yet suddenly, after years of empirical research demonstrating high efficiency in market-pricing mechanisms, we have had the spectacle of large liquid stocks, supposedly efficiently priced, disappearing in merger transactions at 40 percent premiums or more. Initially, these events were dismissed as actions of the lunatic fringe, the raiders; but today, bankers, investment bankers, and corporations are joining in the decisive third phase of the equity market.

Phase III: Global Corporate Valuation

While institutions are often concerned with short-term changes like the direction of earnings per share in the next quarter, corporations tend to focus on long-term "business" values. Using techniques that pay more attention to the balance sheet than the income statement, they look for restructuring opportunities where the replacement cost or "break-up" value exceeds the current stock price. From this perspective, equity prices have seemed low for some time (Federal Reserve statistics show the market value of nonfinancial corporations 25 percent below replacement cost today, compared with a 13 percent premium in 1967). The result has been an increase in corporate activity in the stock market, shown by Figure 18–3. During the 1970s, institutional net purchase of common stocks

FIGURE 18–3
Demand for U.S. Stock from Corporations and Institutions

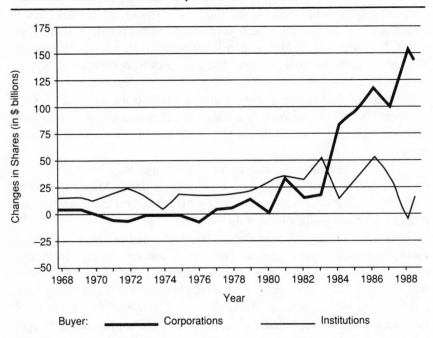

Source: Batterymarch Financial Management.

was high, but it was exceeded in 1983 by corporate demand. Since then, corporate purchases for share buybacks, recapitalizations, and acquisitions have gone on to a new high, while institutional demand has shrunk further. A dramatic divergence occurred following the October 1987 market decline: institutions reacted to high market volatility by increasing their estimate of risk and reducing their holdings. Meanwhile, corporations reacted to the low prices with buybacks. Over 100 companies announced stock repurchase programs before the week of the crash was over, over 400 by the end of the month. And in the subsequent months, a new wave of mergers and restructuring was announced. In 1988, U.S. merger activity reached a new high of $248 billion, up from $164 billion in 1987 and 38 percent above the previous high in 1985.

While the pattern of investment styles in the U.S. market has been evolutionary and sequential, it has been revolutionary and even chaotic in many other markets around the globe. We see all the elements of the three

FIGURE 18–4
Evolution of Global Investing

Era	Philosophy
I. Traditional	Growth orientation
II. Global institutional	Value investing
(1980–Present)	Contrary investing
	Indexing
	Asset allocation
III. Global corporate	Business value:
(1986–Present)	Restructuring
	Acquisition
	Joint venture

Source: Batterymarch Financial Management.

phases of the U.S. market in every market—only the dates differ. Traditional investing with its growth orientation remains popular, particularly in Japan. At the same time, however, new databases are making institutional quantitative investing possible, and this is breeding new styles, such as contrary investing, value investing, indexing, and tactical asset allocation. Meanwhile, corporations are becoming increasingly active. Merger activity has exploded in Europe as companies prepare for open borders in the Common Market in 1992. Even in Japan, Boone Pickens has made headlines, and merger activity seems to be on the rise. The worldwide mosaic of investment styles is summarized by Figure 18–4, with bold type indicating the techniques that may prove most enduring.

IS THE WORLD BECOMING MORE GLOBAL?

The common thread in the development of investment styles around the world is globalization. Victor Hugo said, "Greater than the tread of mighty armies is an idea whose time has come." Indeed, today there are no border guards who can stop the technology of global information. October 19, 1987, signaled the end of one era and the beginning of the next. Some believe the global market decline, first felt in New York in October 1987, may have been precipitated by an interest rate rise in Frankfurt, moderated by financial discipline in Tokyo, and then spread to such remote markets as Sao Paulo. Clearly, all the world's markets are linked to share a common reward or penalty. What happens in Tokyo clues the London market, which is eagerly watched by American investors on morning television as an aid to pricing the New York opening.

Security prices are clearly too important to be set by mindless trading algorithms in institutional computers. Consideration of the underlying values is increasingly done by corporations themselves, with the power to take swift response. In the past, a company that thought its stock too cheap would hold a luncheon for institutional investors and say, in effect, "Please buy my stock." Today, the balance of power has shifted. The lunches are still held out of habit; but now, the market is established by corporate investors acting for themselves.

In 1978, there were $45 billion of large acquisitions worldwide, mostly in the United States. By 1988, this figure had risen to $370 billion. Of that total, $100 billion was outside the United States and another $70 billion involved a non-U.S. buyer.[1] The patterns of cross-border transactions in 1988 (Figure 18-5) show that the United States was a significant net seller (56 percent of sales and only 13 percent of purchases), while the United Kingdom, Japan, France, Switzerland, and Germany were large net buyers.

GLOBAL COMPARABILITY PROBLEMS

While it is easy to claim the future is here today, there are some significant obstacles to global valuation founded on differences in definition, regulation, and accounting. It has been said that English-speaking people are one, yet divided by a common language. In the world of business, English is king, yet the meanings of its words are slanted to suit local custom and practice.

Most obvious are differences in accounting practices, which the International Accounting Standards Committee (IASC) is struggling to address. Today, profit reports can differ by hundreds of percentages, depending on whether they are prepared under U.S. GAAP or German, French, or Japanese accounting standards. The outlook for compromise is bleak indeed, with representatives such as Herbert Lederle of Volkswagen insisting it will only issue statements under "German law" (comparable to U.S. IRS reports). Yet the accountants are being bypassed by corporate investors who are making investment decisions across boundaries of

FIGURE 18–5
International Cross-Border Mergers and Acquisitions, 1988 Data
through December 31, 1988

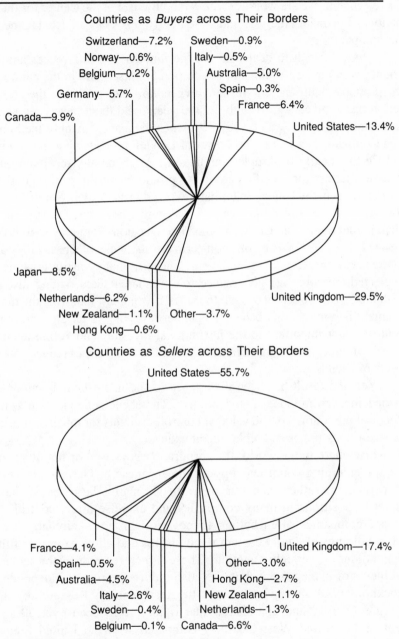

Countries as *Buyers* across Their Borders

Switzerland—7.2%   Sweden—0.9%
Norway—0.6%   Italy—0.5%
Belgium—0.2%   Australia—5.0%
Germany—5.7%   Spain—0.3%
France—6.4%
Canada—9.9%
United States—13.4%

Japan—8.5%
Netherlands—6.2%   United Kingdom—29.5%
New Zealand—1.1%   Other—3.7%
Hong Kong—0.6%

Countries as *Sellers* across Their Borders

United States—55.7%

France—4.1%   United Kingdom—17.4%
Spain—0.5%   Other—3.0%
Australia—4.5%   Hong Kong—2.7%
Italy—2.6%   New Zealand—1.1%
Sweden—0.4%   Netherlands—1.3%
Belgium—0.1%   Canada—6.6%

Source: Salomon Brothers.

country and accounting differences based on their own adjustments. At Batterymarch, we are working with Vinod Bavishi of the Center for International Financial Analysis and Research (CIFAR) to adjust statements for comparability.

More difficult to deal with are the fundamental differences among countries in their definitions of the corporation itself and in the nature of the property right inherent in share ownership. The concept of the corporation has evolved significantly in 300 years, and there have been some false starts along the way (as in 1720, when the management of the South Sea Company was sent to the Tower of London for causing a speculative bubble that nearly bankrupted the nation). After initially receiving only narrow charters for specific activities "promotive of the public good,"[2] corporations in the United States have evolved in an "Adam Smith" environment with considerable freedom. Recently, however, the system of shareholder ownership has been called into question. Some say shareholders are impatient, focusing on short-term profits, while others say they are inattentive, inept, and incompetent. Indeed, many institutions have neglected the corporate governance role of shareholders, voting instead with the "Wall Street rule" (sell the stock if you don't like what the management is doing). This behavior is understandable. After all, corporate control is not important to the institutional investor, and voting against boards of directors and managements on antitakeover issues reduces one's circle of friends.

Yet, the result has been divergence of the interests and actions of management from those of shareholders. The phenomenon known as the "control premium," or the value of control, accounts for much of the gap between stock prices and replacement values.

Elsewhere in the world, the corporation is viewed differently, and we see emerging countries copying the Japanese or German structure of capitalism rather than our own. In Germany, large banks have majority positions in many companies and exercise direct control. In Japan, companies often belong to powerful groups, keiretsu, where cross-holdings of equity cement relationships and allow exercise of the shareholder's oversight function. These structures reduce the agency problems of management, but they also reduce the role of independent stockholders. A survey by the Investor Responsibility Research Center (Figure 18–6) found that shareholder rights are reduced over 50 percent in Japan and West Germany compared with the United States. Unfortunately, we may be losing our advantage. Professor Michael

Jensen of Harvard argues that this is the "eclipse of the public corporation."[3] He believes we will see public companies replaced by powerful private corporations funded by leveraged buyout groups. With large pools of capital available for direct financing, corporations in the United States may now rely less on the volatile public market, where high-powered voting stock presents the risk of a hostile takeover. Some corporations will go private, while others will protect themselves with antitakeover amendments that alter the property rights of shareholders, making their common stock more like a participating preferred stock than an instrument of control.

Investors in the United States are clearly uncertain in dealing with control issues. This is illustrated by their low valuation of their vote in the affairs of the corporation. If offered a slight increase in dividend, U.S. shareholders will freely exchange their voting stock for a new class of

FIGURE 18–6
IRRC World Index of Shareholder Rights

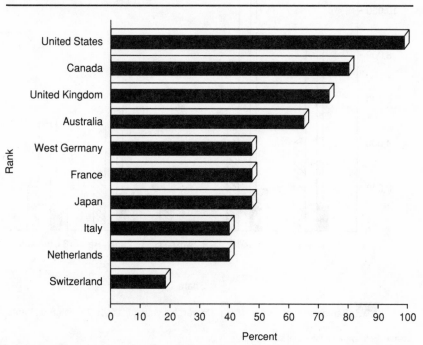

Source: Investor Responsibility Research Center.

stock, minus voting rights. In other markets, however, nonvoting stock sells at a deep discount of 50 percent or more. Figure 18–7 shows the prices of three classes of several Swiss stocks; the nonvoting participating certificates sell for significantly less than the voting bearer and registered shares.

Despite the differences of definition, accounting, and regulation, however, global investors are in our midst and are shaping markets to fit a global valuation model.

FIGURE 18–7
Swiss Stock Prices by Type of Share

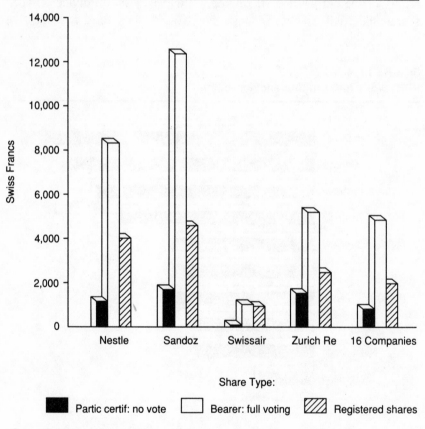

Share Type:

■ Partic certif: no vote □ Bearer: full voting ▨ Registered shares

Source: Batterymarch Financial Management

THE GLOBAL VALUATION MODEL

As investment techniques move from traditional to global, they will incorporate many features of institutional and corporate valuation. There are three elements in this process: proliferation of global databases, blending of institutional techniques, and leadership by global corporations.

1. As *global databases* proliferate, there will be opportunities to exploit inefficiencies in common market-factor characteristics. Where the traditional investor has been limited by time and resources, the computer can compare the universe of stocks within each market and make arbitrage profits—from small stocks that have been overlooked or from low-P/E, low-price/book, and high-yield stocks that are out of favor. At Batterymarch, we use a consolidated database from several sources to rank stocks by their attractiveness along these factor dimensions. Caution is required, however. In the U.S. market, many of these factor opportunities have already been exploited; and in other markets, the windows of opportunity will be much shorter. In fact, exploitation of them, by Batterymarch and others, is now under way even in emerging markets like South America.

2. As *institutional investors* increase their global focus, they will blend their local practices. The universal valuation model will draw on investment disciplines in each area of the globe. Investors in North America have a heavy quantitative orientation; qualitative information is weighted more heavily elsewhere. The most fascinating thing about Japanese investors is the information that they value. A recent study asked Japanese and American businessmen to rate a list of potential goals in order of importance. The list included such things as income, longevity, friendly relations with fellow workers, esteem, price, reputation, and quality. The Japanese rated esteem as the most important goal and income as the least important. The Americans treated income as the most important goal and esteem as the least important. We should not be so chauvinistic to say that our own notion of income maximization must be the primary goal of the Japanese investor; it seems perfectly clear that esteem can be just as important a value as income. Therefore, we cannot subject the Japanese to "the tyranny of the price/earnings ratio" when they do not subscribe to this notion.

3. More important than databases and the influence of institutions, however, will be the *global activities of corporations*. Already, the shares of over 1,200 U.S. companies are listed in at least one other country, with 100 listed in Tokyo. The worldwide record for listings, however, is held by Sony with 18. More important than listings, though, are two contributions of corporations to our universal valuation model: financial valuation and strategic valuation.

Financial Valuation

In the corporation's valuation models, it is unlikely that much attention is paid to the investor's favorite, the dividend discount model. Instead, merger transactions are often based on unused debt capacity, which is provided by free cash flow, or on the theoretical break-up value of individual business units. Cash flow analysis is time consuming and has been unpopular with financial analysts, but it shows a company's ability to finance itself, to diversify, and to compete. Analysis of cash flow has another advantage in our universal valuation model, because it eliminates many of the accounting differences among countries that occur in depreciation, reserves, and taxes.

An example of financial valuation is the cash flow analysis of Philips N.V. in Figure 18–8. This leveraged buyout analysis begins with current

FIGURE 18–8
Batterymarch Global Strategy: Financial Tension—
Philips N.V.

(Country: Netherlands)	
Current pretax	849
× Growth rate (15.2%)	1,127
+ Depreciation	2,770
− ¾ Capital expenses	2,547
+ Provisions to reserves	0
= Free cash flow	1,350
× Multiplier	13.2
Total	17,858
+ Cash	1,429
= Theoretical value	19,287
Market value	11,103
Ratio	1.7
Percentile rank (100 is best)	70.9

pretax earnings, based on the IBES database estimate for future earnings. We apply an estimated growth factor over the next two years and then add depreciation, minus a portion of capital spending. Any provisions of reserves, particularly important in West Germany, are added back to eliminate the impact of arbitrary fluctuations. The total of free cash flow is capitalized at the local corporate borrowing rate, and cash is added to produce an estimate of theoretical value. In this case, Philips is valued at more than its current market price; it is in the top third of our 2,000-company universe.

Analysis of business segment values is more difficult because of limited disclosure. With help from the Center for International Financial Analysis and Research (CIFAR), we have prepared a database of 600 non-U.S. companies with 2,305 business segments in 300 industries. This complements our U.S. Compustat Business Segment database, which covers 6,000 U.S. companies having 12,000 segments. In the United States, segment disclosure is required by *FASB Statement 14*, but elsewhere it is less uniform. Disclosure is good in Canada, the United Kingdom, and Australia, but elsewhere information rarely goes beyond sales (although Japan has proposed full disclosure in 1991). Our segment databases form a sparse matrix, which is reduced to theoretical values for each division and company by using regression and interactive techniques.

Strategic Valuation

While financial values alone are the foundation for many mergers, the highest prices are commanded by companies that offer strategic values as well. Strategic values take many forms, which are subtle and rarely included in accounting data. In Japan, investors talk about "fukumi shisan," or hidden assets, which are often found in Tokyo real estate. Elsewhere, corporate transactions are based on acquiring distribution channels, geographic exposure, and shelf space. These values are hard to measure except after the fact once merger transactions occur. Then, they quickly disappear once more as acquirers write off goodwill. We can, however, apply the values implicit in actual transactions to other companies sharing similar characteristics. This allows us to adjust the accounting treatment of advertising, research, and goodwill expense and to estimate replacement or market values of real estate and intangibles. In addition, a strategic valuation model must make allowances for "soft" assets like market dominance, share change, global stature, joint ventures, alliances, and changes in ownership (including cross-shareholdings, insider holdings, and buybacks).

THE FUTURE PRESENT

Our present universal valuation is a prototype for the future. The enduring investment styles of tomorrow are being practiced by corporations today, and financial markets will not wait for accountants or institutional investors who are not ready. Leadership will go to those who apply uniform models that set the standard, against which markets are measured. In the ultimate universal valuation model, we will balance American quantitative principles with Japanese qualitative ones, balance accounting for hard assets with estimates of soft assets, balance U.S. shareholders' property rights with those in Europe, and balance corporate financial values with corporate strategic values.

As the investor's world continues to grow in terms of capital flows and to shrink in time and distance due to technology, one universal valuation model will emerge as the synthesis of individual, institutional, and corporate investment techniques. It will operate globally, 24 hours each day, with automatic adjustments for currency, country, and local market characteristics, and it will enable the efficient allocation of capital worldwide.

ENDNOTES

1. John M. Hennessy (Vice Chairman, CS First Boston), "The World Catches Takeover Fever," *New York Times,* May 21, 1989, Business Section, p. 1.
2. Robert Erich, "The Corporations and the Nation," *Atlantic Monthly,* May 1988, p. 76.
3. Michael Jensen, "The Eclipse of the Public Corporation," *Harvard Business Review,* September–October 1989, p. 61.

PART 4

THE FOREIGN EXCHANGE EXPOSURE DECISION

CHAPTER 19

UNIVERSAL HEDGING: OPTIMIZING CURRENCY RISK AND REWARD IN INTERNATIONAL EQUITY PORTFOLIOS

Fischer Black

Investors can increase their returns by holding foreign stocks in addition to domestic ones. They can also gain by taking the appropriate amount of exchange risk. But what amount is appropriate?

Assume investors see the world in light of their own consumption goods and count both risk and expected return when figuring their optimum hedges. Assume they share common views on stocks and currencies, and markets are liquid and there are no barriers to international investing. In this perfect world, it is possible to derive a formula for the optimal hedge ratio.

This formula requires three basic inputs—the average across countries of the expected returns on the world market portfolio; the average across countries of the volatility of the world market portfolio; and the average across all pairs of countries of exchange rate volatility. These values can be estimated from historical data.

This chapter is an adaptation of Fischer Black, "Universal Hedging: Optimizing Currency Risk and Reward in International Equity Portfolios," *Financial Analysts Journal*, July/August 1989. Copyright 1989 by the Financial Analysts Federation.

The formula in turn gives three rules: (1) hedge foreign equity, (2) hedge less than 100 percent of foreign equity, and (3) hedge equities equally for all countries. The formula's solution applies no matter where an investor lives or what investments he holds. That's why it's called "the universal hedging formula."

In a world where everyone can hedge against changes in the value of real exchange rates (the relative values of domestic and foreign goods), and where no barriers limit international investment, there is a universal constant that gives the optimal hedge ratio—the fraction of your foreign investments you should hedge. The formula for this optimal hedge ratio depends on just three inputs:

- Expected return on the world market portfolio.
- Volatility of the world market portfolio.
- Average exchange rate volatility.

The formula, in turn, yields three rules.

- Hedge your foreign equities.
- Hedge equities equally for all countries.
- Don't hedge 100 percent of your foreign equities.

This formula applies to every investor who holds foreign securities. It applies equally to a U.S. investor holding Japanese assets, a Japanese investor holding British assets, and a British investor holding U.S. assets. That's why we call this method "universal hedging."

WHY HEDGE AT ALL?

You may consider hedging a zero-sum game. After all, if U.S. investors hedge their Japanese investments, and Japanese investors hedge their U.S. investments, then when U.S. investors gain on their hedges, Japanese investors lose, and vice versa. But even though one side always wins and the other side always loses, hedging *reduces risk* for both sides.

More often than not, when performance is measured in local currency, U.S. investors gain on their hedging when their portfolios do badly, and Japanese investors gain on their hedging when their portfolios do badly. The gains from hedging are similar to the gains from international diversification. Because it reduces risk for both sides, currency hedging provides a "free lunch."

Why not Hedge *All*?

If investors in all countries can reduce risk through currency hedging, why shouldn't they hedge 100 percent of their foreign investments? Why hedge less?

The answer contains our most interesting finding. When they have different consumption baskets, investors in different countries can all add to their expected returns by taking some currency risk in their portfolios.

To see how this can be, imagine an extremely simple case, where the exchange rate between two countries is now 1:1 but will change over the next year to either 2:1 or 1:2 with equal probability. Call the consumption goods in one country "apples" and those in the other "oranges."

Imagine the world market portfolio contains equal amounts of apples and oranges. To the apple consumer, holding oranges is risky. To the orange consumer, holding apples is risky.

The apple consumer could choose to hold only apples and thus bear no risk at all. Likewise, the orange consumer could decide to hold only oranges. But, surprisingly enough, each will gain in expected return by trading an apple and an orange. At year-end, an orange will be worth either two apples or 0.5 apples. Its expected value is 1.25 apples. Similarly, an apple will have an expected value of 1.25 oranges. So, each consumer will gain from the swap.

This isn't a mathematical trick. In fact, it's sometimes called Siegel's paradox.[1] It's real, and it means investors generally want to hedge less than 100 percent of their foreign investments.

To understand Siegel's paradox, consider historical exchange rate data for deutsche marks and U.S. dollars. Table 19–1 shows the quarterly percentage changes in the exchange rates and their averages. Note that, in each period and for the average, the gain for one currency exceeds the loss for the other currency.

Why *Universal* Hedging?

Why is the optimal hedge ratio identical for investors everywhere? The answer lies in how exchange rates reach equilibrium.

Models of international equilibrium generally assume the typical investor in any country consumes a single good or basket of goods.[2] The investor wants to maximize expected return and minimize risk, measuring expected return and risk in terms of his own consumption good.

TABLE 19–1
Siegel's Paradox

	Start-of-Quarter Exchange Rates		Percentage Changes in Exchange Rates	
	Mark	Dollar	Mark	Dollar
Quarter	Dollar	Mark	Dollar	Mark
1Q84	2.75	.362	−5.58	5.90
2Q84	2.60	.384	7.18	−6.69
3Q84	2.79	.358	9.64	−8.79
4Q84	3.06	.326	3.66	−3.52
1Q85	3.17	.315	−1.83	1.84
2Q85	3.11	.321	−2.25	2.30
3Q85	3.04	.328	−13.04	15.01
4Q85	2.64	.377	−7.59	8.21
1Q86	2.44	.408	−4.46	4.67
2Q86	2.33	.427	−6.80	7.29
3Q86	2.17	.459	−7.16	7.73
4Q86	2.02	.494	−5.19	5.46
1Q87	1.91	.521	−5.11	5.41
2Q87	1.81	.549	0.49	−0.49
3Q87	1.82	.547	1.09	−1.08
4Q87	1.84	.541	−14.00	16.28
1Q88	1.58	.629	4.29	−4.12
2Q88	1.65	.603	9.83	−8.95
3Q88	1.82	.549	2.27	−2.22
4Q88	1.86	.537	−4.88	5.12
Average			−1.97	2.47

Given the risk-reducing and return-enhancing properties of international diversification, an investor will want to hold an internationally diversified portfolio of equities. Given no barriers to international investment, every investor will hold a share of a fully diversified portfolio of world equities. And, in the absence of government participation, some investor must lend when another investor borrows, and some investor must go long a currency when another goes short.

Whatever the given levels of market volatility, exchange rate volatilities, correlations between exchange rates, and correlations between exchange rates and stock, in equilibrium prices will adjust until everyone is willing to hold all stocks and until someone is willing to take the other side of every exchange rate contract.

Suppose, for example, we know the return on a portfolio in one currency, and we know the change in the exchange rate between that currency and another currency. We can thus derive the portfolio return in the other currency. We can write down an equation relating expected returns and exchange rate volatilities from the points of view of two investors in the two different currencies.

Suppose investor A finds a high correlation between the returns on his stocks in another country and the corresponding exchange rate change. He will probably want to hedge to reduce his portfolio risk. But suppose an investor B in that other country would increase his own portfolio's risk by taking the other side of A's hedge. Investor A may be so anxious to hedge that he will be willing to pay B to take the other side. As a result, the exchange rate contract will be priced so that the hedge reduces A's expected return but increases B's.

In equilibrium, both investors will hedge. Investor A will hedge to reduce risk, while investor B will hedge to increase expected return. But they will hedge equally, in proportion to their stock holdings.

THE UNIVERSAL HEDGING FORMULA

By extending the above analysis to investors in all possible pairs of countries, we find that the proportion that each investor wants to hedge depends on three averages—the average across countries of the expected excess return on the world market portfolio; the average across countries of the volatility of the world market portfolio; and the average across all pairs of countries of exchange rate volatility. These averages become inputs for the universal hedging formula:[3]

$$\frac{\mu_m - \sigma_m^2}{\mu_m - \frac{1}{2}\sigma_e^2}$$

where

μ_m = Average across investors of the expected excess return (return above each investor's riskless rate) on the world market portfolio (which contains stocks from all major countries in proportion to each country's market value).

σ_m = Average across investors of the volatility of the world market portfolio (where variances, rather than standard deviation, are averaged).

σ_e = Average exchange rate volatility (averaged variances) across all pairs of countries.

Neither expected changes in exchange rates nor correlations between exchange rate changes and stock returns or other exchange rate changes affect optimal hedge ratios. In equilibrium, the expected changes and the correlations cancel one another, so they do not appear in the universal hedging formula.

In the same way, the Black-Scholes option formula includes neither the underlying stock's expected return nor its beta. In equilibrium, they cancel one another.

The capital asset pricing model is similar. The optimal portfolio for any one investor could depend on the expected returns and volatilities of all available assets. In equilibrium, however, the optimal portfolio for any investor is a mix of the market portfolio with borrowing or lending. The expected returns and volatilities cancel one another (except for the market as a whole), so they do not affect the investor's optimal holdings.

Inputs for the Formula

Historical data and judgment are used to create inputs for the formula. Tables 19–2 through 19–8 give some historical data that may be helpful.

Table 19–2 lists weights that can be applied to different countries in estimating the three averages. Japan, the United States, and the United Kingdom carry the most weight.

Tables 19–3 to 19–5 contain statistics for 1986 to 1988, and Tables 19–6 to 19–8 contain statistics for 1981 to 1985. These subperiods give an indication of how statistics change from one sample period to another.

When averaging exchange rate volatilities over pairs of countries, we include the volatility of a country's exchange rate with itself. Those volatilities are always zero; they run diagonally through Tables 19–3 and 19–6. This means the average exchange rate volatilities shown in Tables 19–5 and 19–8 are lower than the averages of the positive numbers in Tables 19–3 and 19–6.

The excess returns in Tables 19–4 and 19–7 are averages for the world market return in each country's currency, minus that country's risk-

TABLE 19–2
Capitalizations and Capitalization Weights

	Domestic Companies Listed on the Major Stock Exchange as of December 31, 1987*		Companies in the FT-Actuaries World Indices℠ as of December 31, 1987†	
	Capitalization (U.S.$ billions)	Weight (percent)	Capitalization (U.S.$ billions)	Weight (percent)
Japan	2,700	40%	2,100	41%
United States	2,100	31	1,800	34
United Kingdom	680	10	560	11
Canada	220	3.2	110	2.1
Germany	220	3.2	160	3.1
France	160	2.3	100	2.0
Australia	140	2.0	64	1.2
Switzerland	130	1.9	58	1.1
Italy	120	1.8	85	1.6
Netherlands	87	1.3	66	1.3
Sweden	70	1.0	17	0.32
Hong Kong	54	0.79	38	0.72
Belgium	42	0.61	29	0.56
Denmark	20	0.30	11	0.20
Singapore	18	0.26	6.2	0.12
New Zealand	16	0.23	7.4	0.14
Norway	12	0.17	2.2	0.042
Austria	7.9	0.12	3.9	0.074
Total	6,800	100	5,300	100

* From "Activities and Statistics: 1987 Report" by Federation Internationale des Bourses de Valeurs (page 16).
† The FT-Actuaries World Indices™ are jointly compiled by The Financial Times Limited, Goldman, Sachs & Co., and County NatWest/Wood Mackenzie in conjunction with the Institute of Actuaries and the Faculty of Actuaries. This table excludes Finland, Ireland, Malaysia, Mexico, South Africa, and Spain.

less interest rate. The average excess returns differ between countries because of differences in exchange rate movements.

The excess returns are *not* national market returns. For example, the Japanese market did better than the U.S. market in 1987, but the world market portfolio did better relative to interest rates in the United States than in Japan.

Because exchange rate volatility contributes to average stock market volatility, σ_m^2 should be greater than $\frac{1}{2}\sigma_e^2$. Exchange rate volatility also contributes to the average return on the world market, so μ_m should be greater than $\frac{1}{2}\sigma_e^2$, too.

TABLE 19–3
Exchange Rate Volatilities, 1986–1988

	Japan	United States	United Kingdom	Can-ada	Ger-many	France	Aus-tralia	Switzer-land
Japan	0	11	9	12	7	7	14	7
United States	11	0	11	5	11	11	11	12
United Kingdom	9	10	0	11	8	8	14	9
Canada	12	5	11	0	12	11	12	13
Germany	7	11	8	12	0	3	15	4
France	7	11	8	11	2	0	14	5
Australia	14	11	14	12	14	14	0	15
Switzerland	7	12	9	13	4	5	15	0
Italy	8	10	8	11	3	3	14	5
Netherlands	7	11	8	11	2	3	14	5
Sweden	7	8	7	9	5	5	12	7
Hong Kong	11	4	11	6	11	11	11	12
Belgium	9	11	9	12	6	6	14	8
Denmark	8	11	8	11	4	4	14	6
Singapore	10	6	10	8	10	10	12	11
New Zealand	17	15	16	15	17	17	14	18
Norway	9	10	9	10	7	7	13	9
Austria	8	11	9	12	5	5	15	7

Source: FT-Actuaries World Indices™ database.

An Example

Tables 19–5 and 19–8 suggest one way to create inputs for the formula. The average excess return on the world market was 3 percent in the earlier period and 11 percent in the later period. We may thus estimate a future excess return of 8 percent.

The volatility of the world market was higher in the later period, but that included the crash, so we may want to use the 15 percent volatility from the earlier period. The average exchange rate volatility of 10 percent in the earlier period may also be a better estimate of the future than the more recent 8 percent.

This reasoning leads to the following possible values for the inputs:

$$\mu_m = 8\%$$
$$\sigma_m = 15\%$$
$$\sigma_e = 10\%$$

Given these inputs, the formula tells us that 77 percent of holdings should be hedged:

TABLE 19–3—Concluded

Italy	Nether-lands	Sweden	Hong Kong	Belgium	Den-mark	Singa-pore	New Zealand	Norway	Austria
8	7	7	11	9	8	10	17	9	8
10	11	8	4	11	11	6	15	10	11
8	8	7	11	9	8	10	16	9	9
11	11	9	6	12	11	8	15	10	12
3	2	5	11	6	4	10	17	8	5
3	3	5	11	6	4	10	17	7	5
14	14	12	11	14	14	12	14	14	14
5	5	7	12	8	6	11	18	9	7
0	3	5	11	6	4	10	17	7	5
3	0	5	11	6	4	10	17	7	5
5	5	0	8	6	4	8	16	6	5
10	11	8	0	11	11	5	14	10	11
6	6	6	11	0	6	10	17	8	6
4	4	4	11	6	0	10	17	7	5
10	10	8	5	10	10	0	15	10	10
17	17	15	14	17	17	15	0	16	17
7	7	5	10	8	7	10	16	0	7
5	5	5	11	6	5	10	17	8	0

$$\frac{0.08 - 0.15^2}{0.08 - \frac{1}{2}(0.10)^2} = 0.77$$

To compare the results of using different inputs, we can use the historical averages from both the earlier and later periods:

$$\mu_m = \text{3\% or 11\%}$$
$$\sigma_m = \text{15\% or 18\%}$$
$$\sigma_e = \text{10\% or 8\%}$$

With the historical averages from the earlier period as inputs, the fraction hedged comes to 30 percent:

$$\frac{0.03 - 0.15^2}{0.03 - \frac{1}{2}(0.10)^2} = 0.30$$

Using averages from the later period gives a fraction hedged of 73 percent:

$$\frac{0.11 - 0.18^2}{0.11 - \frac{1}{2}(0.08)^2} = 0.73$$

Generally, straight historical averages vary too much to serve as useful inputs for the formula. Estimates of long-run average values are better.

TABLE 19–4
World Market Excess Returns and Return Volatilities in Different Currencies, 1986–1988

Currency	Excess Return			Return Volatility		
	1986	1987	1988	1986	1987	1988
Japan	8	−12	21	14	26	15
United States	29	12	14	13	25	11
United Kingdom	23	−14	16	14	26	15
Canada	26	4	5	14	24	11
Germany	8	−5	30	15	27	14
France	11	−7	27	14	26	14
Australia	23	−2	−6	19	25	14
Switzerland	8	−8	36	15	27	15
Italy	2	−6	23	15	27	14
Netherlands	8	−7	30	15	27	14
Sweden	16	−6	19	13	25	13
Hong Kong	30	13	17	13	25	11
Belgium	7	−8	28	15	27	14
Denmark	8	−10	26	15	27	14
Singapore	36	6	16	12	25	12
New Zealand	15	−22	13	20	29	14
Norway	19	−11	15	14	26	12
Austria	7	−6	30	15	27	14

Source: FT-Actuaries World Indices™ database.

Optimization

The universal hedging formula assumes you put into the formula your opinions about what investors around the world expect for the future. If your own views on stock markets and on exchange rates are the same as

TABLE 19–5
World Average Values, 1986–1988

	Excess Return	Return Volatility	Exchange Rate Volatility
1986	17	14	9
1987	−3	26	8
1988	18	13	8
1986–1988	11	18	8

TABLE 19–6
Exchange Rate Volatilities, 1981–1985

	Japan	United States	United Kingdom	Canada	Germany	France	Australia	Switzerland	Italy	Netherlands
Japan	0	12	13	11	10	10	12	11	9	10
United States	11	0	12	4	12	13	11	13	10	12
United Kingdom	12	13	0	12	10	11	14	12	11	10
Canada	11	4	11	0	11	12	10	12	10	11
Germany	10	12	10	12	0	5	13	7	5	2
France	10	13	11	12	4	0	12	8	5	5
Australia	12	10	13	10	12	12	0	13	11	12
Switzerland	11	14	12	13	7	8	14	0	8	7
Italy	9	10	11	10	5	5	12	8	0	5
Netherlands	10	12	10	11	2	5	12	7	5	0

Source: FT-Actuaries World Indices™ database.

TABLE 19-7
World Market Excess Returns and Return Volatilities in Different Currencies, 1981–1985

Currency	Excess Return	Return Volatility
Japan	3	17
United States	−1	13
United Kingdom	10	16
Canada	2	13
Germany	8	15
France	7	16
Australia	7	18
Switzerland	9	16
Italy	4	15
Netherlands	8	15

those you attribute to investors generally, then you can use the formula as it is.

If your views differ from those of the consensus, you may want to incorporate them using optimization methods. Starting with expected returns and covariances for the stock markets and exchange rates, you would find the mix that maximizes the expected portfolio return for a given level of volatility.

The optimization approach is fully consistent with the universal hedging approach. When you put the expectations of investors around the world into the optimization approach, you will find that the optimal currency hedge for any foreign investment will be given by the universal hedging formula.

A Note on the Currency Hedge

The formula assumes investors hedge real (inflation-adjusted) exchange rate changes, not changes due to inflation differentials between countries. To the extent that currency changes are the result of changes in inflation, the formula is only an approximation.

In other words, currency hedging only approximates real exchange rate hedging. But most changes in currency values, at least in countries with moderate inflation rates, are due to changes in real exchange rates.

TABLE 19–8
World Average Values, 1981–1985

Excess Return	Return Volatility	Exchange Rate Volatility
3	15	10

Thus, currency hedging will normally be a good approximation to real exchange rate hedging.

In constructing a hedging basket, it may be desirable to substitute highly liquid currencies for less liquid ones. This can best be done by building a currency hedge basket that closely tracks the basket based on the universal hedging formula. When there is tracking error, the fraction hedged should be reduced.

In practice, then, hedging may be done using a basket of a few of the most liquid currencies and using a fraction somewhat smaller than the one the formula suggests.

The formula also assumes the real exchange rate between two countries is defined as the relative value of domestic and foreign goods. Domestic goods are those consumed at home, not those produced at home. Imports thus count as domestic goods. Foreign goods are those goods consumed abroad, not those produced abroad.

Currency changes should be examined to see if they track real exchange rate changes so defined. When the currency rate changes between two countries differ from *real* exchange rate changes, the hedging done in that currency can be modified or omitted.

If everyone in the world eventually consumes the same mix of goods and services, and prices of goods and services are the same everywhere, hedging will no longer help.

APPLYING THE FORMULA TO OTHER TYPES OF PORTFOLIOS

How can you use the formula if you don't have a fully diversified international portfolio, or if foreign equities are only a small part of your portfolio? The answer depends on why you have a small amount in foreign equities. You may be:

    a. Wary of foreign exchange risk.
    b. Wary of foreign equity risk, even if it is optimally hedged.
    c. Wary of foreign exchange risk and foreign equity risk, in equal
       measure.

In case *(a)*, you should hedge more than the formula suggests. In case *(b)*, you should hedge less than the formula suggests. In case *(c)*, it probably makes sense to apply the formula as given to the foreign equities you hold.

If the barriers to foreign investment are small, you should gain by investing more abroad and by continuing to hedge the optimal fraction of your foreign equities.

Foreign Bonds

What if your portfolio contains foreign bonds as well as foreign stocks?

The approach that led to the universal hedging formula for stocks suggests 100 percent hedging for foreign bonds. A portfolio of foreign bonds that is hedged with short-term forward contracts still has foreign interest rate risk, as well as the expected return that goes with that risk.

Any foreign bonds you hold unhedged can be counted as part of your total exposure to foreign currency risk. The less you hedge your foreign bonds, the more you will want to hedge your foreign stocks.

At times, you may want to hold unhedged foreign bonds because you believe the exchange rate will move in your favor in the near future. In the long run, though, you will want to hedge your foreign bonds even more than your foreign equities.

CONCLUSION

The formula's results may be thought of as a base case. When you have special views on the prospects for a certain currency, or when a currency's forward market is illiquid, you can adjust the hedging positions that the formula suggests.

When you deviate from the formula because you think a particular currency is overpriced or underpriced, you can plan to bring your position back to normal as the currency returns to normal. You may even want to use options, so that your effective hedge changes automatically as the currency price changes.

ENDNOTES

1. J. J. Siegel, "Risk, Interest Rates, and the Forward Exchange," *Quarterly Journal of Economics,* May 1972.
2. See, for example, B. H. Solnik, "An Equilibrium Model of the International Capital Market," *Journal of Economic Theory,* August 1974; F. L. A. Grauer, R. H. Litzenberger, and R. E. Stehle, "Sharing Rules and Equilibrium in an International Capital Market under Uncertainty," *Journal of Financial Economics,* June 1976; P. Sercu, "A Generalization of the International Asset Pricing Model," *Revue de l'Association Française de Finance,* June 1980; and R. Stultz, "A Model of International Asset Pricing," *Journal of Financial Economics,* December 1981.
3. The derivation of the formula is described in detail in F. Black, "Equilibrium Exchange Rate Hedging" (National Bureau of Economic Research Working Paper No. 2947, April 1989).

CHAPTER 20

CURRENCY RISKS IN INTERNATIONAL EQUITY PORTFOLIOS*

Lee R. Thomas

If you own foreign equity shares, it is natural to separate their total return into two components. First is the local dividend yield plus the appreciation or depreciation of the stock, measured in its local currency. Second is the change in the associated foreign exchange rate. Analyzing returns this way highlights an opportunity that you may not know you have: to choose the equity risks you bear separately from the foreign exchange rate risks you bear. How? By currency hedging your foreign stock holdings.

Most equity investors hold foreign stocks without hedging away the embedded exchange rate risks.[1] But, nothing prohibits you from doing so. If you sell forward (for your own currency) the foreign exchange you anticipate receiving when you dispose of your foreign shares, your total return will consist of the appreciation or depreciation of the stock in its local currency, plus or minus a (previously known) forward exchange premium or discount.[2]

So, as an international investor, you must make two decisions. First, which equity should you buy? The local currency return to a foreign stock represents the outcome of this, your first financial decision. Next, you decide whether to sell foreign currency forward against your foreign stock

*The author, without implicating, thanks Fischer Black, Ronald A. Krieger, and William J. Marshall for their helpful comments on an earlier draft. An earlier version of this manuscript was published in *Financial Analysts Journal*.

holdings. If you decide not to hedge this way, your total return also includes any appreciation that accrues to the foreign currency. Your profit or loss on the currency conversion represents the outcome of your second choice—not to immunize your portfolio against exchange rate changes.

If you consider the total return to a foreign equity position without separating it into its components, you may blur the effects of the two distinct financial decisions you made. Moreover, failing to distinguish between hedged and unhedged foreign equity returns obscures the fact that taking on currency risks in a stock portfolio should be an active decision. You should never back into a foreign exchange exposure without subjecting it to the same scrutiny that you insist on when you buy stocks or bonds.

This chapter investigates the risk associated with investing in foreign stock markets, comparing the unhedged and currency-hedged approaches. Our perspective is that of a dollar-based investor who initially holds only U.S. equities but is otherwise well diversified.

HOW RISKY ARE FOREIGN EQUITIES?

The analysis is based on monthly data from January 1975 through March 1987, encompassing most of the floating-rate period. We examine the riskiness of 15 nondollar equity markets.

Let's start by looking at foreign shares' volatility. (Later we will look at risk in a more sophisticated way.) The dollar volatility of foreign shares depends on (1) the local currency volatility, (2) the volatility of exchange rates, and (3) the correlation between stock price movements and exchange rate changes. Table 20–1 summarizes the data.

The first column shows the variability of returns in foreign and U.S. stock markets, measured in local currencies. Accordingly, these results do not include the effects of exchange rate changes. Even so, in 12 of 15 cases, foreign stock prices are more volatile than U.S. stock prices. In most cases, the difference is substantial. Thus, even ignoring the risk contributed by exchange rates, a U.S. equity investor who measures risk by the volatility of return will generally find foreign stock returns to be more volatile than domestic shares' returns.

The second column shows the volatility of the foreign exchange rate (against the U.S. dollar) for each country covered in the study. In most cases, equity prices are much more volatile than their associated exchange rates, and none of the exchange rates examined are as volatile as U.S. stock prices.

TABLE 20–1
Volatilities of Stock Prices and Exchange Rates

(Annualized)

Currency	Volatility of Stock Prices in Local Currency (Percent)	Volatility of U.S. Dollar Exchange Rate (Percent)	Volatility of Stock Prices in U.S. Dollars
Australia	20.0%	10.5%	$22.5
Austria	13.8	11.9	19.0
Belgium	15.4	13.5	21.1
Canada	18.2	4.9	18.8
Denmark	16.1	11.5	18.9
France	20.9	11.4	24.7
Germany	15.7	11.9	20.4
Italy	25.7	10.8	29.6
Japan	14.2	12.1	19.3
Netherlands	16.0	11.7	20.0
Norway	25.6	9.7	26.9
Spain	20.3	11.0	24.0
Sweden	20.2	10.2	21.4
Switzerland	12.5	13.6	19.9
United Kingdom	19.6	11.3	23.2
Average (Non-U.S.)	18.3	11.1	22.0
United States	14.4	—	—

For 10 of the 15 countries examined, equity price changes and the dollar value of the local currency are positively correlated. But, the correlations are low, and none are statistically significant. This means exchange rate changes tend to amplify the variability of foreign stock prices, but the effect is small.

By comparing the first and third columns, you can see that foreign stock returns were more volatile measured in U.S. dollars than they were in their local currencies. The average difference was 3.7 percentage points, or about 20 percent. The differences were the greatest in Europe and Japan, and smallest in Canada and Scandinavia.

While foreign stock prices have clearly been *more volatile* than U.S. stock prices, whether measured in their local currencies or in dollars, it is not clear that they are *riskier*. Volatility is not a good measure of an asset's risk, because it does not tell us how much the asset contributed to the volatility of a portfolio of equities. To find out, we must separate the asset's risk into its nonsystematic component—the diversifiable risk that vanishes when the asset is added to the investor's portfolio—and the systematic risk that remains after diversification, contributing to portfolio volatility.

Conventional financial analysis "explains" the return that accrues to a stock, or a portfolio of stocks, by comparing it with the return posted by a portfolio that is taken to represent the overall market. The sensitivity of the stock (or portfolio) to changes in the value of the market portfolio, which is a measure of the stock's systematic risk, is called its *beta*. Beta can be measured by estimating a simple regression equation of the following form:[3]

$$\begin{array}{c}\text{Rate of return to the}\\ \text{stock or portfolio}\end{array} = a + b \begin{bmatrix}\text{Rate of return}\\ \text{to the market}\end{bmatrix} + \begin{array}{c}\text{Random}\\ \text{error}\\ \text{term}\end{array} \quad (1)$$

To assess the risk of foreign equities, we will adapt the method commonly used to measure the risk of a domestic stock. That is, we empirically estimate Equation (1) after selecting a proxy for the market portfolio.

The first problem is identifying the rate of return to the "market." We cannot directly observe the true market portfolio, which is the value-weighted average of the return to all assets, domestic and foreign, including equities, bonds, real estate, collectibles, and human capital. The usual practice is to use a comprehensive index of U.S. equities as a proxy for the market portfolio. This practice is clearly deficient in principle, unless the omitted nonequity components of the market portfolio are highly correlated with the movements of U.S. equity prices.[4]

Fortunately, we can adopt this convention here with more than the usual justification. In the first place, one of the objectives of this study is to compare the betas of foreign stocks with the betas of U.S. stocks, which are measured in the same way. Further, our perspective is that of a U.S. equity investor considering expanding his portfolio into foreign markets. Beta as estimated here accurately measures how much foreign stocks would contribute to the risk of an otherwise well-diversified portfolio containing only U.S. equities. This measure of beta is relevant to the many U.S. equity investors who hold few foreign shares.

Table 20–2 gives the regression estimates under the assumption that the U.S. investor does not hedge away his exchange rate exposure. That is, these estimates were calculated using the U.S. dollar values of foreign

TABLE 20–2
Unhedged Foreign Equity Regression Results

Country	Beta Estimate	Adjusted R-Squared	Residual Volatility (Annualized Percent)
Australia	0.86	0.13	21.0%
Austria	0.42	0.05	18.5
Belgium	0.58	0.07	20.4
Canada	1.16	0.45	14.0
Denmark	0.38	0.05	18.4
France	0.90	0.14	22.9
Germany	0.49	0.05	19.7
Italy	0.56	0.04	29.0
Japan	0.59	0.11	18.0
Netherlands	0.80	0.19	18.0
Norway	0.76	0.13	25.2
Spain	0.50	0.03	23.7
Sweden	0.67	0.09	20.4
Switzerland	0.66	0.12	18.7
United Kingdom	0.65	0.14	20.7
Average	0.62		

equities. All the beta estimates are positive and significantly differ from zero at the 95 percent level. When U.S. stocks were appreciating, the dollar values of foreign stocks were generally appreciating too. This suggests the existence of an important worldwide business cycle, to which most of the world's equity markets respond.

Although all of the estimated betas are positive, they are less than 1 for all but one of the foreign equity markets (Canada). This difference is statistically significant for nine countries. The average beta for the 15 foreign equity markets examined is 0.62. That is, a 1 percent change in U.S. stock prices is associated with a change of about two thirds of 1 percent in the average foreign market index. Stated another way, as measured by systematic risk, most foreign equity markets are only about two thirds as risky as the average U.S. stock when considered from the perspective of an otherwise well-diversified investor who holds only U.S. equities and does not currency hedge.

In summary, Table 20–2 indicates that an investor holding U.S. equities will reduce his portfolio's systematic risk by including some foreign equities, even though foreign shares are generally more volatile than

U.S. shares. This conclusion must be tempered by looking at the nonsystematic, or diversifiable, risks of foreign stocks. [Nonsystematic risk is indicated by the standard error of estimate (SEE) of the regression.] The annualized SEEs of all the regression equations exceed the annualized total volatility of U.S. stocks (14.4 percent). But, because the errors from the foreign beta regressions are statistically independent of U.S. stock price changes, a U.S. investor who is adding a small amount of foreign equities to his U.S.-only portfolio can essentially neglect them.

THE EFFECT OF HEDGING EXCHANGE RATE RISK

Now consider the systematic riskiness of adding foreign stocks to your U.S. portfolio when the exchange rate risk is hedged away. Table 20–3 presents the estimates of Equation (1) when foreign equity returns are purged of their exchange rate components and measured in local currency values.

The major conclusion of the previous section—that, from the perspective of a U.S. equity investor, foreign stocks carry relatively low

TABLE 20–3
Unhedged Foreign Equity Regression Results

Country	Beta Estimate	Adjusted R-Squared	Residual Volatility (Annualized Percent)
Australia	0.90	0.19	18.0%
Austria	0.26	0.03	13.6
Belgium	0.34	0.07	14.8
Canada	1.06	0.46	13.5
Denmark	0.21	0.07	15.6
France	0.70	0.14	19.4
Germany	0.34	0.04	15.2
Italy	0.42	0.03	25.4
Japan	0.45	0.12	13.2
Netherlands	0.66	0.26	13.8
Norway	0.66	0.15	23.7
Spain	0.38	0.02	20.1
Sweden	0.56	0.07	19.5
Switzerland	0.50	0.23	11.0
United Kingdom	0.53	0.17	17.2
Average	0.53		

amounts of systematic risk—holds here as well. Again, in all but one case (Canada) the estimated beta of foreign markets is less than 1. In 11 of 15 cases, the difference is statistically significant.

Two conclusions emerge from comparing Tables 20–2 and 20–3. First, for all the foreign markets examined save one, hedging to eliminate foreign exchange risk succeeds in reducing the systematic risk of foreign stocks. The beta for the average foreign equity index in this sample declines by about 15 percent, from 0.62 to 0.53. Second, in each case, the SEE also declines, indicating that nonsystematic risk also falls when exchange rate risk is hedged away.

The evidence indicates that hedging the exchange rate exposures embedded in foreign equities can reduce the risk, both systematic and nonsystematic, for U.S. investors who are considering diversifying into any of the 15 foreign equity markets examined.

CONCLUSION

From the perspective of a U.S. investor, during the 1975–87 period exchange rate changes accounted for about 20 percent of the volatility of foreign stock market returns. Historically, the foreign exchange component contributed most to total return volatility in Switzerland, Austria, the Netherlands, Belgium, and Japan.

Nevertheless, even without hedging, a U.S. equity investor holding a diversified portfolio containing only domestic stocks would have found the systematic risk of foreign stocks to be low. The beta of the average foreign market examined was only 0.62. Protecting foreign shares against adverse exchange rate changes eliminated an average of 15 percent of a U.S. investor's systematic risk, compared with buying foreign equities without such a hedge. Hedging reduced the average beta to 0.53.

The conclusion that hedging reduces foreign equities' systematic risk has important implications for constructing internationally diversified equity portfolios. Investors should always hedge if they believe foreign currencies are likely to be worth less than the value indicated by the forward exchange rate. In this case, the currency hedge not only reduces risk but also increases the portfolio's expected return. Investors should also hedge if they believe forward rates fairly value foreign currencies. In this case, the hedge leaves the expected return to the portfolio unchanged but (as our results show) reduces the portfolio's risk. Investors who expect a foreign currency to appreciate relative to the forward rate should balance the risk reduction afforded by hedging (approximately 15 percent) against the anticipated reduction in the portfolio's return.

We noted earlier that most U.S. investors in foreign stock markets prefer not to hedge their foreign exchange risk. Our results indicate that, in general, this is not a wise practice. Unless an investor expects the currency in question to appreciate beyond the value indicated by the forward rate, he is well advised to hedge. And even if he is bullish on the currency, he may wish to consider trading off some expected return to secure some risk reduction.

ENDNOTES

1. This presumes foreign stocks carry exchange rate risk. This is not theoretically obvious; unlike a bond, an equity share is not a claim to a stream of cash flows denominated in a particular currency but, rather, a claim to a real asset with no natural currency of denomination. Recent empirical work, however, indicates that the behavior of equities is similar to that of nominal assets. See M. Adler and D. Simon, "Exchange Risk Surprises in International Portfolios," *Journal of Portfolio Management*, Winter 1986, pp. 44–53.
2. Because it is customary to enter into a forward contract for a specified amount of foreign currency, it may seem that the investor would need a perfect forecast of foreign stock prices to hedge accurately. However, there is little *practical* difference between (1) currency hedging the initial value of your foreign equities, then rebalancing the hedge monthly and (2) a theoretically perfect accounting hedge, which sells forward the future value of your foreign shares. The former is easy to execute—and the latter, impossible.
3. Sophisticated multifactor models better characterize the evolution of share prices. But the single-factor, or Sharpe, model is more commonly used by portfolio managers.
4. Both returns refer to excess rates, or returns after subtracting the riskless rate of return.

CHAPTER 21

AN INTRODUCTION TO CURRENCY INSURANCE[1]

David F. DeRosa

INTRODUCTION

Anyone who has invested internationally has faced the dilemma of what to do about foreign exchange risk. Often, the exchange rate component of total return is as large—or larger—than the portion attributable to the underlying foreign securities markets in their local currency. For example, a U.S. investor's compound annual return in dollars on Japanese equities was 59 percent from 1985 through 1987. Only 24.8 percent was due to the Japanese stock market; 27.6 percent was caused by the falling U.S. dollar.

The picture on the other side of the Pacific was not so happy. Despite the favorable performance of the U.S. markets, especially in the late 1980s, an unhedged (or uninsured) yen-based investor would have suffered tremendous foreign exchange translation losses. In three consecutive years beginning with 1985, the dollar lost more than 20 percent per year. From 1981 to the end of 1988, exchange losses would have cut the gain on the S&P 500 almost in half, from 14.2 percent dollar-based down to 7.4 percent yen-based.

Currency risk has always been important; but now, because the flow of international investments has become so great compared to the past and because experience has been so dramatic, many more investors are aware of the need to manage their foreign exchange exposures. New ideas and methods, like currency insurance, are in demand.

THE NOMENCLATURE OF HEDGING
AND INSURANCE

Discussions of handling currency risk often get confused on terminology, so it is best to make our definitions at once.

We define *hedging* as an attempt to completely immunize some currency's risk. A hedged portfolio of yen 100 million worth of Japanese equities might consist of the stocks plus a short position in yen forwards, calling for the delivery of yen 100 million in exchange for dollars at some future date. Over time, the currency forward position might have to be rolled over as it approaches maturity, and the face value would have to be adjusted periodically for changes in the yen value of the portfolio. A properly implemented hedging program would seek to completely immunize against currency movements, with no losses but also no profits, due to exchange rate movements.

Insurance means something different. By insurance, we mean a program that limits but does not eliminate potential downside losses due to adverse currency movements. Most definitely, potential upside profits are still possible when currencies move favorably. In reality, the insured investor is giving up a portion of the upside profit potential (some of the "right-hand side" of the probability distribution of currency returns) for putting a limit on the potential downside losses (truncating the distribution at, say, -10 percent).

In some circles, insurance has become pseudonymous with *dynamic hedging*, and, in an attempt to make terminology less ambiguous, the hedging that was described above (which seeks to immunize against all movements in currencies, both up and down) is called *static hedging*.

A few more pieces of terminology are useful. Both hedging and insurance programs can operate *bilaterally* (dealing with a single foreign currency) or *multilaterally* (working on a multicurrency exposure), as would have an investor in an EAFE index portfolio. Multicurrency exposures either can be treated using a separate static or dynamic hedge for each and every currency exposure, a method called *matched hedging*, or they can be managed by creating a *basket* or proxy portfolio, consisting of a small number of major currencies—which, hopefully, tracks the actual currency exposure closely.

Finally, practitioners usually refer to the underlying portfolio of stocks and bonds as the "primary portfolio." The collection of instruments that accomplishes the currency hedging or insurance program is called the "overlay portfolio."

WHAT IS CURRENCY RISK?

The term *currency risk* will refer in this chapter to the risk of a foreign exchange translation's gains or losses on an international investment. The other component of risk is *local market risk*. Consider two examples:

> An unfortunate U.S. dollar-based investor buys a bond denominated in French francs just before the franc falls sharply against the dollar. The bond's price, however, is unchanged, measured in francs.

> A fortunate U.S. dollar-based investor buys the shares of a Swiss pharmaceuticals company that exports the majority of its production to Japan. The Swiss franc falls relative to the yen, thereby enriching the firm and its shareholders.

The first example is currency risk—meaning exchange translation risk, because if the bond were sold, the proceeds would convert back into fewer dollars even though the bond's price in francs had not changed. The second—even though it is currency induced—is local market risk.

The distinction can be seen in terms of an algebraic decomposition:

$$R_{Investor} = (1 + R_{Local}) \times (1 + R_{Currency}) - 1$$

Where

$R_{Investor}$ = Total rate of return translated into the home country currency.

R_{Local} = Rate of return in the currency of the country in which the investment is made.

$R_{Currency}$ = Percentage return on the pure currency movement.

CURRENCY BASICS

Currencies are traded on two levels: spot and forward. Spot is cash for cash, usually on a two-day settlement calendar.

A forward contract is an agreement struck at trade date to exchange one currency for another at a time in the future, referred to as the *settlement date*. The price and amount are fixed by the two parties on the trade date, but no currency changes hands until the settlement date. A forward contract can be closed fully or partially prior to settlement by doing a second transaction with a matching settlement date. As the closing transaction is almost always done at a new and different price than the original trade, net differences will need to be cleaned up on settlement date.

For example, suppose an investor wishes to buy $1 million U.S. worth of Japanese securities and implement a static hedge on this exposure to the Japanese yen using two-month forward contracts (see Figure 21–1). The investor would have to first exchange the dollars for yen, say, at a spot yen/dollar exchange rate of 140.00, yielding 140,000,000 yen, and second, implement the hedge by selling 140,000,000 yen forward for two months at an assumed forward price of 139.40. What would happen if the investor wished to close the forward position, for whatever reason, after 30 days, when the spot exchange rate has risen to 142.00? The closing transaction would be to buy 140,000,000 yen against the dollar forward to the same settlement date, now 30 days away. The net difference of $16,301 will be collected on the settlement day. It represents the dollar difference between 140,000,000 yen sold on day 1 forward for settlement in 60 days at a forward rate of 139.40 and the same amount of yen bought 30 days later forward for delivery in 30 days at the forward rate of 141.70. Note that had the dollar fallen against the yen, a net dollar payment, instead of collection, would have been required on settlement day.

Why is the forward price assumed to be below the spot in this example? Because at the time of this writing, interest rates denominated in yen were below those denominated in dollars, making the yen a "premium" currency with respect to the dollar. The spot rate, working in terms of number of yen per each dollar, must lie above or be at premium to the forward rate. Otherwise, one could risklessly borrow in yen at the lower interest rate, convert to dollars, invest at the higher dollar interest rate, and seal up the transaction with a nice profit by selling dollars forward against the yen.

Currencies that have higher interest rates than the investor's currency have spot rates that lie below or are at discount to their forward rates (but remember to work in terms of number of units of the foreign currency per one unit of home currency!). What would happen if the foreign currency's yield curve were lower at the short end but then rose steeply, crossing and then rising above the investor's yield curve? At the short maturities, the spot rate would be at premium, above the short-maturity forward rates; at the cross-over maturity, spot would equal forward; and at long maturities, the spot exchange rate would be at discount to the long-maturity forward.

The significance of the distinction of premium and discount currencies is this: Whenever an investor goes for a higher yield by switching into

FIGURE 21–1
Opening and Closing a Forward Transaction

Day 1

(a) The spot transaction: Buy $1,000,000 worth of yen spot

Dollars	$1,000,000
Spot	140.00
Yen	140,000,000

(b) The forward transaction: Sell 140,000,000 yen versus dollars forward for settlement in 60 days

60-Day Forward	139.40
Dollar Value	$1,004,304

Day 31

The closing transaction: Buy 140,000,000 yen forward versus dollars to close position

Spot	142.00
30-Day Forward	141.70
Dollar Value	($988,003)

Day 60: Settlement

	Dollar Position	Yen Position
Day 1	$1,004,304	(140,000,000)
Day 31	($988,003)	140,000,000
Net	$16,301	0

FIGURE 21–2
Schematic Diagram of Implementation of Currency Insurance

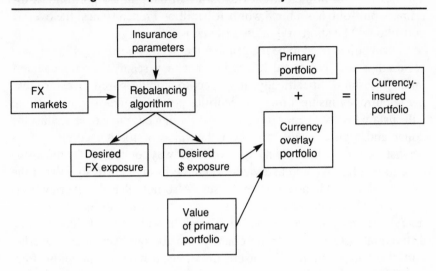

a discount currency, a hedging (or insurance) program—by virtue of the spot exchange rate being at discount to the relevant forward rate—"gives up" some or all of the yield advantage. The opposite is true for premium currencies: a hedging, or insurance, program "picks up" some of the yield disadvantage of the premium currency.

THE OVERLAY PORTFOLIO

As was stated, by definition, currency insurance takes place in the overlay portfolio. Figure 21–2 presents a schematic diagram of how it can be implemented. The right-hand side of the figure shows the conceptual division of the currency-insured portfolio into the portion that contains the stocks, bonds, and other foreign securities, called the *primary portfolio,* and the portion where the currency insurance transactions are done, called the *currency overlay portfolio.*

The idea is to use the overlay portfolio to take short positions in the same currency or currencies of the primary portfolio. In currency insurance programs, the size of the short position in the overlay portfolio varies between zero and 100 percent of the primary portfolio's exposure. (In contrast, with static hedging, the overlay portfolio's short position matches the size of the currency exposure of the primary portfolio: if the primary portfolio has a bond worth 100 million French francs, the overlay portfolio will be short 100 million francs.)

Two points need to be made about the overlay portfolio. First, it will accumulate real gains and losses in what may seem at first a counterintuitive fashion. Specifically, in respect to a dollar-based investor seeking to currency insure a foreign securities portfolio, the overlay portfolio will sustain losses whenever the value of foreign currency rises against the dollar and register gains whenever the value of foreign currency falls against the dollar. It would have to work that way, of course, for the insurance to be effective and add value when the foreign currency falls at the cost of taking some away when it rises. Also note that the overlay portfolio may accumulate gains and losses even if the value of the foreign currency does not change, provided there is a wide enough interest rate differential between the home country and foreign currencies. Overlay portfolios of programs that insure investments made in premium (discount) currencies will accumulate gains (losses) even when no change in the exchange rate occurs.

A second point concerns what is done about the overlay portfolio's gains and losses. If gains and losses directly feed into and out of the primary portfolio, the program is said to be *invasive*. This may not be desirable, especially to the manager of the primary portfolio, who may then be forced to buy and sell securities at times not of his or her own choosing. Also, measurement of the performance of the primary portfolio manager becomes more complicated because there is a need to isolate the effects of the cash flows between the primary and overlay portfolios. As an alternative, the program can be made *noninvasive* by establishing a reserve fund of liquid assets that can be used to pay and collect cash flow from the overlay portfolio. As long as the value of the foreign exchange does not rise too much and too fast, the primary portfolio will be isolated from the overlay portfolio.

REBALANCING ALGORITHMS

The rebalancing algorithm is the heart of a currency insurance program. It does the job of reducing exposure to a falling currency and adding exposure to a rising currency so as to preserve the value of the aggregate portfolio above a predetermined minimum, the "floor," while allowing for upside profit potential during favorable foreign exchange rate environments. The rebalancing algorithm is constrained by two predetermined *insurance parameters* (the level of the floor and the speed of rebalancing) and is driven by movements in exchange rates.

There are two main categories of rebalancing algorithms. Neither relies on making forecasts of foreign exchange markets. The first is based on the theory of option pricing. The key theoretical work was done by Garman and Kohlhagen (1983), who modified the Black-Scholes (1973) model to handle currency options.

The second type of rebalancing algorithm is called *constant proportion portfolio insurance* (CCPI). This approach was first developed as an alternative to option-theoretic portfolio insurance as applied to the stock market—see Black and Jones (1986) and Perold (1986). In that context, CPPI divides the total portfolio into two compartments: (1) a "risky asset" and (2) a "safe reserve asset." The amount by which the market value of the total portfolio exceeds the floor is called the *cushion*. CPPI calls for the exposure to the risky asset to be adjusted periodically, to maintain a constant proportion to the cushion. The constant proportion itself, which we shall call k, is the speed at which the rebalancing takes place. Also, provided rebalancing takes place before the risky asset drops by more than the reciprocal of k, the floor will be preserved. For example, for $k = 5$, rebalancing must occur before the risky asset falls by more than 20 percent. Larger values of k capture more of the upside potential in good markets but often involve more trading and transactions costs, and they expose the portfolio to a greater probability of violating the floor when markets move discontinuously. In applying CPPI to currency risk, the "risky asset" becomes the exposure to the foreign currency, and the "safe reserve asset" is the exposure to the home currency.

Figure 21-3 shows 100 simulations of CPPI. Each simulation is a 10-step path generated by random normal shocks with zero mean and standard deviation corresponding to an annual level of 9.5 percent (approximately the same as what it is for major currencies). The insurance parameters are a floor of 90 percent, which is never broken, and k of 5. As can be seen from these simulations, a CPPI program produces a rate of return pattern similar—but not identical—to adding a put option on the risky asset to the portfolio. Black and Rouhani (1987) report that CPPI dominates traditional option-theoretic portfolio insurance in quiet and turbulent markets but is inferior in moderately fluctuating markets.

FIGURE 21–3
100 Simulations of CPPI

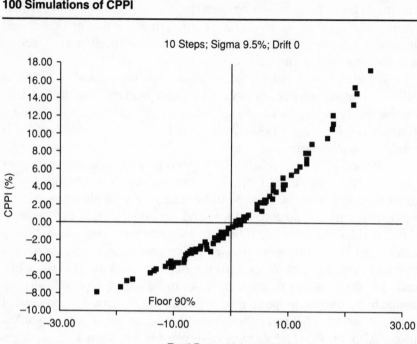

10 Steps; Sigma 9.5%; Drift 0

Although one cannot say with certainty that CPPI will outperform option-theoretic programs, it is certainly easier to implement. Another reason for preferring CPPI is that it does not require an option-pricing model and does not need volatility forecasts.

BACKTESTS OF CURRENCY INSURANCE

Figure 21–4 displays the results from backtests of the currency insurance working on a U.S. dollar-based investor's portfolio of Japanese equities and on a Japanese yen-based investor's portfolio of U.S. equities, measured as the total rate of return on the S&P 500. The basic results show that CPPI currency insurance affords significant downside protection from adverse movements in exchange rates (see the years 1985

FIGURE 21-4
Backtests of Currency Insurance

Japanese equities with currency insurance
$-based investor: Annual total rates of return

| | Currency Alone | | Japanese Equities—Hedged | | Japan Insured |
	Unhedged	Insured	$	Yen	$
1981	−7.60%	−4.49%	12.86%	22.26%	22.32%
1982	−6.35	−4.66	−0.14	6.63	4.86
1983	1.29	0.14	27.17	25.54	27.62
1984	−7.91	−3.84	17.12	27.17	25.60
1985	25.64	16.49	44.16	14.74	35.79
1986	26.50	17.38	96.38	55.24	87.96
1987	30.56	20.18	42.37	9.05	32.64
1988	−2.99	−2.86	36.05	40.24	38.53
Average	6.26%	4.29%	31.98%	24.22%	32.75%

S&P 500 with currency insurance
Yen-based investor: Annual total rates of return

| | Currency Alone | | S&P 500—Unhedged | | S&P 500 Insured |
	Unhedged	Insured	$	Yen	Yen
1981	8.22%	−0.92%	−4.92%	2.90%	−6.65%
1982	6.78	−0.21	21.55	29.79	22.91
1983	−1.28	−2.42	22.56	20.99	20.06
1984	8.59	0.51	6.27	15.39	7.29
1985	−20.41	−8.01	31.71	4.83	18.46
1986	−20.95	−8.59	18.65	−6.21	6.96
1987	−23.41	−8.85	5.25	−19.39	−1.66
1988	3.08	−1.71	16.55	20.15	15.36
Average	−5.89%	−3.85%	14.16%	7.44%	9.88%

through 1987 for the yen-based investor) while preserving the possibility of upside gains when currencies move favorably (see the results for the U.S. dollar-based investor).

These tests were done with very simple rules: monthly rebalancing using yen currency futures with calendar rollover two weeks prior to

FIGURE 21–5

Example of the Rebalancing Algorithm: 1981 Yen-Based Investor in U.S. Securities

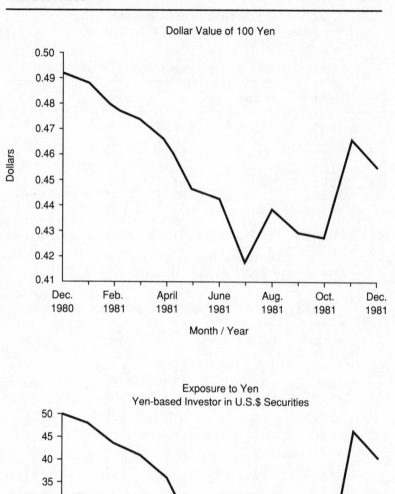

FIGURE 21–6
Dynamic Currency Hedging of EAFE Index; Three-Currency Basket;
U.S. $-Based Investor

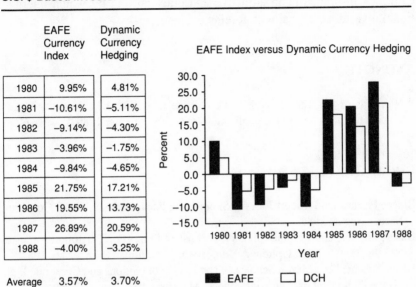

	EAFE Currency Index	Dynamic Currency Hedging
1980	9.95%	4.81%
1981	−10.61%	−5.11%
1982	−9.14%	−4.30%
1983	−3.96%	−1.75%
1984	−9.84%	−4.65%
1985	21.75%	17.21%
1986	19.55%	13.73%
1987	26.89%	20.59%
1988	−4.00%	−3.25%
Average	3.57%	3.70%

EAFE Index versus Dynamic Currency Hedging

■ EAFE   □ DCH

delivery date and 25 basis points of transactions costs. In practice, simple monthly rebalancing is often sufficient to implement currency insurance. However, some clients like the added protection requiring an immediate rebalancing after a 5 percent movement in either direction in the spot exchange rate.

Figure 21–5 shows the month-by-month rebalancing of the overlay portfolio's position in yen futures. Note the algorithm pulls away from the yen as it falls relative to the dollar (December 1980 through June 1981) and pushes it back as the yen rises (July 1981 through November 1981).

Figure 21–6 shows a backtest of a CPPI program on the EAFE currency exposure from the point of view of a U.S. dollar-based investor. This program uses a three-currency basket (Japanese yen, British pound, and German mark) designed to replicate the entire index with low tracking error. Rebalancing was done against the basket in spot currency markets. The results again show the advantages of currency insurance in the way of limited downside risk with upside profit potential.

CONCLUSION

Currency insurance is an attractive and practical tool by which international investors can deal with foreign exchange risk.

ENDNOTE

1. Portions of this chapter appeared under the title "What Is Currency Insurance" by the author in the publication *Investing,* Summer 1989, pp. 56–62.

BIBLIOGRAPHY

Black, Fischer, and Robert Jones. "Simplifying Portfolio Insurance." Goldman Sachs, August 1986.

Black, Fischer, and Ramine Rouhani. "Constant Proportion Portfolio Insurance and the Synthetic Put Option: A Comparison." Goldman Sachs, May 1987.

Black, Fischer, and Myron Scholes. "The Pricing of Options and Corporate Liabilities." *Journal of Political Economy* May/June 1973, pp. 637–54.

DeRosa, David F. "What Is Currency Insurance." *Investing,* Summer 1989, pp. 56–62.

DeRosa, David F. *Managing Foreign Exchange Risk: Strategies for Global Portfolios.* Chicago: Probus, 1991.

Garman, M., and Steven W. Kolhagen. "Foreign Currency Option Values." *Journal of International Money and Finance* 2, December 1983, pp. 231–37.

Perold, Andre F. "Constant-Proportion Portfolio Insurance." Harvard Business School, August 1986.

CHAPTER 22

THE CASE FOR NOT HEDGING

Remi J. Browne

Pension plan sponsors fortunate or foresighted enough to have invested some of their plan assets in international equities during the last few years have enjoyed extraordinary returns, especially as compared to the S&P 500. The MSCI Europe, Australia, and Far East index (EAFE) rose in U.S. dollar terms 56.2 percent in 1985, 69.4 percent in 1986, and 24.6 percent in 1987—an astounding 229.7 percent in just three years. For the same period, the 71.1 percent increase in the S&P 500 was strong but pales in comparison to EAFE's return.

Yes, those brave souls who ventured into this new world of international investments could certainly address their boards with puffed chests and chins held high—until recently. Some latter-day Cotton Mathers of the investment world have been telling these proud performers, "Repent, for the Lord doth find unrewarded risk vile in his eyes." These killjoys are spoiling everyone's fun and insisting that assets held in currencies other than the currency in which the corresponding liabilities are denominated are bearing exchange rate risk, for which the expected return is zero.

Their argument runs something like this. A portfolio of international equities with all foreign exchange exposure hedged out will be less volatile than the same portfolio left unhedged. Because the expected return on currencies should be zero for international interest rate arbitrage relationships to hold, the more volatile, unhedged portfolio should have the same expected return as the hedged portfolio (except for transaction costs necessary to execute the hedge). They recommended hedging away currency exposure to reduce portfolio risk while keeping expected

FIGURE 22–1
Annual Standard Deviation of S&P 500, International Mix

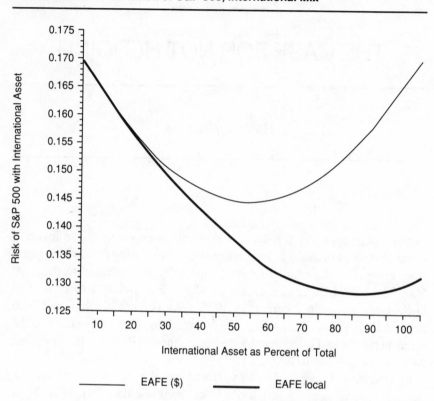

EAFE ($)   EAFE local

return constant. And, shame on those who experienced 20 percent currency gains and more in 1985, 1986, and 1987. Repent now, lest thine portfolio be rent asunder by the vicious claws of modern currency markets.

This argument falls one step short of completion, however. It is true that a hedged portfolio of international securities is less risky than its unhedged twin. Monthly data for the EAFE index from January 1978 through December 1987 show that the annual standard deviation of returns of a hedged EAFE portfolio was 13.1 percent, while the comparable risk figure for an unhedged EAFE portfolio was 17.1 percent. The annualized return for both portfolios for the period was approximately 22 percent, showing that the zero expected return of the currency exposure is also reasonable. The missing variable, however, is correlation of those returns with the rest of the pension plan assets.

Any equity investment analyzed in isolation can look scary. Modern portfolio theory has taught us to analyze total portfolios for risk and return, rewarding some otherwise risky investments for their diversification potential. Indeed, an unhedged EAFE portfolio has much lower correlation of returns with the domestic portion of a pension plan's assets than does a hedged EAFE portfolio. For instance, the correlation with the S&P 500 returns for the same 10-year period (1978 to 1987) was 0.61 for a hedged EAFE portfolio and 0.45 for an unhedged EAFE portfolio.

Figure 22–1 shows the standard deviation of returns for various mixes of the S&P 500 with unhedged or hedged EAFE portfolios. The standard deviations were calculated using the formula for the standard deviation of a two-asset portfolio. The period used to estimate the standard deviations and correlations was the 120 months from January 1978 through December 1987. The analysis was performed for other periods with similar results. Actual standard deviations and correlations for this period were:

Assets	Annual Standard Deviation (Percent)	Correlation with S&P 500
S&P 500	16.9575%	1
EAFE (hedged)	13.1403	0.6082
EAFE (unhedged)	17.0585	0.4464

The figure shows that at heavy levels of the international asset (EAFE hedged or EAFE unhedged), total portfolio risk is lower than with EAFE unhedged. This is the area of the figure on which those who are encouraging hedging have been focusing. Yet, the critical point is that at the actual international equity target levels of U.S. pension plans (0 to 15 percent), the reduction in total portfolio risk virtually disappears. At the levels most frequently targeted by U.S. plan sponsors for international equity exposure—5 percent and 10 percent—total portfolio risk is:

Level of International Investment (Percent)	Portfolio Risk Hedged (Percent)	Portfolio Risk Unhedged (Percent)
5%	16.51745%	16.50800%
10	16.09478	16.09577

With risk differences so low (and inconsistent) and similar expected returns, the burden switches to those who propose to hedge international equity exposure to show they can do this in a "frictionless" manner—accurately and at low or no cost.

Such a hedge could prove difficult and costly. To do it, one would need to adjust the hedge as the equities appreciate or depreciate. The less frequent those adjustments, the less accurate the hedge. If one were to attempt to adjust every month, and if one market rose 10 percent while another dropped 10 percent (not uncommon these days), the hedge would be fairly seriously out of line until corrected. Futures contracts are available on only a few currencies, and forward contracts on some of the less-liquid currencies (such as the Austrian schilling) are difficult to obtain without paying up due to very wide bid-ask spreads. Quick, accurate determination of the exposure is also a problem with large international portfolios. Accurate "next-day" portfolio valuation could be very costly, perhaps necessitating the sort of fees (or staff) one sees in international mutual fund accounting. Most portfolios are valued only monthly, and accurate figures frequently take two weeks to generate.

In short, it is doubtful that the added expense to a pension plan incurred in hedging international equity exposure is worth the possible reduction in total-portfolio risk that may (or may not) be realized. Pension plan sponsors can thus savor their recent gains due to the drop in the U.S. dollar without assuming any puritanical guilt.

INDEX

Abnormal equity risk premium, 42, 50
Accounting practices in global investment, 292, 294
Active portfolio management
  emerging country investment, 265, 281–82
  international bonds, 123, 159, 162, 163–69
  quantitative strategy, 77
  traditional versus quantitative, 199
Aliber, Robert Z., 1, 16, 227
Anomalies in stock returns; see Stock return anomalies
Arbel, Avner, 242
Arbitrage pricing theory factor analysis model, 214
Argentina, 272, 275
Arnott, Robert, 15, 33, 197, 243
Asset allocation
  bottom-up investing, 63
  changing equilibrium measurement, 52–55
  comparison of equity markets, 33–38, 40–41
  currency allocation committee, 66–68, 71–72
  currency-driven investing, 63–64
  versus currency selection, 42–47
  emerging markets, 264
  errors in, 34–38
  index weight basis, 26, 28
  international investing principles, 64
  macroeconomic influence, 55–60
  manager evaluation, 101–9, 264–65
  market capitalization weights, 27
  objective measures of future returns, 47–52
  quantitative forecasting, 76–99
    QUØT, 84–98
    RS2, 82–83
  returns and P/E ratios, 41–42
  risk management, 23, 26, 28–30
  rules for, 65–68
    example, 68–73
  selective investing, 64–65
  setting policy, 21, 23
    full optimization, 24
    global indices, 23
    partial optimization, 23–24, 26
  U.S. versus non-U.S. assets, 22–23
Asset allocation committee (AAC), 65–67
  choices, 70–71
Asset class returns, 42–43
  allocation, 70
Attribution analysis, 107, 109

Australia
  bond yield minus cash yield, 51
  equity performance characteristics, 29
  market value and national income, 7
  rate of return on corporate bonds, 5
  rate of return on government bonds, 4
  rate of return on national equities, 6
  security menu, 69, 71
  stock earnings minus bonds, 49
  stock earnings minus cash, 50
Austria
  bond yield minus cash yield, 51
  market value and national income, 7
  rate of return on national equities, 6
  stock earnings minus bonds, 49
  stock earnings minus cash, 50

Banz, R., 254
Barksdale, Edgar W., 15, 101
BARRA, 267
Basis risk, 151
Basket portfolio, 327
Basu, Sanjoy, 242
Bauman, W. Scott, 242
Bavishi, Vinod, 294
Bekin, Ricardo, 227
Belgium
  bond yield minus cash yield, 51
  market value and national income, 7
  stock earnings minus bonds, 49
  stock earnings minus cash, 50
Benchmark approach to development of portfolio, 14
Benesh, Gary A., 243
Bergstrom, Gary, 16, 241
Beta, 321–23
Bilateral hedging, 327
Black, Fischer, 17, 303, 318, 333
Black box, 211, 214
Black-Scholes model, 333
  option formula, 308
Bohan, James, 244
Boles, Keith E., 244
Bombay Stock Exchange, 271
Bonds; see International bonds
Book/price ratios, 242
Bottom-up investing, 63
Brazil, 275
Brealey, Richard A., 243

Breen, William, 242
Brinson, Gary, 15, 21
Brinson Partners, 266
Brown, Remi, 17, 200
Bruce, Brian R., 1, 16, 197
Brush, John S., 244
Bulldog bond issue, 146
Business segment valuation, 299
Buybacks, 290

Canada
    bond yield minus cash yield, 51
    equity performance characteristics, 29–30
    government bond market performance, 115–16
    market value and national income, 7
    rate of return on corporate bonds, 5
    rate of return on long-term bonds, 4
    rate of return on national equities, 6
    security menu, 69, 71
    stock earnings yield minus bond yield, 49
    stock earnings yield minus cash yield, 50
Capital asset pricing model (CAPM), 214
Capital gains tax, 15
Capitalization-weighted indices, 27–29, 32
Capitalization weighting, 207–9
Center for International Financial Analysis and
    Research (CIFAR), 294
Chile, 272
Chisholm, John R., 16, 241
Colombia, 272
Common Market 1992, 291
Comovements; see Market comovements
Consensus earnings forecasts, recent trends in, 241,
    242–43
Constant proportion portfolio insurance (CCPI),
    333
    100 simulations, 334
Consumer price index (CPI), 58
Control premium, 294
Corporate bonds, rate of return by country, 3, 5
Corporation
    country differences in concepts, 294
    evolution of, 294
    financial valuation, 298–99
    global activities, 297–98
    public replacement by private, 295
Correlations; see also Market comovements
    government bond markets, 17
    history of, 80
    outliers, 80
    trailing, 82–83
    trimmed, 80, 81
Country allocation funds, 199
Country market, 184–87
Country weight decision, 14
Covariance structure of emerging markets, 271–79
Cross-currency predictor models, 90
Cross-currency synthetic bonds, 141

Currencies
    forward contract, 328–29
    spot trading, 328–29
Currency allocation committee (CAC), 66–68, 71–
    72
Currency-driven investing, 63–64
Currency forecasting, 63–65
Currency hedging, 66–68, 314–15
    approximating real exchange rate hedging, 314–
    15
    cost and rewards, 46
    on forward market, 47
    international bonds, 119–23
    international equity portfolios, 318, 323–24
Currency insurance, 192, 326–38
    backtests, 334–36
    implementation, 331
    Japanese equities, 335
    overlay portfolio, 331–32
    rebalancing algorithms, 332–34, 337
Currency overlay portfolio, 70, 331–32
Currency risk, 328
    foreign equities, 319–23
    hedging exchange rate risks, 318, 323–24
    volatility of stock prices and exchange rates,
    320
Currency selection versus global asset allocation,
    42–47
    hedging, 46
Currency swap, 123, 132, 154–55
Cushion on total portfolio value, 333

DeBondt, Werner F. M., 244
Delta of an option, 152
Denmark
    bond yield minus cash yield, 51
    market value and national income, 7
    rate of return on national equities, 6
    stock earnings yield minus bond yield, 49
    stock earnings yield minus cash yield, 50
Derivative securities, 150–56
    exchange-traded, 150–54
DeRosa, David, 17, 192
Diversified international portfolio
    share of foreign equities in investor portfolios,
    12–13
    U.S. multinational firms, equities of, 13
Dividend discount model of corporate valuation,
    40, 298
Dowen, Richard J., 242
Dremen, David, 242
Dynamic hedging, 327, 338

EAFE; see Europe Australia Far East Index
Earnings estimates, recent trends in, 241, 242–43
Efficient frontiers, 90, 92, 117, 120
Elton, Edwin J., 243

Emerging markets, investment in, 264
  allocation of funds, 264–66
  correlation of returns, 273–79
  covariance structure, 271–79
  definition, 267, 269
  list of stock markets, 268–70
  management style, 281–82
  market capitalization, 266–71
  potential, 269
  relation to developed world, 275–79
  within-market and cross-market analysis, 279–81
Equilibrium
  changing, 52
  real interest rates, 53–54
  relationship between asset classes, 52
  short-term definition, 52
Equilibrium theory, 40
  asset allocation, 42
Equity market values, 7
  national differences, 7–12
Equity performance characteristics by country, 29–30
Equity portfolios; see International equities portfolio
Equity risk premium, 34, 37
  abnormal, 42
  versus bonds, 50
  comparison of equity markets, 41–42
Erickson, Hans, 16, 211
Eurodeposit, 64
Europe Australia Far East (EAFE) Index, 34, 200, 211–12, 222–23
  hedged, 340–41
  relative performance measurement, 108
  three-year increase, 339
Exchange rate volatility, 309–10, 312, 313, 314

FASB Statement 14, 299
50-state equity and bond portfolio, 10–13, 17
Filatov, Victor, 136
Financial Times Europe-Pacific Basin index (FT-A), 199, 266
Financial valuation model, 298–99
Finland, 71
First Chicago Investment Advisors, 266
Fong, Gifford, 15, 125
Fong-Pearson-Vasicek model, 125
Foreign equity market risk, 319–23
Foreign exchange exposure, 16
  hedging, 17, 227, 230–31
Formosa fund, 270
Forward contract, 328
  global asset allocation, 62, 68
  opening and closing transaction, 330
  risk of nondollar bonds, 119
France
  bond yield minus cash yield, 51
  market value and national income, 7

France—(continued)
  rate of return on corporate bonds, 5
  rate of return on long-term government bonds, 4
  rate of return on national equities, 6
  security menu, 69, 71
  stock earnings yield minus bond yield, 49
  stock predictor, 88
  total return of international equities, 44
Frashure, Ron, 16, 241
Friedman, Benjamin, 173
Fukumi shishan (hidden assets), 299
Full optimization in asset allocation policy, 24–25

Garman, M., 333
Germany
  bond yield minus cash yield, 51
  equities and bond performance characteristics, 29–31
  government bond markets, 114–15
  market value and national income, 7
  portfolio optimization, 217–19
  rate of return on corporate bonds, 5
  rate of return on long-term government bonds, 4
  rate of return on national equities, 6
  security menu, 69, 71
  stock earnings yield minus bond yield, 49
  stock earnings yield minus cash yield, 50
  stock predictor, 88
  total return on international equities, 44
Global asset allocation; see Asset allocation
Global bonds; see also International bonds
  historical data, 25–32
  performance characteristics, 31
Global corporation valuation, 289–300
  comparability problems, 292–96
  global valuation model, 297–300
    financial, 298–99
    strategic, 299–300
Global databases, 297
Global equities; see also International equities portfolio
  historical data, 24–32
  performance characteristics, 29–30
Global indices, 23, 26, 27, 28
Global information, 291
  Japan versus American values, 297
Global managers
  currency naiveté, 36, 38
  domestic comparisons, 35, 37
  errors, 35
  failure of global comparisons, 40–41
  reckless conservatism, 36
  subjective judgment, 36–37
Global securities market, 22
Goodman, David A., 242
Government bond markets, 115–19
  correlations, 117

Government bond markets—(*continued*)
  performance, 115, 119
  risk, 116
Great Britain
  bond performance characteristics, 31
  bond yield minus cash yield, 51
  equity performance characteristics, 29–30
  government bond market performance, 115
  market value and national income, 7
  rate of return on corporate bonds, 5
  rate of return on long-term government bonds, 4
  rate of return on national equities, 6
  security menu, 69, 71
  small company portfolios, 254
    expected return, 256
  stock earnings yield minus bond yield, 49
  stock earnings yield minus cash yield, 50
  stock predictor, 88
  total returns of international equities, 44
Green, William, 15, 101
Gruber, Martin J., 243
Gutelkin, Mustafa, 243

Hagin, Robert L., 242, 243, 244
Hedging
  bonds, 151
  cost and rewards, 46
  currency; *see* Currency hedging
  definition, 327
  exchange rate risk, 323–24
  foreign exchange exposure, 17, 227, 230–31
  global asset allocation, 46–47, 66–68
  optimal ratio, 303–4
  reasons for hedging, 304–7
  reasons for not hedging, 339–42
  universal, 304
  universal formula, 307–16
    currency, 314, 315
    example, 310–12
    input, 308–9
    optimization, 312, 314
  world markets, 191–92
  world portfolio volatility, 46, 310–14
Henriksson, Roy D., 33
Hong Kong
  market value and national income, 7
  rate of return on national equities, 6

Ibbotson, Roger, 16, 173
Individual investing, 287–88
Inflation, 58
Information trade, 202
Institutional investing, 288–89
  global focus, 297
Insurance of currency; *see* Currency insurance
Integrated world market, 188

International Accounting Standards Committee
  (IASC), 292
International Bond Indices (Salomon Brothers), 115
International bonds
  active management, 123
    enhancing returns, 162
    managing risk, 162
    option strategy, 159, 163–69
  benchmark approach to portfolio development,
    14, 136
  benefits from international diversification, 117–
    18
  currency hedging, 119–23
  development of, 13–17
  diversification, 12–13
  efficient frontier, 117
  50-state, 10–13, 17
  historical record, 115–16
  investment in, 113–15
  management contribution, 127–29, 131–32
  passively managed, 136
    currency decision, 139–41
    duration decision, 142–44
    issue decision, 147–49
    market decision, 141–42
    sector decision, 145–47
    yield curve decision, 144–45
  performance measurement, 125–35
    multiple-currency bond portfolio, 126–35
    single-currency bond portfolio, 126–29
  performance records, 119, 120, 121
  returns, 2–5, 132–35
  risks, 2, 159–69
  universal hedging formula, 316
  world bond market, 114
International Finance Corporation (IFC) composite
  index, 268
International equities portfolio
  beta, 321–23
  choice of country weights, 277
  comparative returns on performance portfolio,
    235
  compared to domestic portfolio, 1, 9
    rate of return, 2, 3
    risk, 1–2
  construction of performance portfolio, 231–33
  currency risks, 318–23
  development of, 13–17
  50-state, 10–13
  hedged U.S. dollar return, 235
  hedging exchange rate risks, 323–24
  hedging foreign exchange exposure, 230–31
  local currency returns, 233–34
  performance based compared to market value
    weighted, 230, 233–38
  risks, 236–38, 318–23
  scope of diversification, 12–13
  unhedged U.S. dollar returns, 234–35
  volatility of stock prices and exchange rates, 320

International portfolio
  bonds; *see* International bonds
  development of, 13–17
  diversification, 12–13
  equities; *see* International equities portfolio
Investable capital market, 266–67
Investment management styles, 197–99
Investment styles
  global corporate valuation, 289–91
  individual investing, 287–88
  institutional investing, 288–89
Investor Responsibility Research Center, 294
Investors Map of the World, 285–86
Ireland, rate of return on national equities, 6
Italy
  bond yield minus cash yield, 51
  market value and national income, 7
  rate of return on corporate bonds, 5
  rate of return on long-term government bonds, 4
  rate of return on national equities, 6
  stock earnings yield minus bond yield, 49
  stock earnings yield minus cash yield, 50
  total return of international equities, 44

Jacobs, Bruce J., 241
Japan
  bond performance characteristics, 31
  bond yield minus cash yield, 51
  equity market, 1990, 268
  equity performance characteristics, 29–30
  global information values, 297
  government bond market performance, 115
  Pacific X index, 219–20
  rate of return on corporate bonds, 5
  rate of return on long-term government
    bonds, 4
  rate of return on national equities, 6
  security menu, 69, 71
  stock model, 89
  stock predictor, 88
Jensen, Michael, 294
Jones, Robert, 333
Jorion, Philippe, 15, 113, 123

Kaplan, Paul, 16, 173
Karnosky, Denis, 15, 21
Keiretsu, 294
Kerrigan, Thomas J., 242
Kolhagen, Steven W., 333
Korea, 269
  covariance structure, 275
  market capitalization, 271
Krieger, Ronald A., 318

Lanstein, Ronald, 242, 244
Large company portfolio, 254
  diversifying U.S. portfolio, 260

LeBaron, Dean, 16, 285
Lederle, Herbert, 292
Legendre, Adrien Marie, 80
Levy, Kenneth N., 241
Little, I. M. D., 243
Local market risk, 328
Long straddle, 153–54
Long-term government bonds, rate of return, 4
Lorie, James, 136
Luxembourg, 287

Macroeconomic influence on asset performance,
  55–60
McWilliams, James D., 242
Madura, Jeff, 120
Malaysia
  market value and national income, 7
  rate of return on national equities, 6
Management style; *see* Active portfolio manage-
    ment *and* Passive portfolio management
Manager evaluation
  interview topics, 103
  qualitative criteria, 102–4
  quantitative criteria, 104
  relative performance measures, 107–9
Market capitalization
  East Asian markets, 271
  emerging markets, 266–71, 286
  global asset allocation policy, 27
  world map, 286
Market comovements, 78–80
  downward drift, 81
  forecasting
    financial market price/value variables, 87
    future of, 82
    macroeconomic series, 86
    technical variables, 87
  future of forecasts, 82
  history of correlation, 80
  maps, 79
  QUØT, 84
  RS2, 82–83, 85
  trend in local markets, 81
Market-value weighted portfolios, 230, 233–38
Marshal, William J., 318
Martin, Larry, 16, 197
Matched hedging, 327
Mergers and acquisitions, cross-border, 292
  293
Mexico
  covariance structure, 272
  rate of return on national equities, 272
Mezrich, Joseph, 15, 76
Miller, Paul F., 242
Morgan, Kelly, 197
Morgan Stanley Capital International (MSCI)
  cross-border indices, 211
  equity versus nonequity index, 21, 25

Morgan Stanley Capital International (MSCI)—
(*continued*)
   Europe Australia Far East Index; *see* Europe Australia Far East Index
   market capitalization, 266
Multifactor regression risk model, 214
Multilateral hedging, 327
Multiple markets index (MMI), 266
Mutual funds, 13

Netherlands
   bond yield minus cash yield, 51
   government bond market performance, 115
   market value and national income, 7
   rate of return on corporate bonds, 5
   rate of return on long-term government bonds, 4
   rate of return on national equities, 6
   security menu, 69, 71
   stock earnings yield minus bond yield, 49
   stock predictor, 88
New York Stock Exchange (NYSE), 173
   inefficient prices, 242
New Zealand, rate of return on national equities, 6
NIKKEI 225 (equity index), 211
Nondollar bonds, 113; *see also* International bonds
Nonsystematic risk of foreign stocks, 323
Normal portfolio, 105–6
Norway
   market value and national income, 7
   rate of return on national equities, 6

Optimal bond portfolio decision, 15
Optimal equity portfolio decision, 16
Optimal hedge ratio, 304
Optimization of portfolio; *see* Portfolio optimization
Option pricing theory, 333
Options
   active portfolio bond management, 163–69
   delta, 152
   derivative securities, 152
   long straddle, 153–54
   over-the-counter market, 154
   price spread, 152–53
Orndorff, Christopher N., 16, 136
Outliers, 78, 80–81
Overlay portfolio, 327, 331
   gains and losses, 332
   invasive or noninvasive program, 332

Pakistan, 272
Paris Bourse, 173
Partial optimization approach to asset allocation, 24–25, 26
Passive portfolio management
   cost, 200
   diversification, 200
   emerging country investment, 265, 281–82

Passive portfolio management—(*continued*)
   international bond portfolio, 136–49
   performance, 206
   quantitative strategy, 77
   strategies, 207–9
Pearson, Charles, 125
Peavy, John W., III, 242
Pension plans, 339
   hedging, 339
   international equity exposure, 342
Perold, Andre, 120, 333
Peterson, Pamela P., 243
Philippines, 275
Pogue, Jerry, 197
Portfolio optimization, 211
   black box, 211, 212
   example of trade-off, 217–24
   indexing, 211
   process, 212–16
Portfolio theory, 116
   asset allocation, 70
Price/book ratios, 242
Price/earnings ratios (P/E ratios), 40–42
   return prospects of low P/E, 41
   stock earnings anomalies, 242
Price/sales ratios, 242
Primary portfolio, 327, 331
Producer price index (PPI), 58–59
Producer prices rate of change, 58, 59
Program trade, 202
Purchasing power parity, 17

Quantitative asset allocation forecasting, 76–99
   active strategy, 77
   efficient frontiers, 90, 92
   market comovements, 78–81
   passive strategy, 77
   QUØT model, 84–98
   return forecast models, 84–90
   robust series, two stages, 82–84
   universal currency predictors, 90
Quantitative optimization algorithms, 76
Quantitative return forecasts, 84–90
QUØT (quantitative underweight overweight tilt) model, 84–98
   currency forecasts, 91
   efficient frontier, 90
   forecasts for world equity market, 88–89
   test results, 92–98

Real interest rates, 53–54
Rebalancing algorithm
   constant proportion portfolio insurance (CCPI), 333–34
   example, 337
   option pricing, 333
Reid, Kenneth, 242, 244

Reiff, Wallace, 120
Relative strength as selective factor for domestic stock, 244
Retail sales rate of change, 57
Risk management
  asset allocation policy, 23, 26, 28–30
  common measure of, 160–61
  managing, 162–69
  option strategy, 159, 163–69
  redefining, 161
Risk model, 213–14
Risky asset, 333
Robeco, 173
Robust series, two stage (RS2), 82–83, 85
ROC Taiwan fund, 270
Roll, Richard, 176
Rosenberg, Barr, 242, 244
Rosenberg, Michael, 136
Rouhani, Ramine, 333
RS2 (robust series, two stage), 82–83, 85
Rudd, Andrew, 16, 264
Russell, Frank, 35

Safe reserve asset, 333
Salomon Broad Investment Grade bond index, 25
Salomon Brothers treasury index, 127
Salomon-Russell extended market index (EMI), 77
Salomon-Russell primary market index (PMI), 77, 199
Samurai bond issue, 146
Scholes, Myron, 333
Schulman, Evan, 36, 120
Security Analysis (Graham and Dodd), 288
Security analyst neglect, 242
Security menu, 69, 71
Selective investor, 64
Settlement date, 328
Shearson-Lehman Treasury bond index, 127
Siegel, Laurence B., 173
Siegel's paradox, 305–6
Singapore
  market value and national income, 7
  rate of return on national equities, 6
Sinquefield, Rex, 16, 254
Small country portfolios, 254
  comparing large and small companies, 257–61
  data sources, 262–63
  effects of diversification, 257
  expected returns, 255–57
  historical returns, 255–57
Sorensen, Eric, 15, 76
South Africa, rate of return on national equities, 6
Spain
  bond yield minus cash yield, 51
  market value and national income, 7
  rate of return on national equities, 6
  stock earnings minus bond yield, 49
  stock earnings minus cash yield, 50

Specific return reversal strategy, 242, 244
Speidell, Lawrence S., 285
Spot currency trading, 328
Standard and Poor (S&P) 500, 211, 216
  large U.S. asset class, 255
Standard error of estimate (SEE), 323
Static hedging, 327
Stock market comovement maps, 79
  trends in global markets, 81
Stock market crash (1987), 290, 291
Stock return anomalies, 241–49
  empirical evidence, 247–49
  equity selection, 242
  methodologies for testing, 245–46
  non-U.S. equity markets, 246–47
Stock return variance, 56–57
Strategic valuation model, 299–300
Strebel, Paul, 242
Sweden
  bond yield minus cash yield, 51
  market value and national income, 7
  rate of return on national equities, 6
  stock earnings yield minus bond yield, 49
  stock earnings yield minus cash yield, 50
Switzerland
  bond earnings minus cash, 51
  government bond performance, 115
  market value and national income, 7
  stock earnings yield minus bond yield, 49
  stock earnings yield minus cash yield, 50
  stock predictor, 88
Synthetic security, 149–56
  cross-currency, 149–50
  derivative security, 150–56

Taipei fund, 270
Taiwan, 287
  emerging market, 269, 270, 271
Taiwan fund, 270
Tang, Eric, 15, 125
Thaler, Richard, 244
Thomas, Lee, 15, 17, 62, 318
Torpedo stock, 243–44
Tracking error, 104
Trailing correlation measure, 82–83
Traub, Heydon, 16, 197
"Trimming" the data, 80, 81
Tukey, John, 98
Turkey, 272
20-country portfolio, 16–17

Unemployment, 59
  by country, 60
United Kingdom; *see* Great Britain
United States
  bond earnings yield minus cash yield, 51
  bond performance characteristics, 31

United States—(*continued*)
  equity performance characteristics, 29–30
  government bond performance, 115–16, 118
  market value and national income, 7
  rate of return on corporate bonds, 5
  rate of return on long-term government bonds, 4
  rate of return on national equities, 6
  security menu, 69, 71
  small companies, 255
    expected returns, 256
  stock earnings yield minus bond yield, 49
  stock earnings yield minus cash yield, 50
  total return of international equities, 44
Unit labor costs, 59, 61
Universal currency predictors, 90
Universal hedging, 304
Universal hedging formula
  application to other types of portfolios, 315–16
  foreign bonds, 316
  inputs, 308–12
  optimization, 312–14
Universal valuation; *see* Global corporation valuation
U.S. Compustat Business Segment data base, 299
USALL portfolio, 257, 259–61
  diversifying U.S. portfolio into international
    large companies, 260
  diversifying U.S. portfolio into international
    small companies, 259
U.S. equity market, stages of, 287–88
  evolution, 291
USTR5 (Treasury note), 255

Vann, Peter, 16, 158
Vasicel, Oldrich, 125
Venezuela, 272

"Wall Street rule," 294
Widman, Ernest R., 242
Wilshire 500 index, 25
WM Company, 35, 38
World bond markets, 14
  performance, 119–21
World equity market
  economic issues in, 188
  future of investing, 184
  historical returns, 180–84
  market capitalization, 178
  QUØT forecasts, 88
  stock markets of the world, listed and character-
    ized, 176–77
  transnational benchmarks, 179
  values, 174
Worldtrack, 212

Zacks, Leonard, 243
Zimbabwe, 272